IMAGES
*of America*

# ALBION

## IN THE 20TH CENTURY

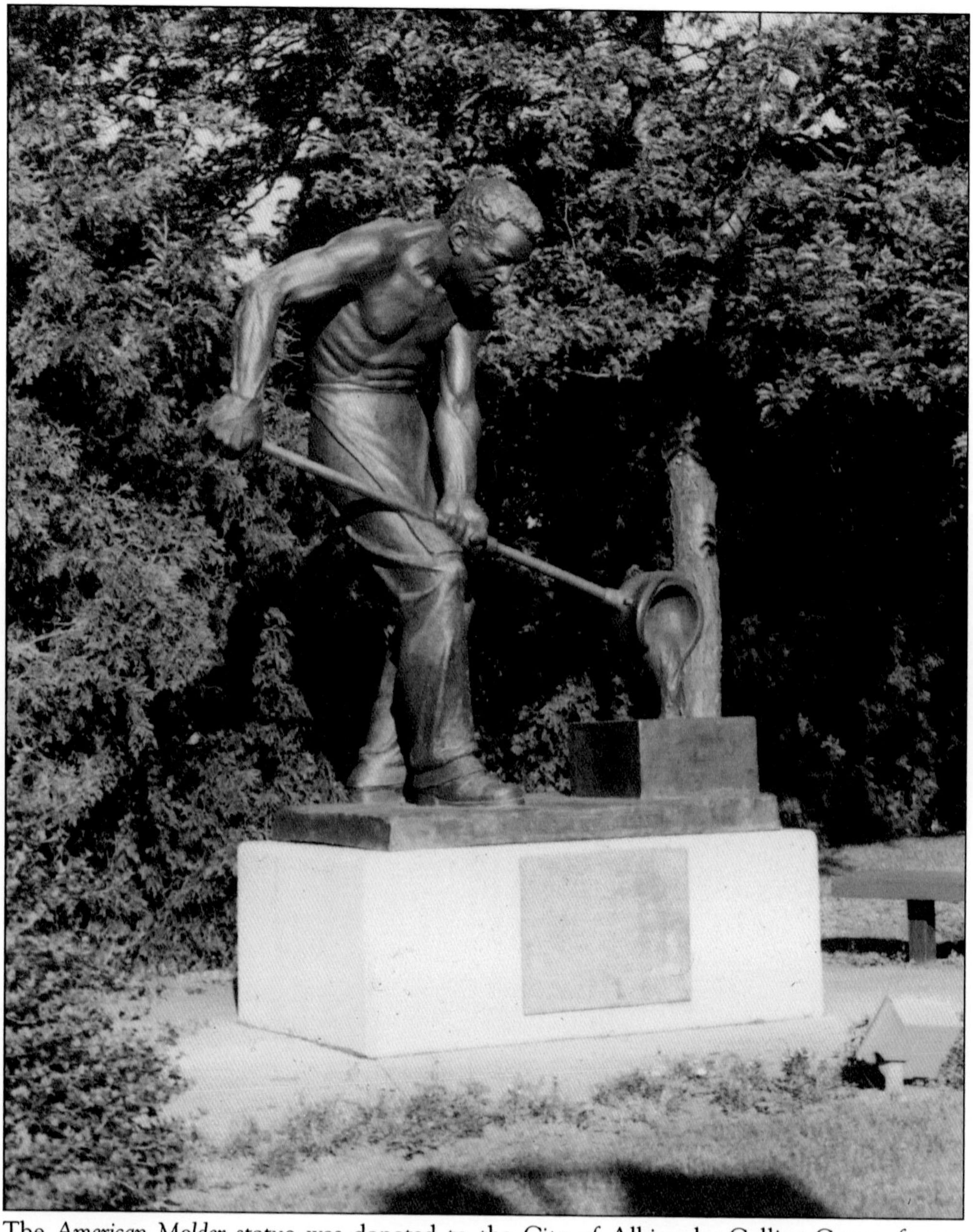

The *American Molder* statue was donated to the City of Albion by Collins Carter, former president of the Albion Malleable Iron Company and his wife Mary. It was dedicated on November 9, 1974, "as a tribute to the craftsmen and laborers of this community," as stated on the plaque below. The statue was designed by sculptor Ed Chesney, based upon an earlier creation of Frederick C. Hubbard. The casting was done by foundryman Fred Petrucci.

Molder Statue Park is located on the southwest corner of North Superior Street and West Michigan Avenue, at the entrance to downtown Albion. The plaque below contains a quote from James Russell Lowell: "No man is born unto the world of work whose work is not borne with him. There is always work and tools to work with for those who will; and blessed are the thorny hands of toil." (Photo courtesy of Gordon Pahl.)

IMAGES
*of America*

# ALBION

## IN THE 20TH CENTURY

Frank Passic

ARCADIA
PUBLISHING

ISBN 978-0-7385-1981-4

Published by Arcadia Publishing,
Charleston, South Carolina

Printed in the United States of America

Library of Congress Catalog Card Number: 2002104368

For all general information contact Arcadia Publishing at:
Telephone 843-853-2070
Fax 843-853-0044
E-mail sales@arcadiapublishing.com
For customer service and orders:
Toll-Free 1-888-313-2665

Visit us on the Internet at www.arcadiapublishing.com

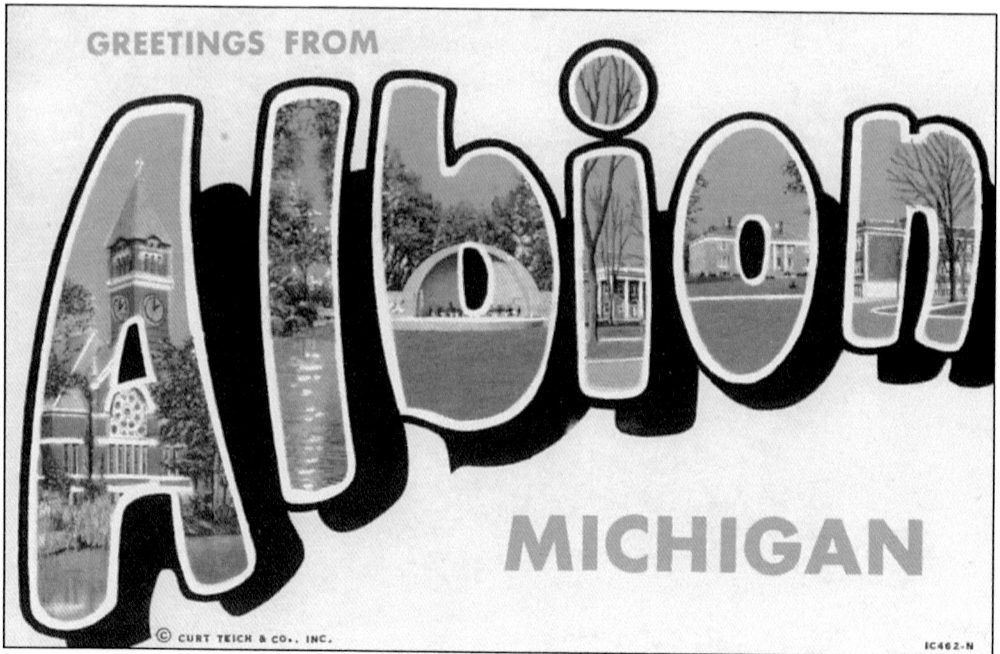


This tourist postcard from the 1940s features various Albion landmarks.

# Contents

# ACKNOWLEDGMENTS

This book has been made possible by the generous support of the citizens of Albion, who have graciously donated photographs and historical materials to this author's personal Albion history archives over the past ten years. It has enabled this author to provide a fresh blend of images that better reflect our community and its people. Not one photograph in this book has been published anywhere in this author's previous books. Also included in the mix are photographs that residents have let me borrow from their own family photograph albums especially for this work. Others have helped with photo identifications.

Such persons, businesses, and institutions who have helped make this book possible include: the Greater Albion Chamber of Commerce, the *Albion Recorder* newspaper, the City of Albion, Albion College, the Albion Public Schools, the Patrick Leo Hanlon Post No. 55 of the American Legion, Austin Professional Portraiture, Dr. Amy Bearman, Michael Bearman, Craig Brown, Cathy Campbell, James Curtis, Ulysses Curtis, Ruth (Dean) Romanchuk, Peg Eckmyre, Dave Eddy, Mike and Carol Egnatuk, David Farley, Tim Felisky, Tom and Barbara Gladney, Frances Gideon, Harvard Industries, Keith Havens, Frederick Heidenreich, Nancy Held, Gardner Lloyd, David Locke, Ralph E. Locke, Sue Marcos, Ray and Dorothy Martin, Steve Mills, Polly S. Moore, Michelle Mueller, Nina Nesselroad, Clifford C. Ott, Gordon Pahl, James Baader Pahl, Bruce Rapp, Lena Ruff, Dr. M. Rashid Saddiqui, Bernadine Sears, Jerry Sacharski, Howard Schatzberg, Barbara Shaffer, the Smithsonian Institution, Starr Commonwealth Schools, Bill Stoffer, Trillium Hospital, Jim Utter, Anne Veramay Thompson, Jack H. Vaughn, Guy Vitale, William M. Wheaton, and Lucille (Mymochod) Wickens. This author thanks you, and so do the readers of this book.

# INTRODUCTION

Albion, Michigan, was originally settled in the 1830s by pioneers from New York State. Located along Interstate-94, 100 miles west of Detroit, Albion is the home of Albion College, a four-year private liberal arts school whose roots go back to the beginning of the town.

Albion's 19th century economy was primarily based upon agriculture. One industry, the Gale Manufacturing Company, came in 1864 and began manufacturing agricultural implements. Many workers from Germany came to Albion and worked at the Gale, thus beginning the basis for Albion's diverse ethnic population. Other factories and industries were also established in the last half of the 19th century, setting the foundation for Albion's reputation as an industrial town for most of the 20th century.

The most significant factor in the growth and development of Albion in the 20th century was the presence of the Albion Malleable Iron Company from 1888 to 1967. Albion's largest employer, the Malleable produced automotive castings in the growing automotive age, and became one of the largest such concerns in the country. Many nationalities were represented in its workforce. The Malleable recruited hundreds of workers from Eastern and Southern Europe from 1900 through World War I, and many African-American workers from U.S. Southern states were recruited beginning in 1916. The Malleable initially housed its workers in company housing in the vicinity of the plant. It also assisted in their welfare by providing philanthropic aid for the establishment of churches and other worthwhile causes.

These workers established their own businesses, churches, clubs, organizations, and built their own homes throughout town. As time passed and families grew, workers at the Malleable assimilated into American life and became active in Albion civic, political, social, and religious organizations. It is in their memory and honor that we include numerous photographs of Albion Malleable workers, union officials, sports teams, ethnic churches and businesses, and related topics throughout this work.

Chapter One presents old-time photographs of what Albion looked like nearly a century ago, and features many unique views of the downtown section. Also included are photographs of several small villages surrounding Albion that have close ties to our community.

Chapter Two reveals the common bonds Albion's residents had as they participated in community life in their churches, organizations, schools, businesses, and celebrations. Several unique photographs are found in this section, dating back to the 1920s and the Great Depression era.

Chapter Three focuses on Albion's involvement in World War II, and how Albion's citizens and factories worked together to help win the War. Following the War there were a variety of activities Albion residents participated in through the booming 1950s, when Albion reached its peak in population and industrial output.

Chapter Four moves through the time of transition, when the "baby boomer" generation grew up during the 1960s and 1970s, and economic and business changes were occurring locally. Chapter Five brings the reader into the 21st Century, featuring recent occurrences in Albion's history that are worth noting for future generations.

Several persons from Albion that gained state or national notoriety in their lifetimes are featured throughout the book. Readers will also discover several "collectable objects" illustrated in various places, such as pool hall tokens, food stamp tokens, banknotes, dog tags, and milk bottles and caps. These serve as nostalgic mementos of the period.

Although there are a variety of historical buildings illustrated throughout the book, the reader will find that the emphasis however is upon the citizens of 20th century Albion who lived, worked, played, and raised their families here. Individuals have been identified wherever possible, and the numerous group photographs found in this book provide a healthy mix of Albion's ethnic diversity. Readers wishing to learn more about Albion history are welcome to visit the www.albionmich.com web site for further information.

—Frank Passic, Albion Historian. April 2002.

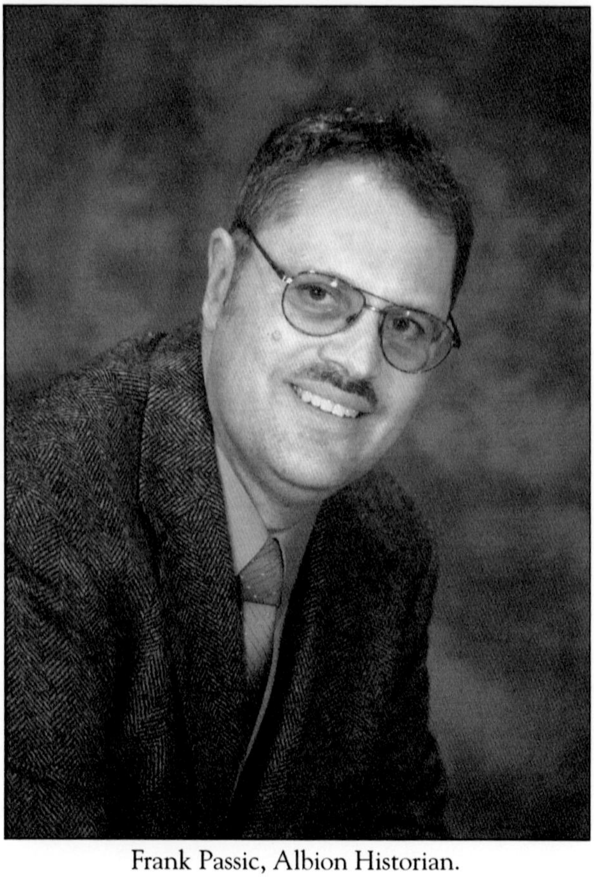

Frank Passic, Albion Historian.

# *One*

# Old Albion

## 1900–1919

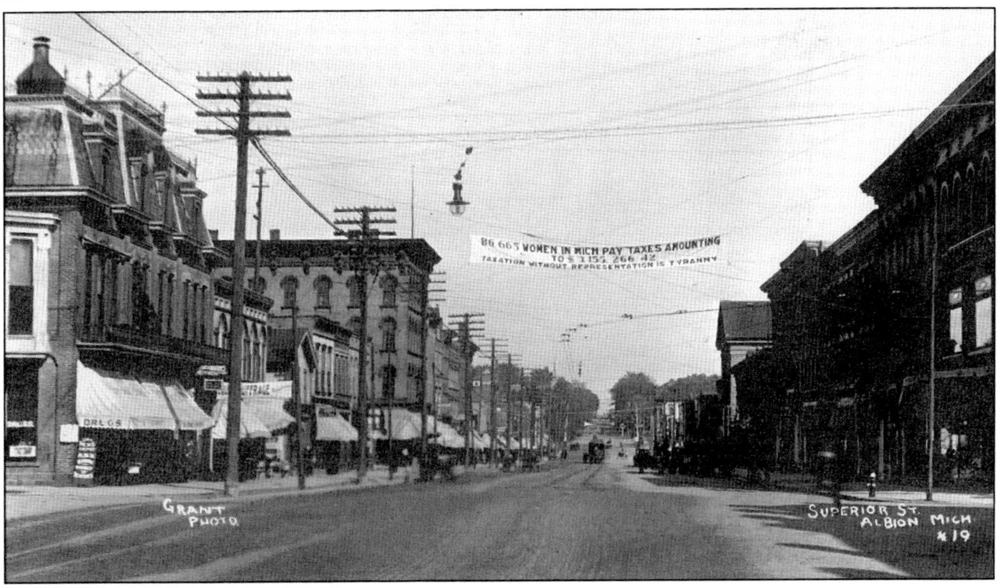


Albion's women banded together in the fall of 1912 and formed a "Suffrage Campaign" in their quest for the right to vote. A large banner (enlarged above) was hung across Superior St, which stated, "86,665 WOMEN IN MICH PAY TAXES AMOUNTING TO $3,155,266.42. TAXATION WITHOUT REPRESENTATION IS TYRANNY." An "EQUAL SUFFRAGE HEADQUARTERS" banner appears in front of the florist shop of the Dysinger sisters, located on the left at 314 South Superior Street.

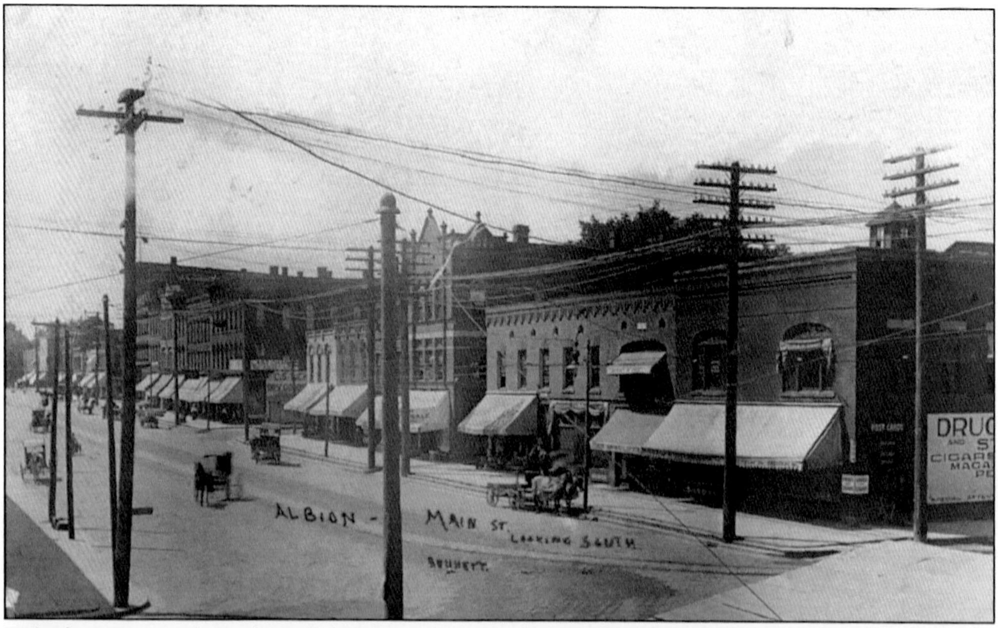


Telephone wires abound while horse and buggies roam the west side of the 100 block of South Superior Street, c. 1908. On the right corner (100) is the Homer Blair Drug Store; followed left by (102) Walter Rogers Shoes; (104) John McAuliffe Meat Market with Harvey Sweet Optician upstairs; (106) unidentified; (108) William H. Rodenbach Grocery; and across the alley, (112) the Morse Clothing store with the Michigan Bell Telephone Company upstairs.

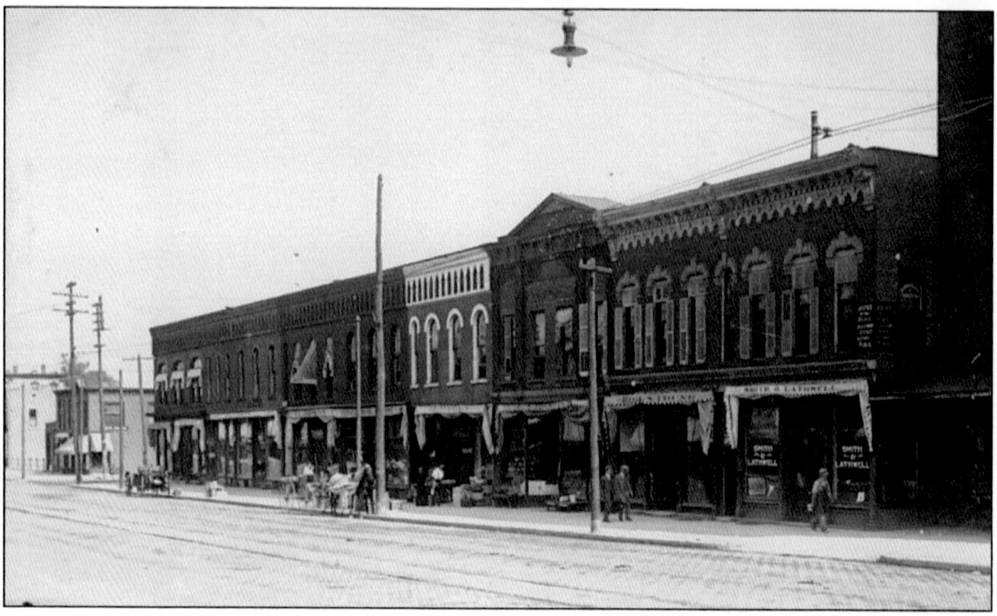

Businesses were thriving on the east side of the 100 block of South Superior Street, c. 1908. Starting from the left corner are: (101-103) Wochholz & Gress Grocers; (105-107) George P. Griffin Hardware; (109) E.C. Carrington Grocery; (111) Randall Novelty store; (113) Sibley & Clark Grocery; (115) Edgar J. Emmons Grocery in the old fire station (peaked roof); (117) Hill & Young Shoes; (119) Smith & Lathwell Tailors; and (119) Arza McCutcheon, real estate.

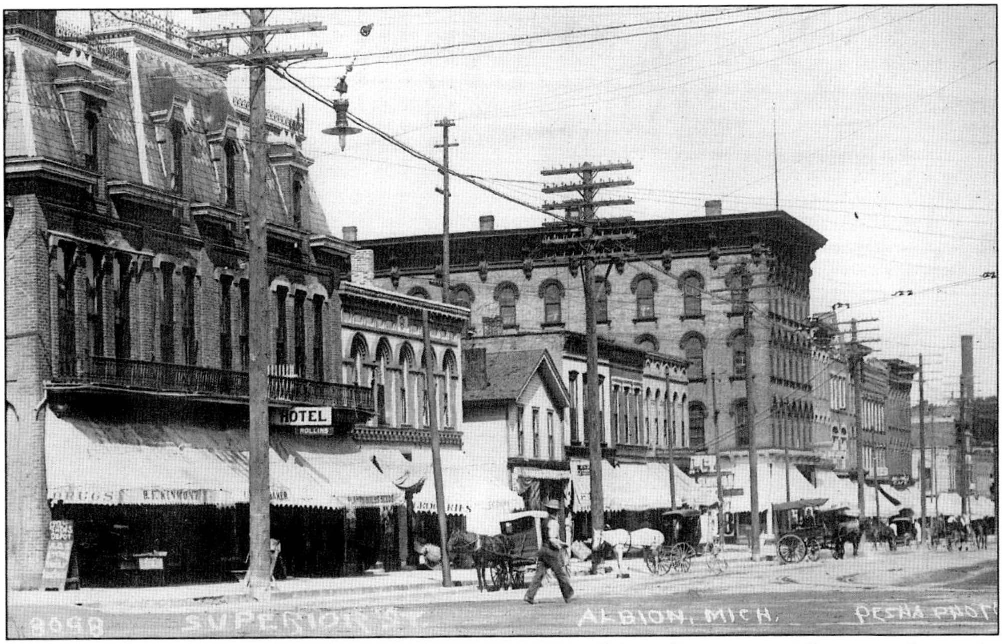


Utility and overhead interurban wires were once plentiful in downtown Albion, as shown in this 1915 photograph of the west side of the 300 block of South Superior Street. The Bruce Kinmont Drugstore is located on the left in the Sheldon Block, with the Rollins Hotel upstairs. Notice that horse and buggies still reigned as the primary transportation in town.

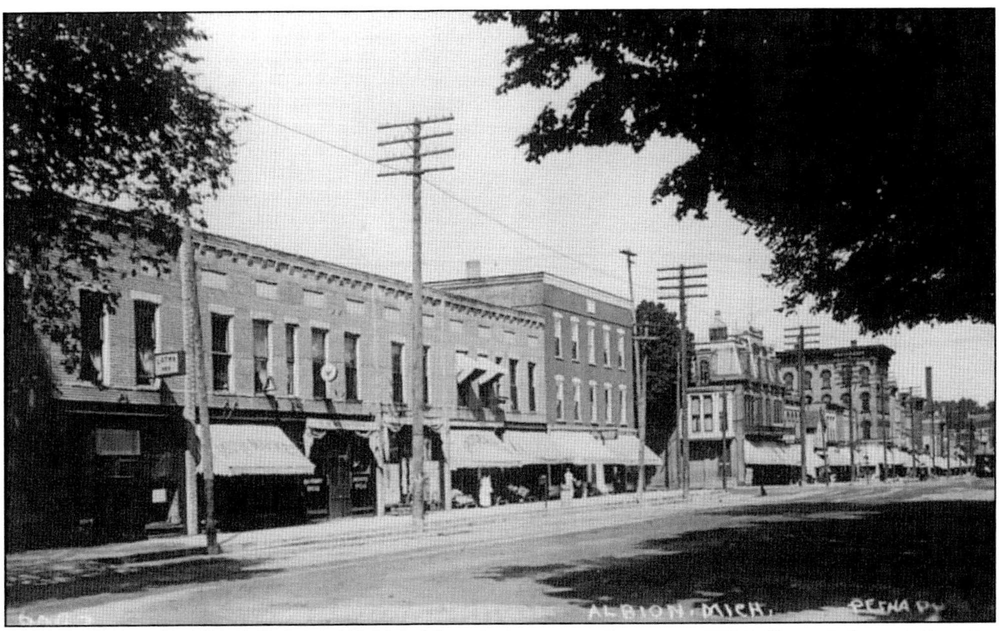


This is the west side of the 400 block of South Superior Street, *c.* 1908. From left to right, the businesses are as follows: (414) Albert Thornton, photographer; (412) South Market; (410) Mounteer's Bakery; (408) unidentified; (406) Ben Franklin Grocery; (404) Franklin & Davis Grocery; (402) People's Cash Grocery; and (400) Mounteer's Bakery on the corner, twice in the block.

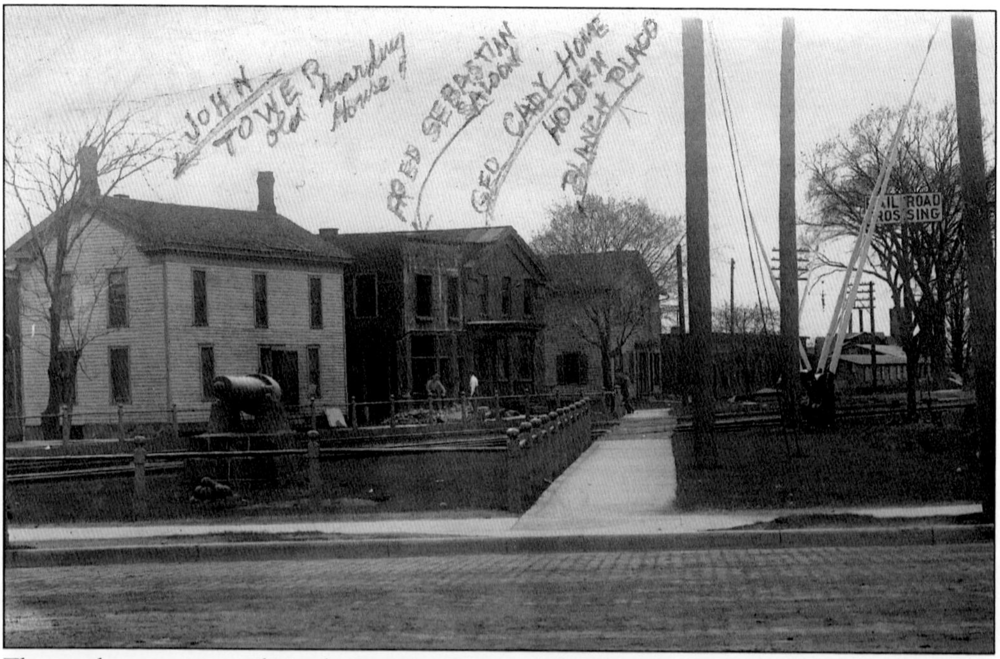


The southwest corner of North Superior Street and Michigan Avenue, along the Michigan Central Railroad tracks, was once known as Cannon Park. The Civil War cannon can be seen in this 1912 photograph. It was later moved to the Albion National Guard Armory on North Clark Street. In the distance, from left to right are: the John Tower Boarding House, the Sebastian Saloon/Restaurant, the George Cady home, and the Blanche Holden Tavern.

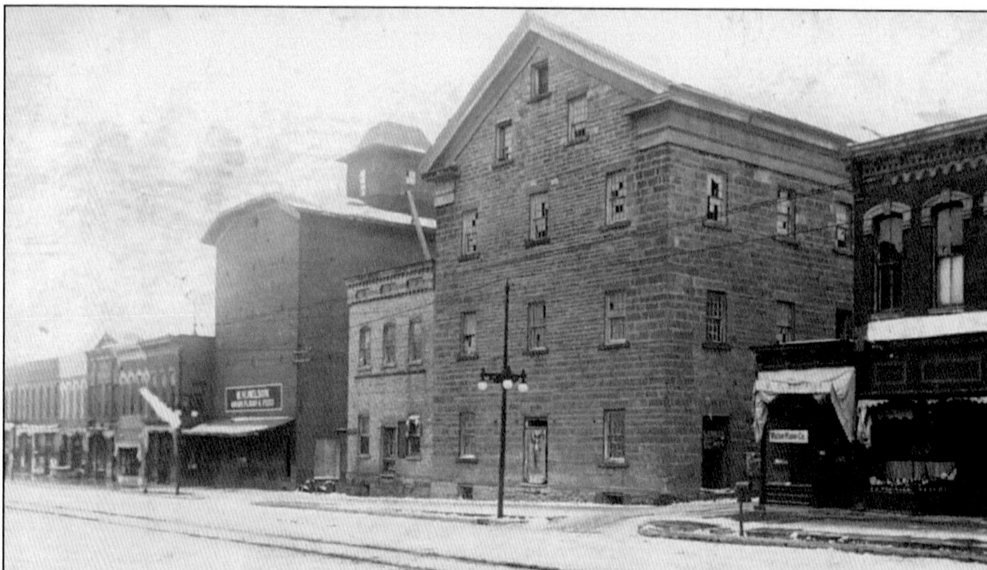

The landmark Stone Mill was erected in 1845 by Jesse Crowell. The structure was remodeled into the Commercial & Savings Bank, which opened on January 1, 1917. The small building on the right was the original location of the Byron D. Robinson Jewelers, which bears a "Victor Piano Co." sign in the window. The new Robinson location is next door on the right. The large Nelson Albion Elevator building (left) was moved eastwards in 1917.

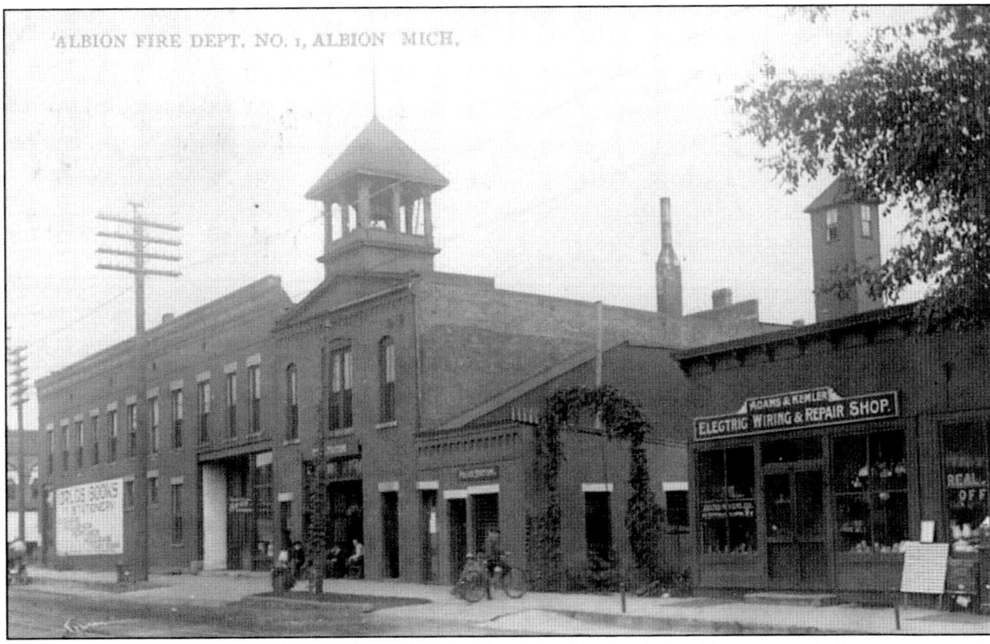


Albion's city offices were located on the south side of West Cass Street until the present City Hall complex opened in 1936 across the street. The fire station (the building with the tower) was originally a warehouse for the Gale Manufacturing Company. The police station was attached on the right. The complex was demolished in the summer of 1958 to make way for a parking lot. On the right is the Adams & Kemler Electric Shop, followed by a real estate establishment. This photo is from c. 1915.

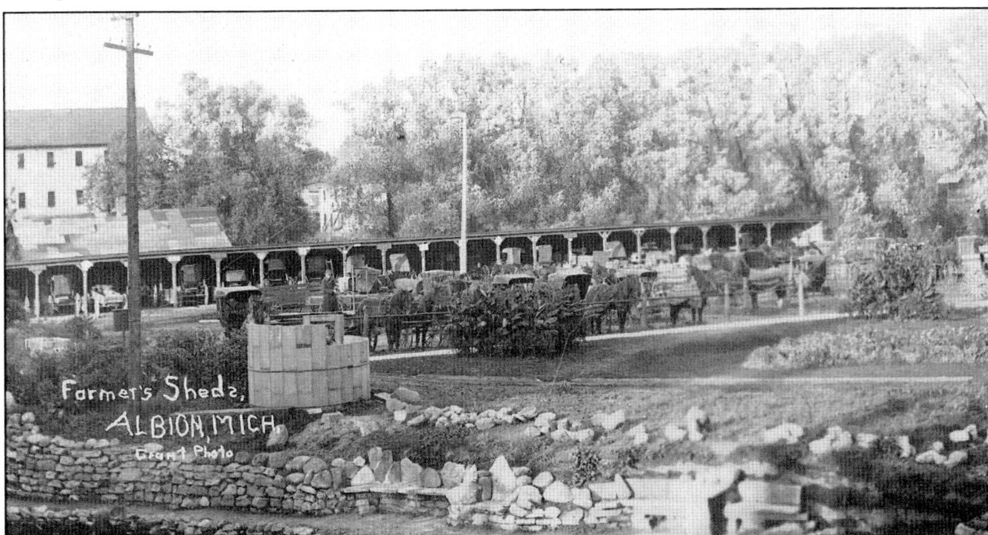


A Farmers Market was begun in the Market Place in 1900 and still operates today on the site known as Stoffer Plaza. Farmers would bring their produce into town to sell, and park their wagons in the sheds while doing business in downtown Albion. This scene from c. 1910 shows the horse-watering trough, with the raceway of the Kalamazoo River flowing from the Commonwealth Power House below. In the distance are the sheds, with the White Mill on the far left.

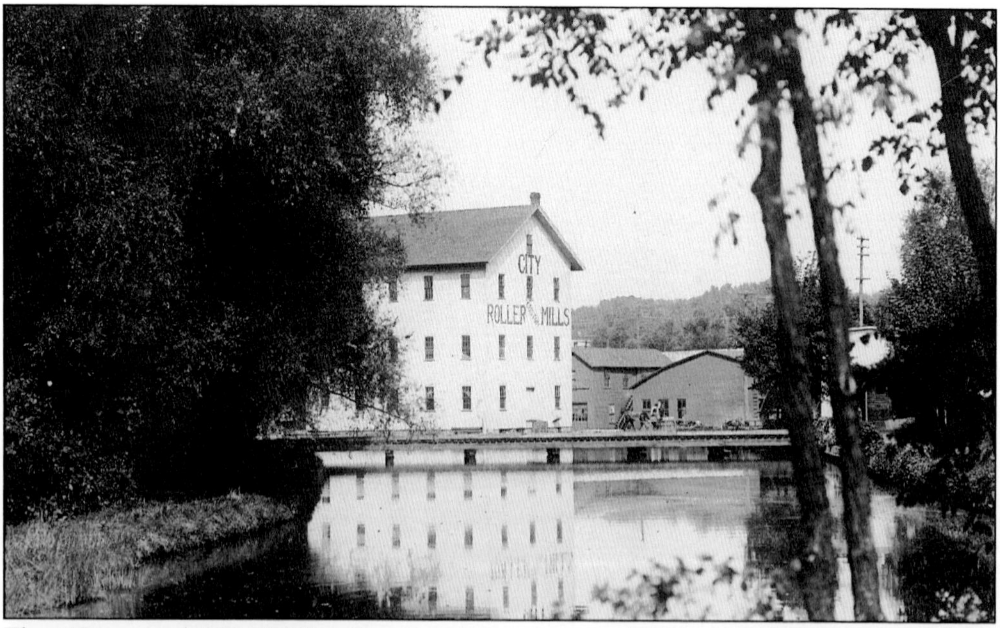


The 1876-erected White Mill on East Cass Street was an Albion landmark for many years, and produced "Victor" brand flour. The Mill was Albion's last water-powered business, and closed on August 24, 1957. The building was demolished in 1974, and Lloyd Park was subsequently erected on the site. This picturesque view, c. 1910, looks north from the Porter Street footbridge. It shows the Mill in the distance, and its reflection in the water below. In front is a railroad spur (removed in December 1948) that led to the Albion Elevator.

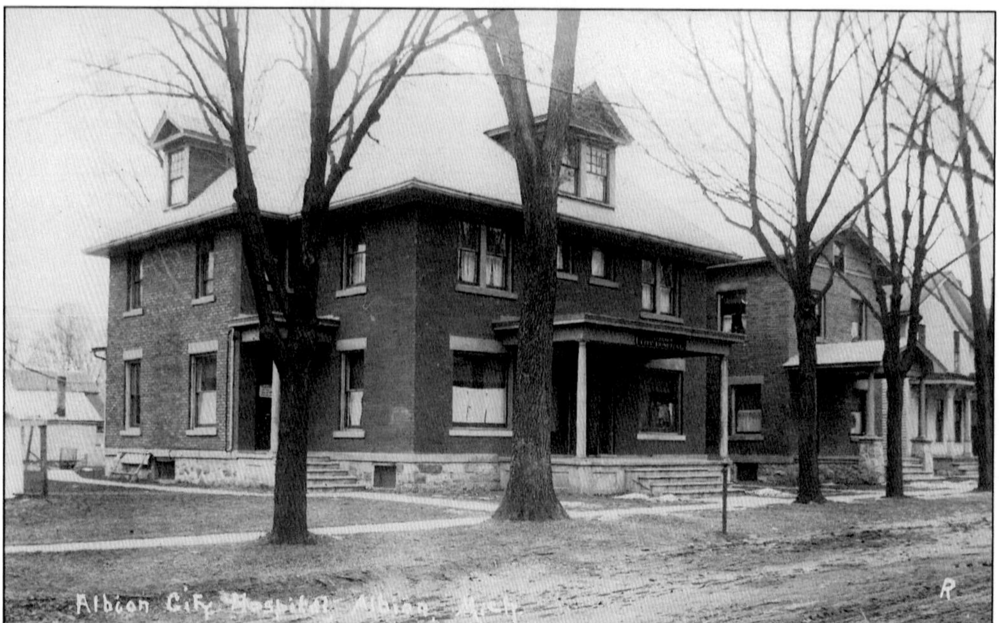


The Albion City Hospital was located at 111–113 West Ash Street from December 1910 until the James W. Sheldon Memorial Hospital opened in May 1924. The house on the right (115) was purchased as an annex in 1912 and used as the nurses' training school until 1921.

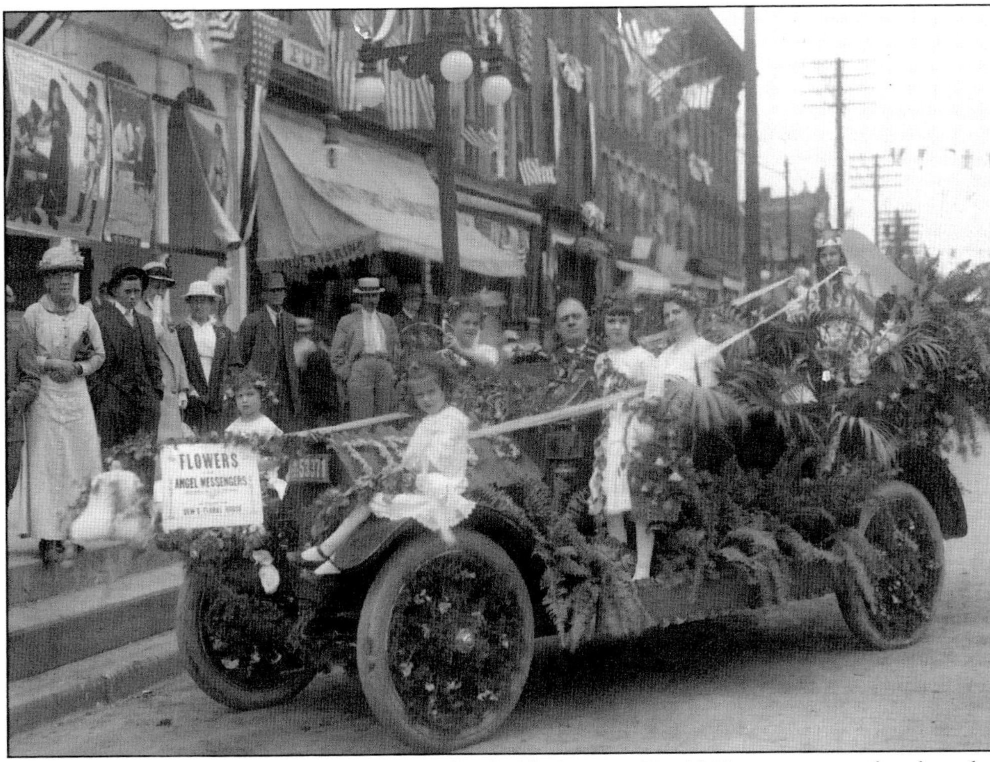



The Albion College Homecoming Parade, held August 20, 1915, was part of a four-day celebration by the entire community, which featured numerous floats, bands, and various events. The "Angels Messengers" float of Dews Flowers is shown here, parked in front of the Bijou Theatre. The adults in the auto are florist Arthur Dew (1873–1950) and his wife Eliza (1873–1953). Their daughter Gwendolyn Dew (1903–1993) is seated in the rumble seat, dressed as an angel with wings.

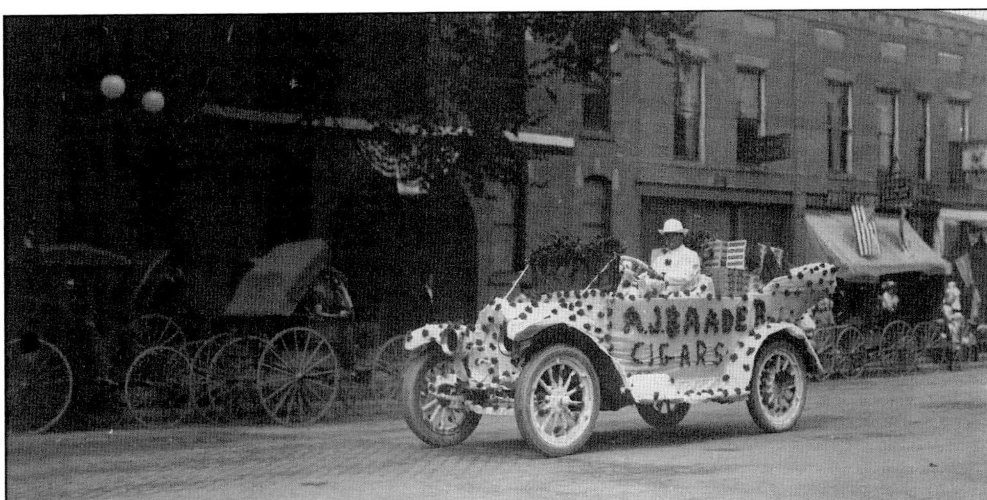



August J. Baader (1863–1939) operated a cigar-making firm in Albion from 1894 to 1939, and employed up to 15 persons. He is shown riding solo in this 1915 homecoming parade float, which features stacks of cigar boxes in back. (Photo courtesy of James Baader Pahl.)

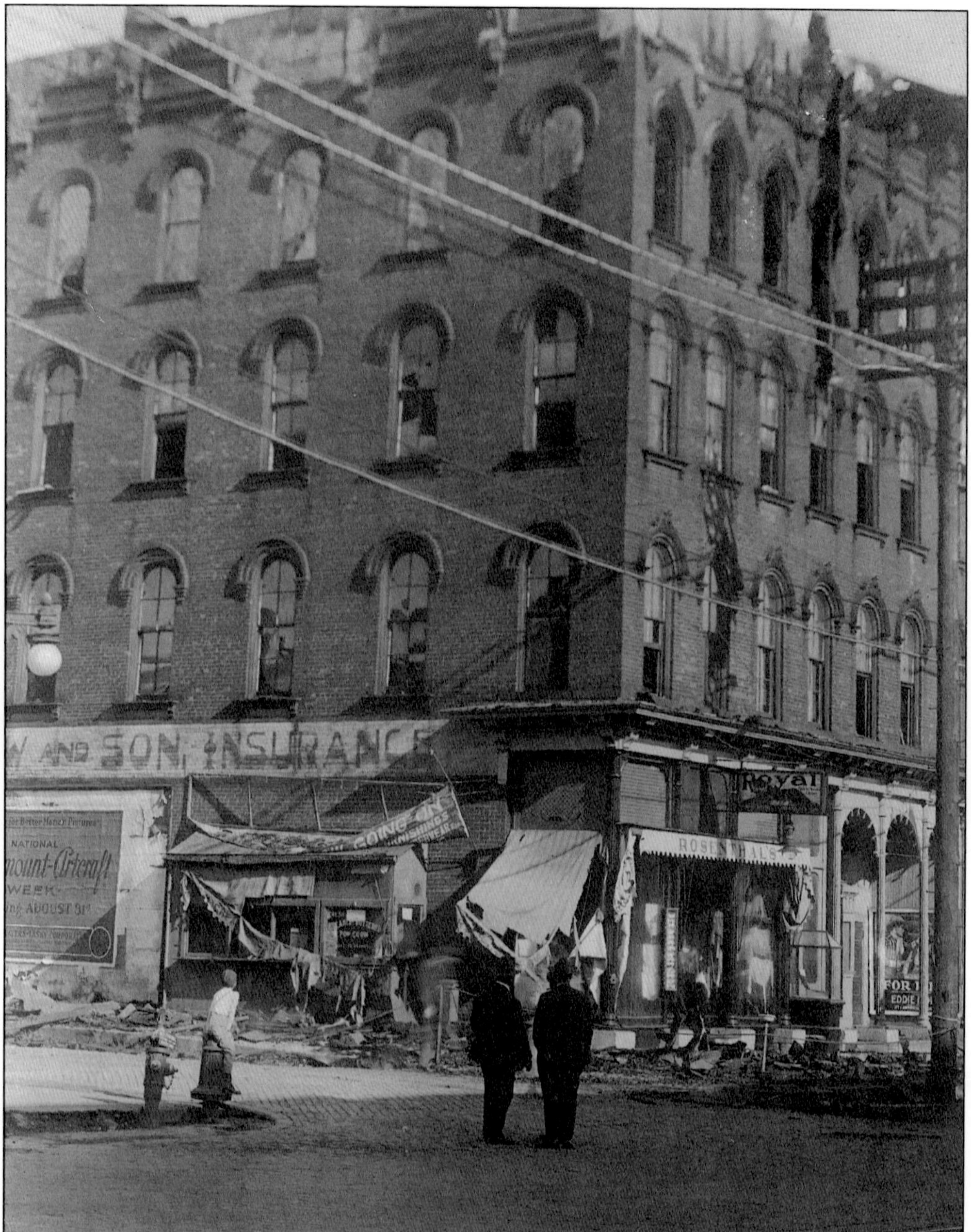


The four-story Eslow Block, at 214–218 South Superior Street, suffered a major fire on August 31, 1919. Fueled by a strong draft from an elevator shaft, the fire began about 3 p.m. on the second floor, during the showing of the film *For Life* in the Bijou Theatre below. A half-ton elevator balance weight came crashing through the ceiling amidst the front row seats occupied by children. A near riot erupted as nearly 200 patrons attempted to flee out the front door. Miraculously, no one was hurt. Over 4,000 feet of hose was used by the Albion Fire Department to put out the fire. The fourth story was subsequently removed. Here, onlookers view the remains of the Rosenthal Clothing store and the Bijou Theatre. On the left is a small "popcorn" newsstand that used to sit at the side of the building. (Photo courtesy of the Albion Department of Public Safety.)

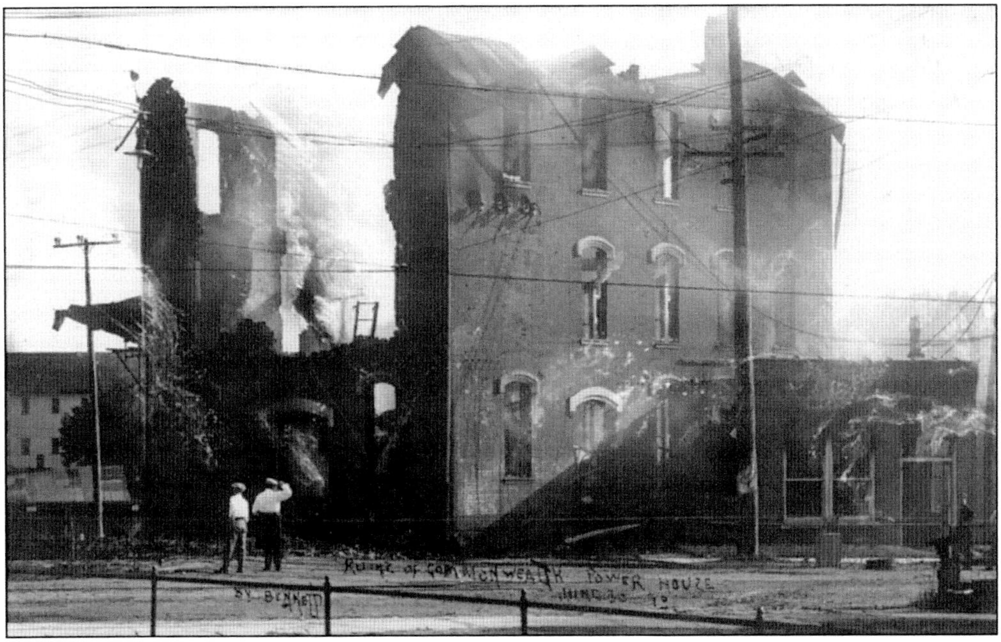


The Commonwealth Power Company water-powered electric generating station on East Erie Street was destroyed by fire on June 30, 1913, causing over $100,000 in damage. The building had been erected in 1883 as a flour mill, and was a prominent Albion landmark for many years.

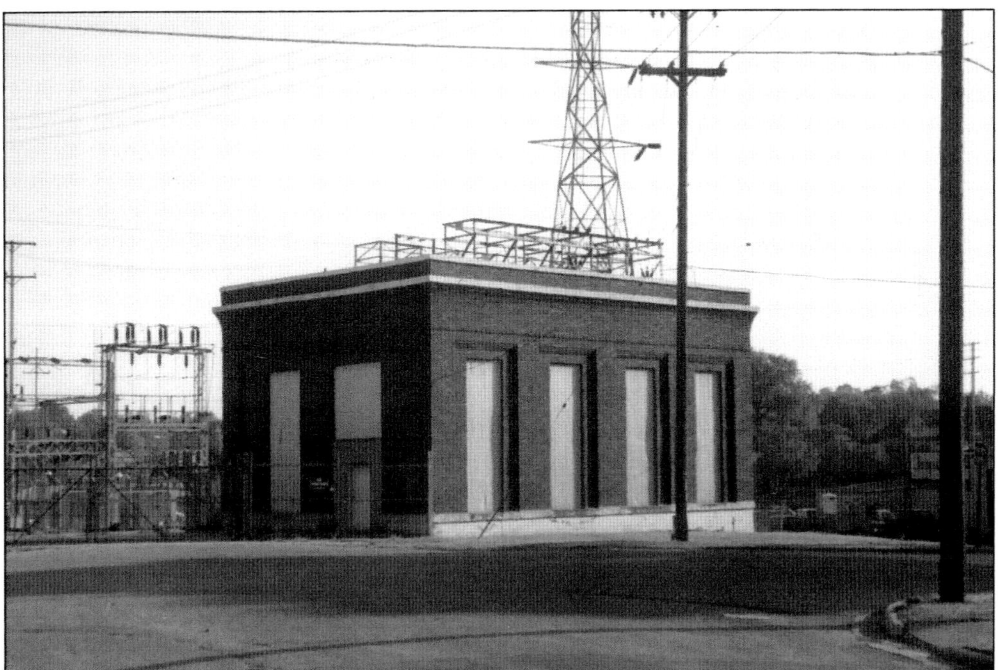

This building replaced the original electric "Power House" that burned in 1913. It was used as an electric water-powered generating station until shortly after World War II. It was subsequently used as an electric power substation by Consumers Power Company until it was abandoned in 1993. The photo was taken in 1993.

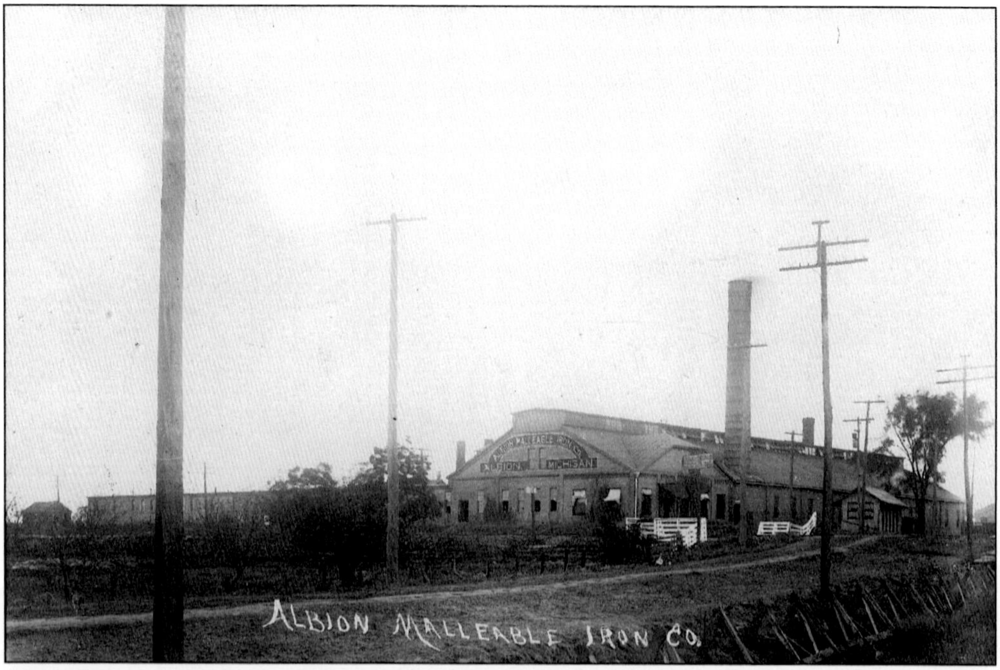


The Albion Malleable Iron Company moved into its new quarters on North Albion Street in 1897. This 1909 photograph of the plant looks northwards from unpaved North Albion Street. The Michigan Central Railroad tracks are located between the white fences.

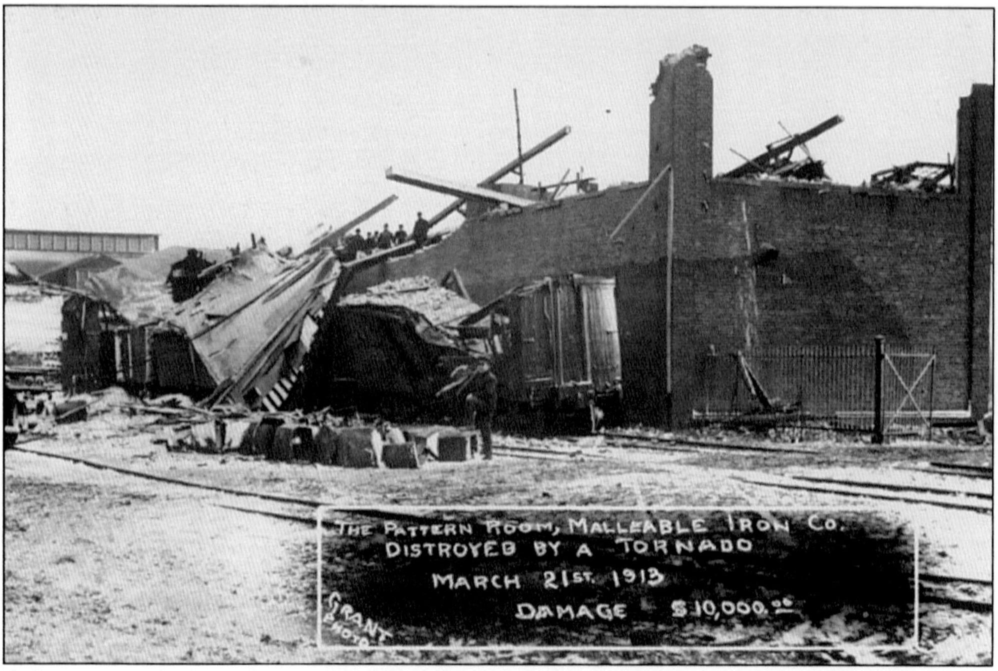


Calamity struck the Albion Malleable Iron Company on March 21, 1913, when a tornado destroyed the pattern room at the plant. The damaged exceeded $10,000. Workmen stand on top of the remains of the building, observing the damage and the crushed rail cars below.

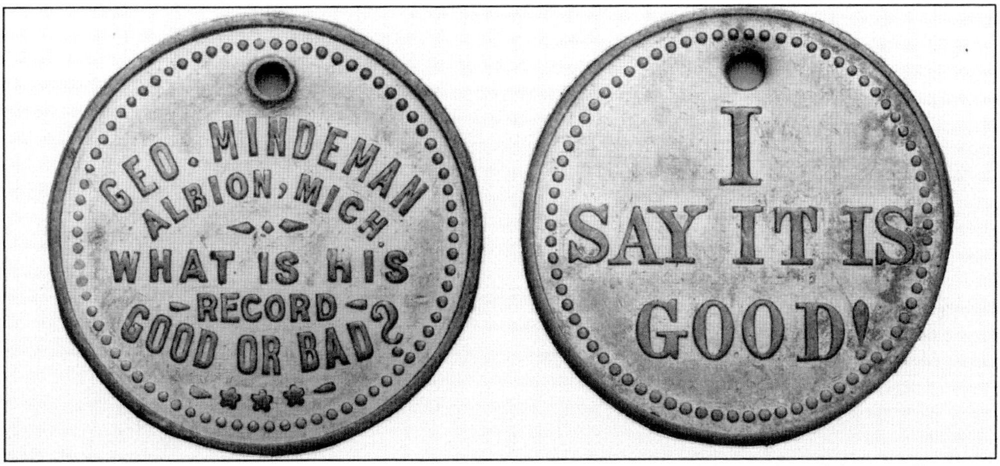


George Mindeman came to Albion in 1907 to raise funds to build a railroad from Albion to Charlotte. The following year he was convicted of stealing $2,050 worth of diamonds and earrings from Mrs. Sarah (Huxford) Murdock. The conviction was overturned on a technicality, and in a new 1909 trial Mindeman was acquitted of the charges. He thereby issued and distributed this unusual 29-mm diameter aluminum token to clear his name.

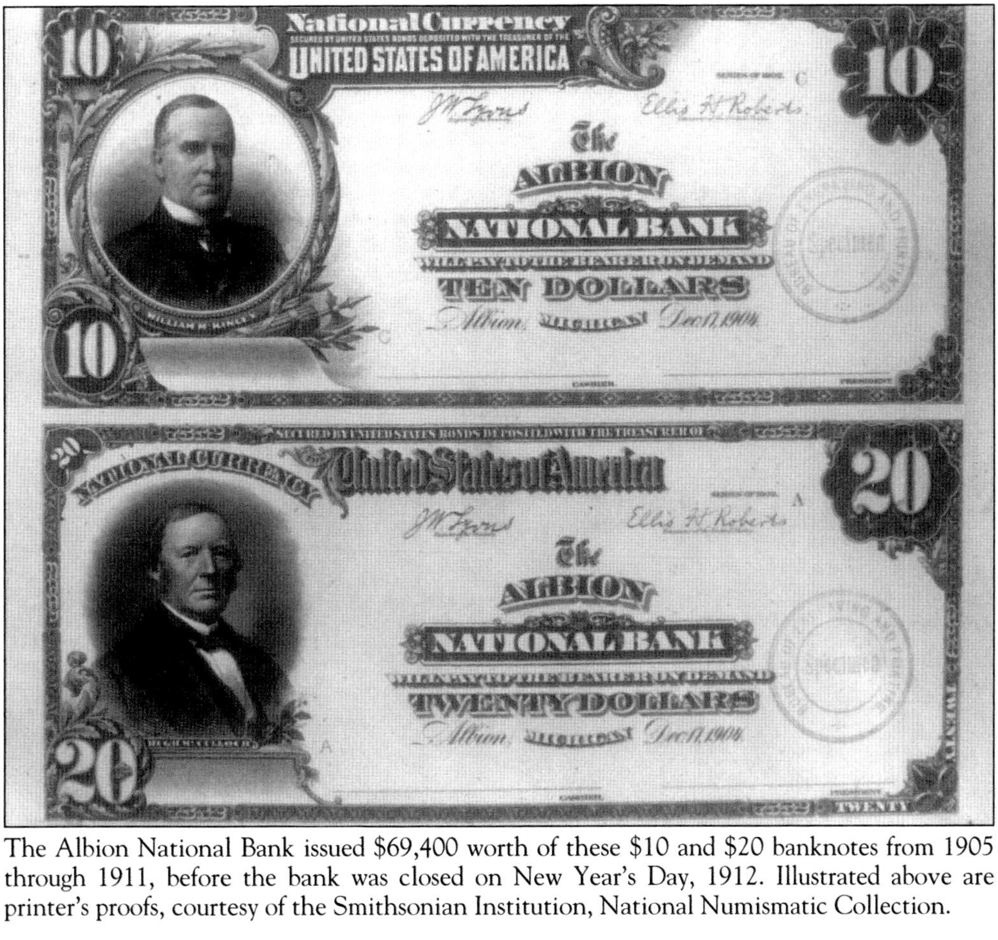


The Albion National Bank issued $69,400 worth of these $10 and $20 banknotes from 1905 through 1911, before the bank was closed on New Year's Day, 1912. Illustrated above are printer's proofs, courtesy of the Smithsonian Institution, National Numismatic Collection.

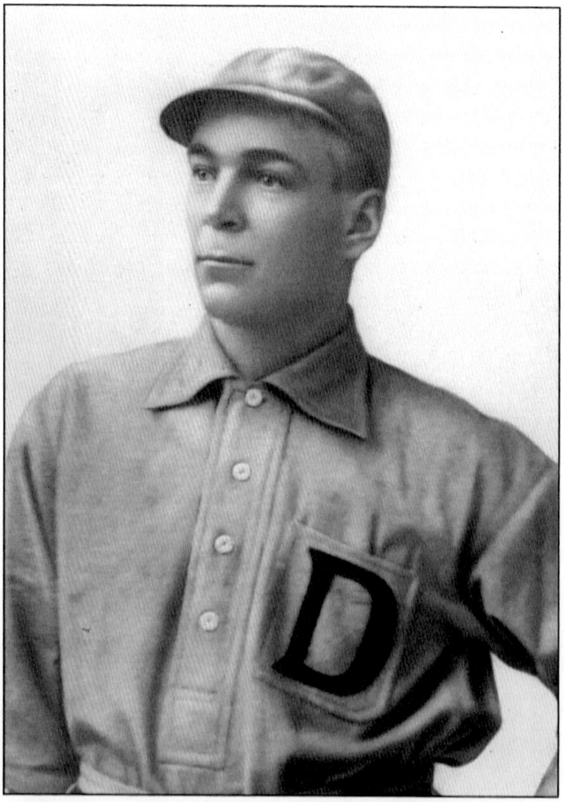

James T. "Deacon" McGuire (1863–1936) was a professional baseball player for 26 years. He set a record for catching in every inning of 132 games played by the Washington Nationals in 1895. McGuire played for the Detroit Tigers in 1903 and in 1912. He lived in Albion and during the off-season operated the McGuire Brothers Saloon with his brother George (1858–1943).

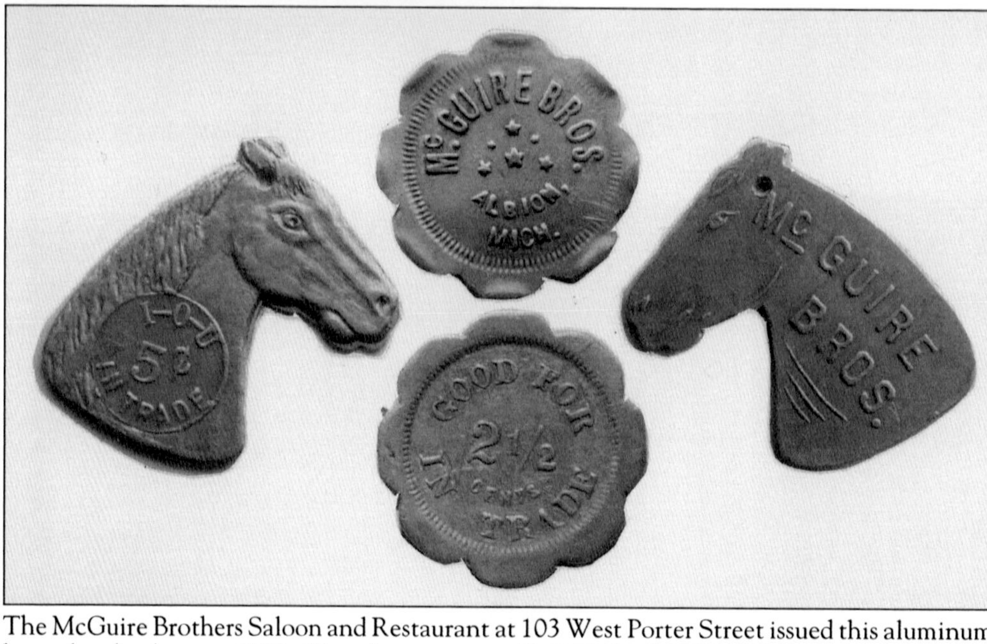


The McGuire Brothers Saloon and Restaurant at 103 West Porter Street issued this aluminum horse-head token, c. 1912. The obverse states "I-O-U 5¢ IN TRADE," while the reverse declares "McGUIRE BROS." In the center is a token with the unusual denomination of 2 1/2¢, also issued by the firm.

Lynn Bogue Hunt (1878–1960) was one of this country's greatest periodical wildlife artists. An 1897 graduate of Albion High School, Hunt studied art at Albion College. He went on to draw wildlife scenes for the covers of national magazines such as *Better Homes and Gardens*, *Colliers*, *Field & Stream*, and the *Saturday Evening Post*. Hunt illustrated more than 50 books in his lifetime. He designed the 1939 Migratory Waterfowl stamp, 19 National Wildlife Federation stamps, and numerous works for Ducks Unlimited. This is a 1909 photo.

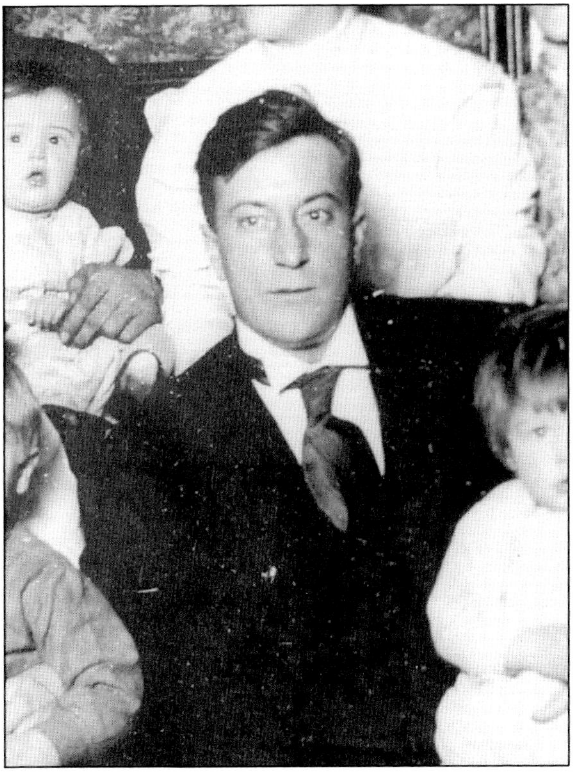

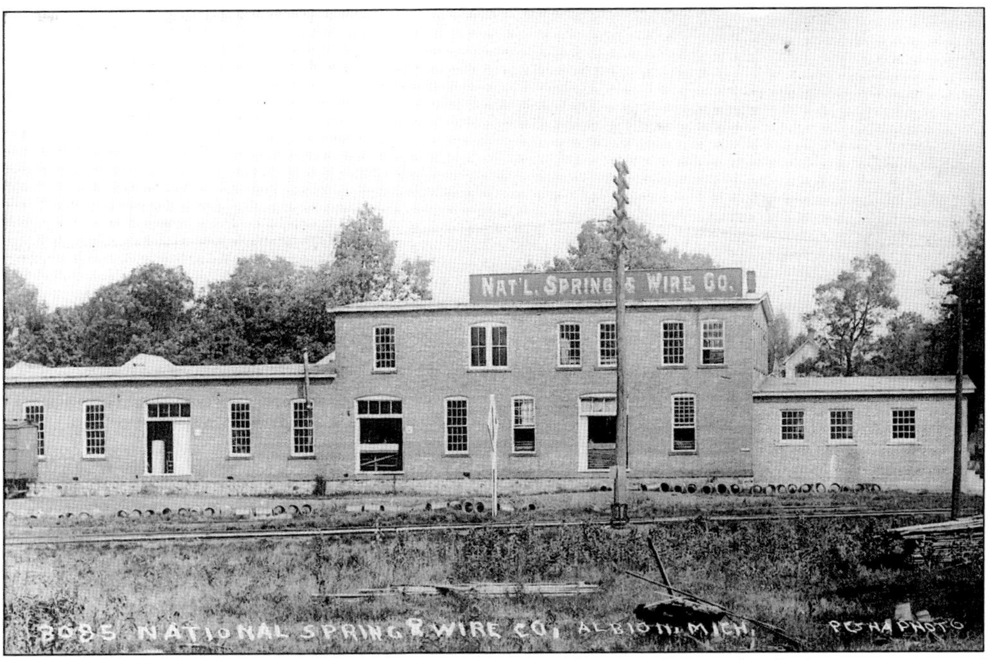


The National Spring and Wire Company manufactured automobile and upholstering springs of all types in Albion from 1902 until the early 1920s. This view, c. 1912, depicts the plant on the northwest corner of East Mulberry and North Berrien Streets. The tracks of the Lake Shore & Michigan Southern Railroad are in the foreground.

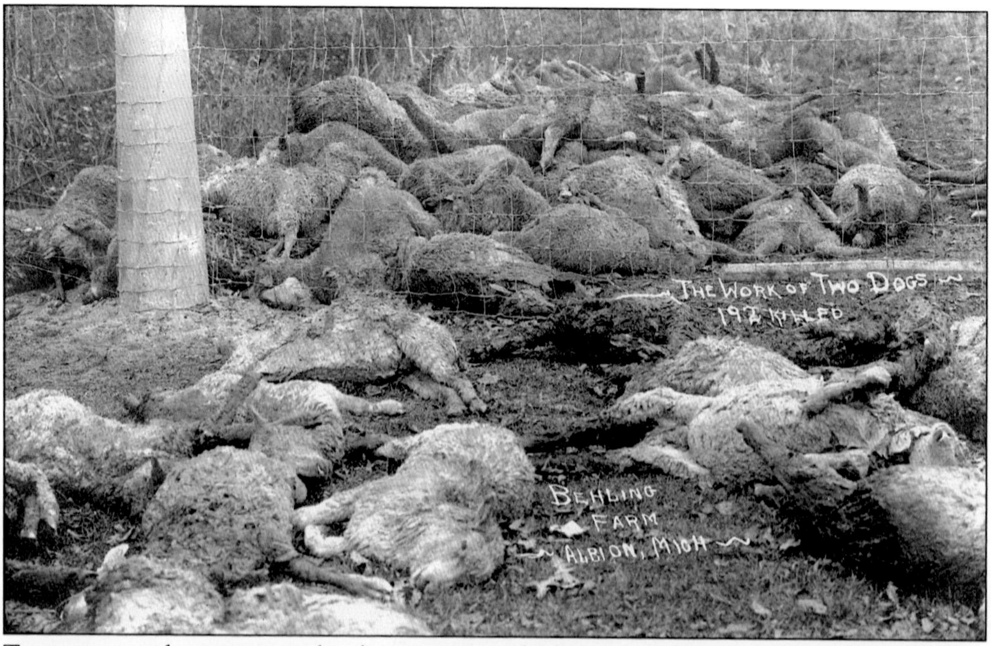


Two ravaging dogs ran into the sheep pasture of Albert C. Behling on West Erie Street on the night of November 13, 1913. They chased his flock under a fence into a "V" shaped ditch near the Kalamazoo River. The panic-stricken sheep were smothered as they jumped upon each other in order to try and escape the dogs. One hundred ninety-two sheep were killed in this manner. The huge pile of dead sheep created an instant tourist attraction and made news headlines across the state.

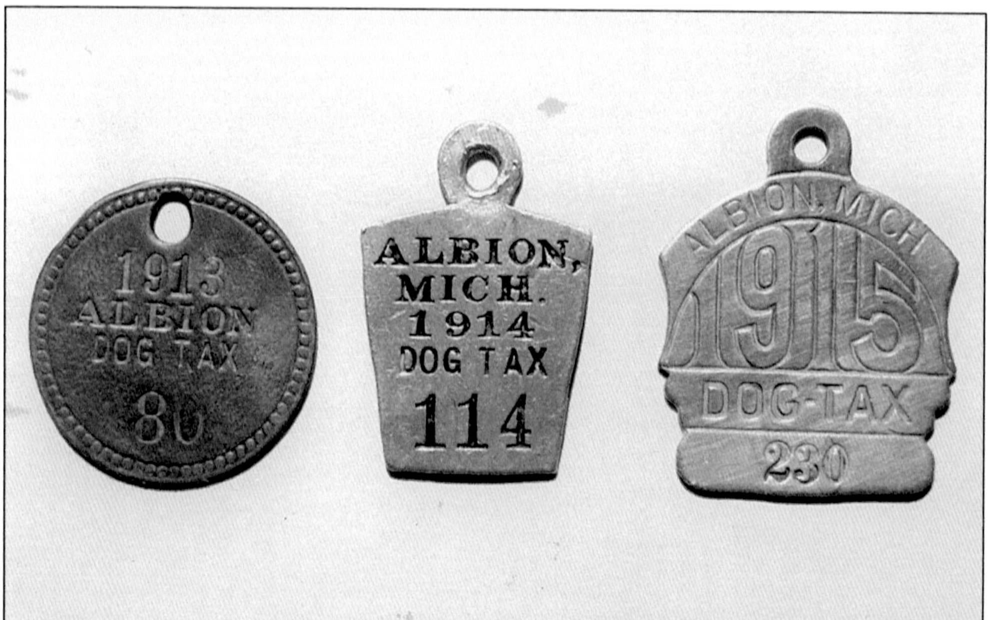


Even the dogs in Albion had to pay taxes, if you believe these "Dog Tax" tags of 1913, 1914, and 1915. These were issued during the 1910s in a variety of sizes and shapes.

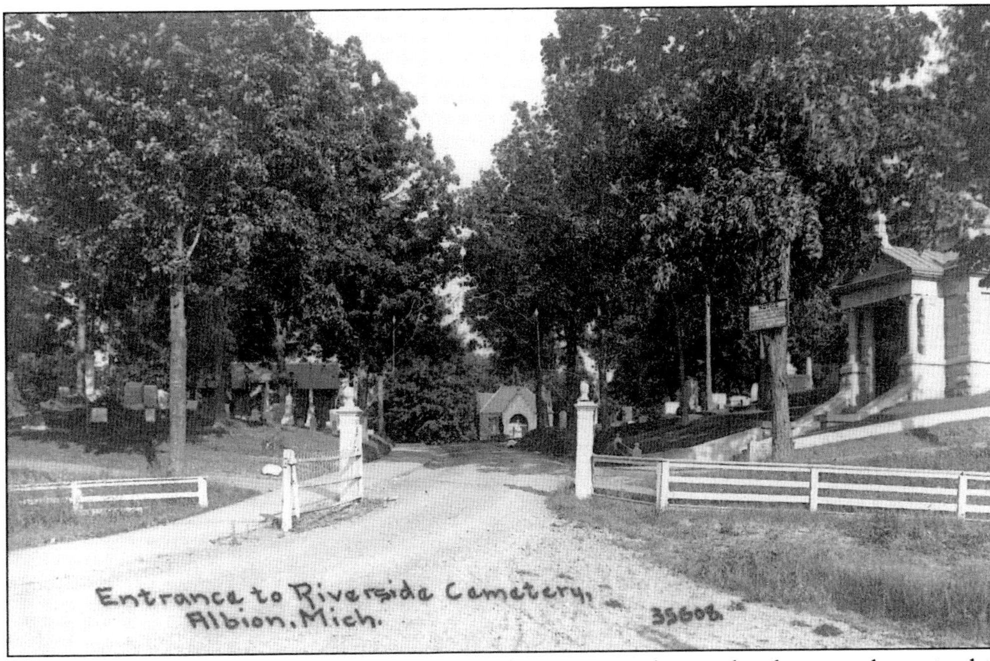


Riverside Cemetery was once enclosed by a gated entrance and a wooden fence, as shown in this c. 1913 photo. The small sign posted to the tree on the right states, "NOTICE. ALL PERSONS ARE FORBIDDEN TO WILLFULLY PLUCK FLOWERS OR TO DISTURB OR INJURE PROPERTY ON THESE GROUNDS UNDER PENALTY."

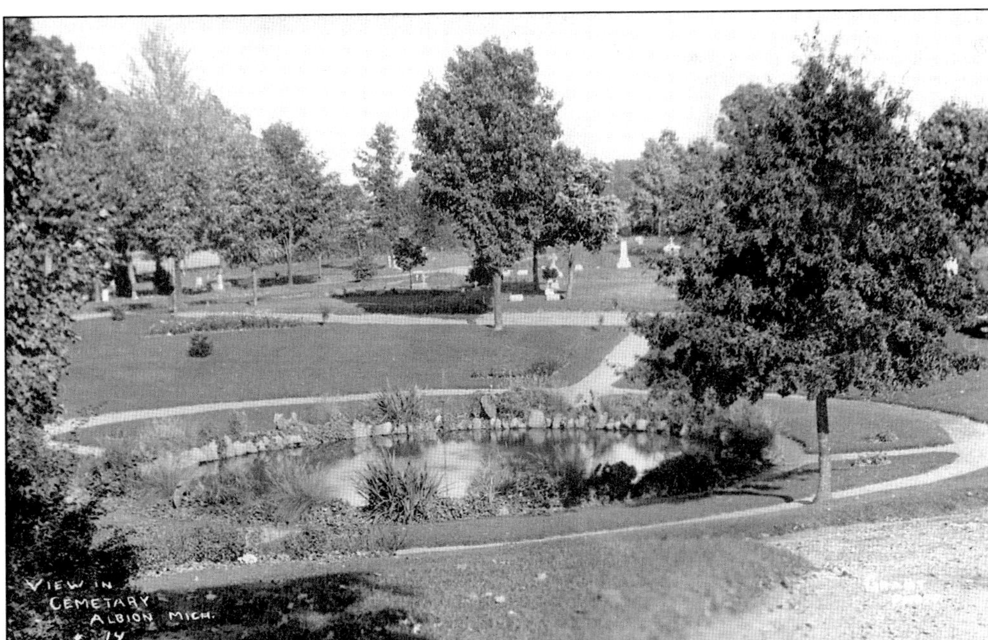


A decorative fishpond was constructed in Riverside Cemetery in May 1902 by Sexton Otto Pahl and his brother F. Albert Pahl. Goldfish were placed in the water, and a circular sidewalk surrounded the pond. This photo is c. 1913.

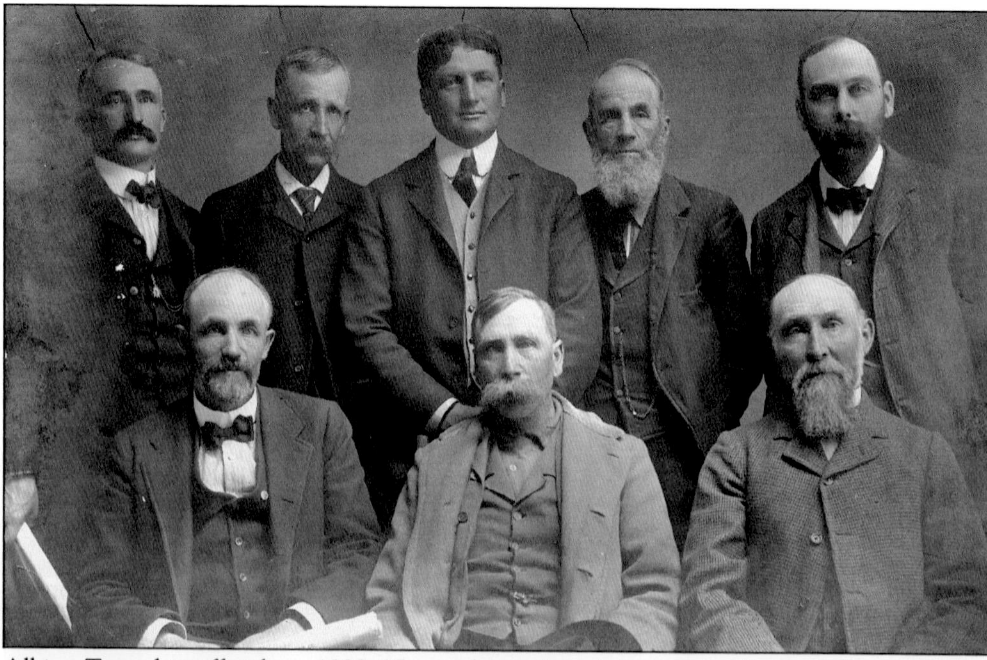

Albion Township officials, *c.* 1900–05, are shown from left to right: (front row) Commodore Perry Belcher (1851–1935), William Ed Ansterburg (1856–1943), and William Anderson (1847–1921); (back row) bridge engineer Robert Raymond (1867–1918), clerk Delos D. Snyder (1844–1933), unidentified, Justice of the Peace Wesley Snyder (1834–1915), and unidentified.

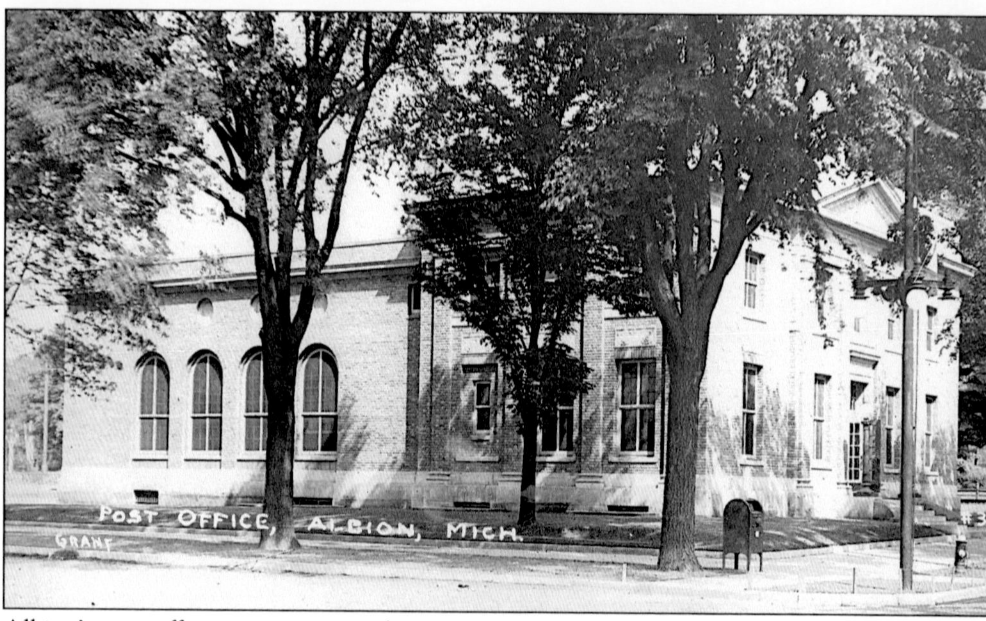


Albion's post office was constructed in 1916-17 under the supervision of Lowell W. Baker (1869–1933). At the time, Mr. Baker was the only African American to ever hold the rank of government consulting engineer. The cost of the project was $70,000. The large stately elm trees in front were typical of many which once lined the streets of Albion until Dutch elm disease wiped out the species in the 1960s.

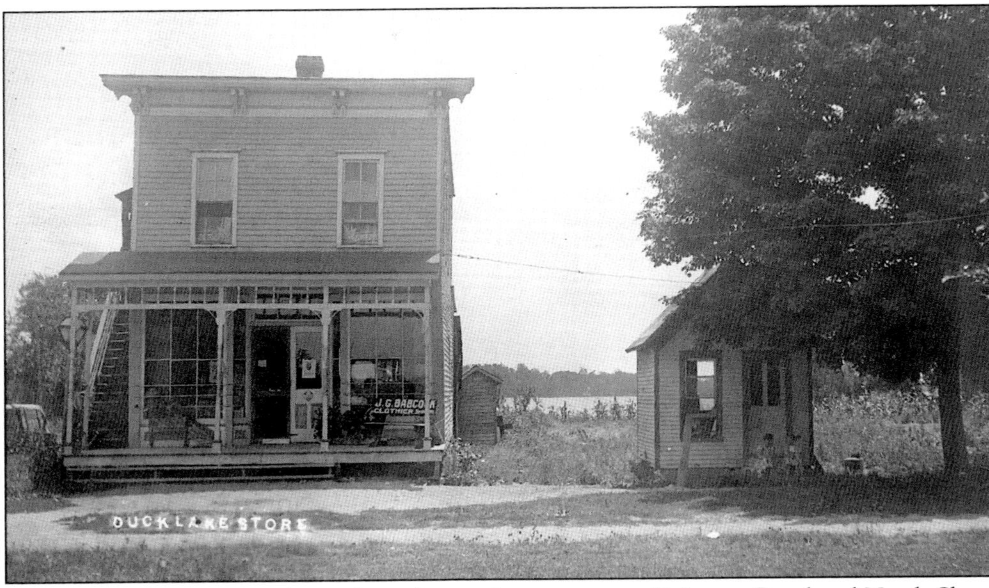


The Duck Lake Store was located on the southwest corner of Monroe Road and North Shore Drive, as shown in this 1911 photograph. This general store was operated by Betsey (Monroe) Leonard (1838–1914). Her husband William H. Leonard (1840–1919) served as Duck Lake postmaster from 1889 to 1893, and the post office was located here during that time. The advertisement on the bench states "J.G. BABCOCK, Clothier, Springport." The small building on the right was Duck Lake's barbershop.

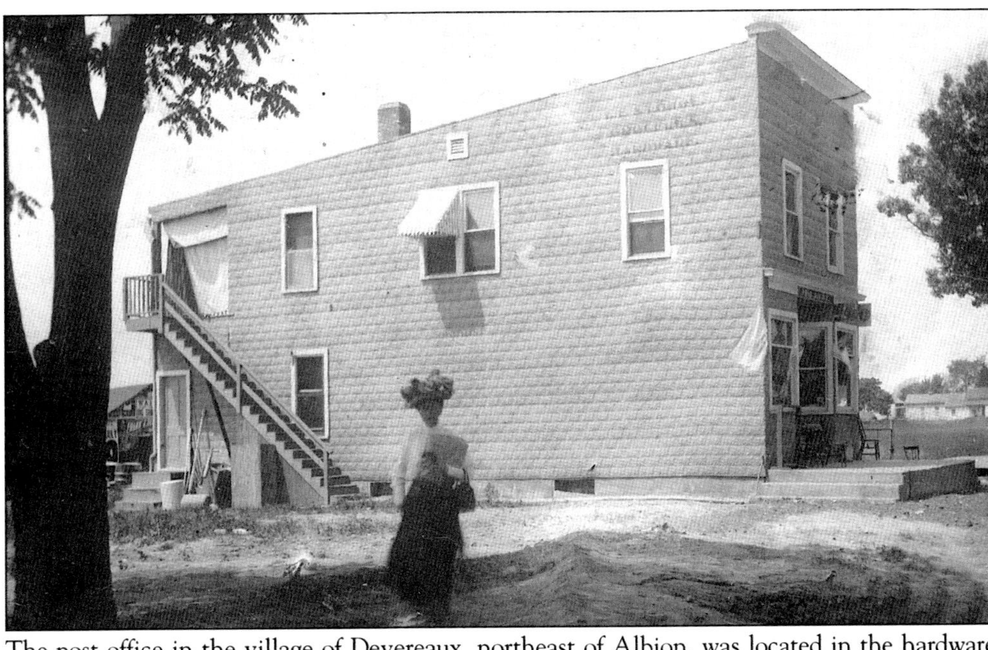

The post office in the village of Devereaux, northeast of Albion, was located in the hardware and grocery store of Ernest E. Stoke (1880–1960), who served as postmaster during the 1910s, before it was closed and consolidated with Albion. Mr. Stoke's mother, Helen, lived upstairs and is shown walking in the center. This building was later demolished after Mr. Stoke erected a new hardware store on the left in 1948. This 1912 photo is courtesy of Ray and Dorothy Martin.

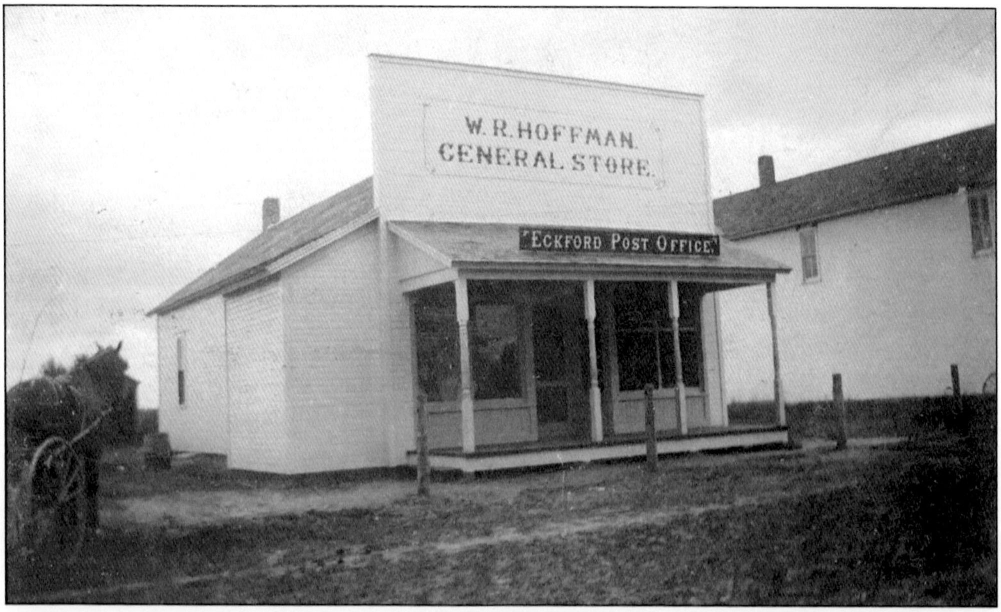


The Eckford Village Post Office was located at 304 Maple Street in the general store of William R. Hoffman, as shown in this photo c. 1913. Mail arrived by train and was delivered via two rural routes that were established in 1899. The Eckford Post Office was closed on June 15, 1934. On the right appears the Maccabbees Hall, later known as the Eckford Community Club building. (Photograph courtesy of Bruce Rapp.)

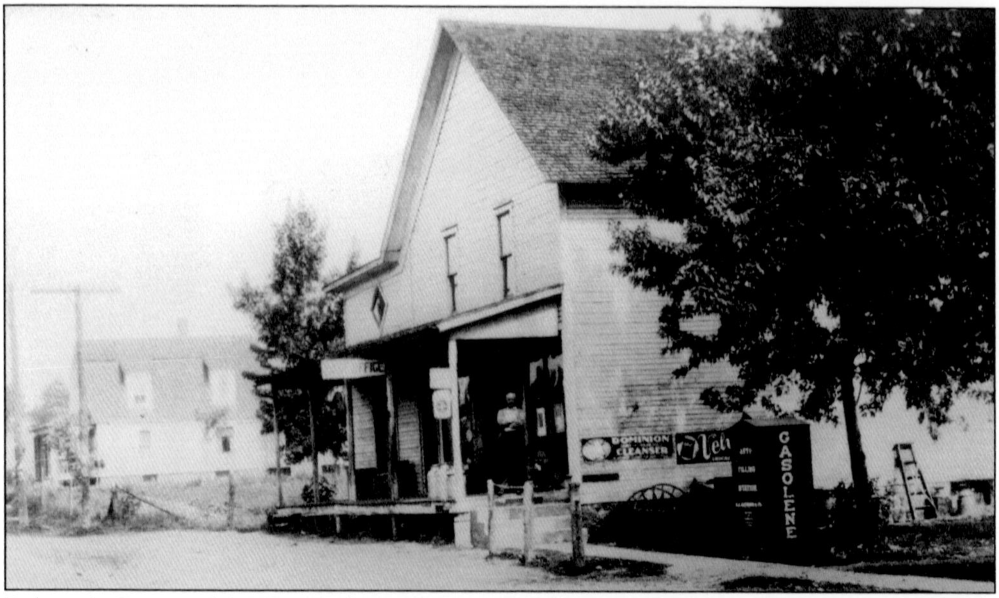


Robert A. Raymond (1867–1918) operated a general store at 412 State Street in the village of Marengo, beginning in 1911. His wife Mary (Garfield) Raymond (1868–1960) served as Marengo postmaster during those years, and the post office sign is shown hanging out front in this photo c. 1915. Mr. Raymond is standing on the porch near large milk containers. To the right is the store's first gasoline pump which states, "Gasolene, Auto Filling Station. R.A. Raymond & Co." The Marengo Post Office was closed on October 31, 1933, and assigned to Albion.

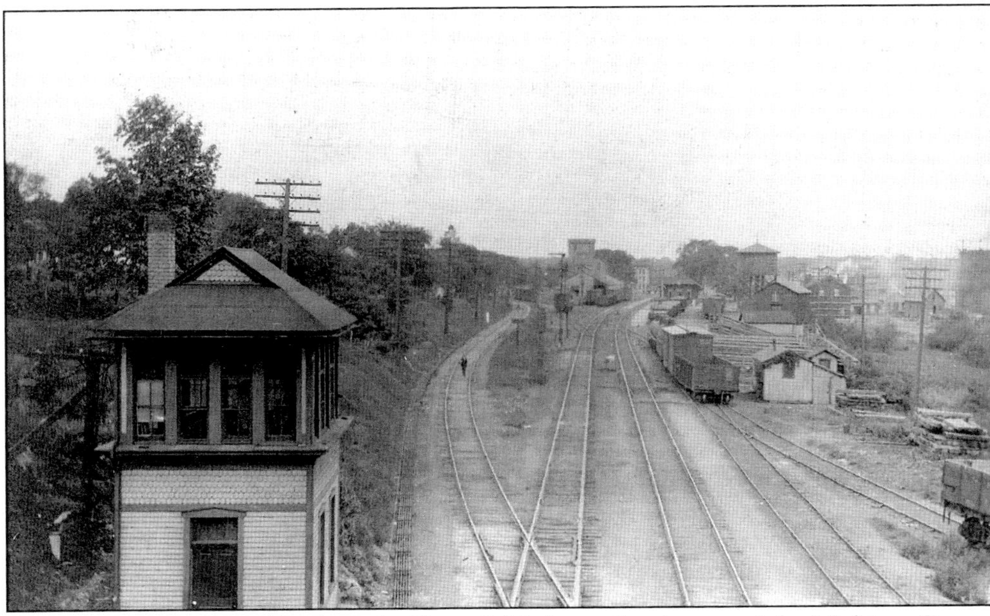

Albion was once serviced by the Lake Shore & Michigan Southern, and the Michigan Central Railroads. Their tracks crossed each other just east of North Albion Street, and a switching tower coordinated rail traffic between the two lines until 1930. This photo was taken from atop of the interurban trestle looking east towards town. On the left is the switching tower. The Lake Shore track crosses on the far left, with the others belonging to the Michigan Central. The photo is c. 1915.

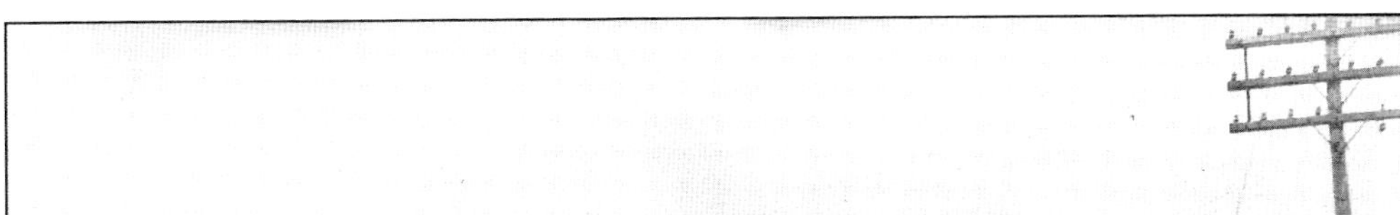

This photo (c. 1915) is the opposite view, facing west. The curved Lake Shore track on the far left serviced the Gale Manufacturing Company, and went to Homer, Jonesville, and Hillsdale. The building, alongside the Michigan Central tracks to the right of the two silos, is the Standard Oil Company. On the far right is the Albion Malleable Iron Company. A sidetrack can be seen leading to the plant. North Albion Street crosses in the distance.

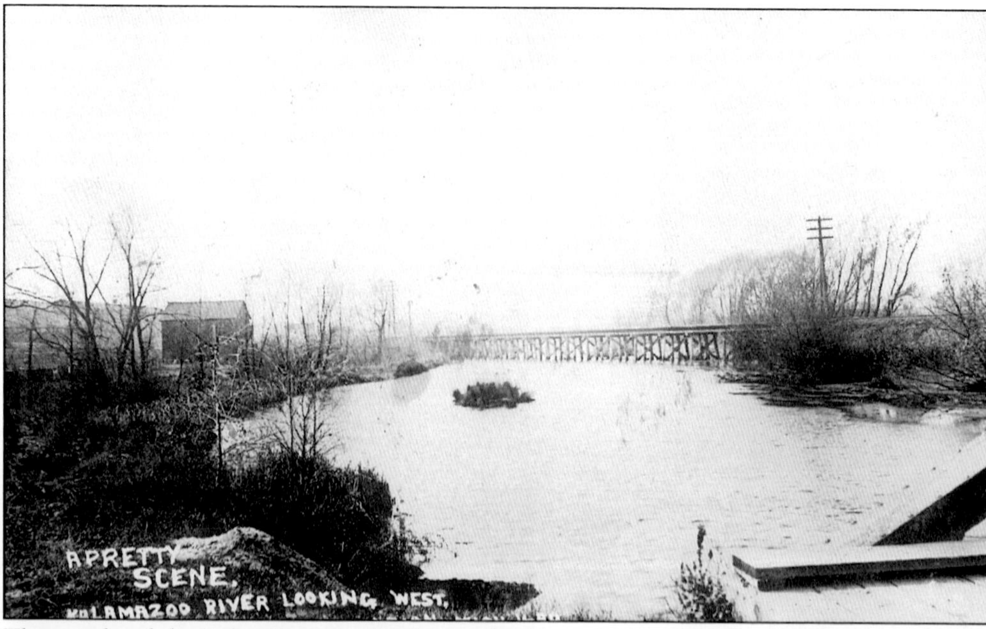


The trestle of the Lake Shore & Michigan Southern Railroad, over the Kalamazoo River, was in use until the tracks were removed in 1976. This scene faces west from the North Albion Street bridge, c. 1910.

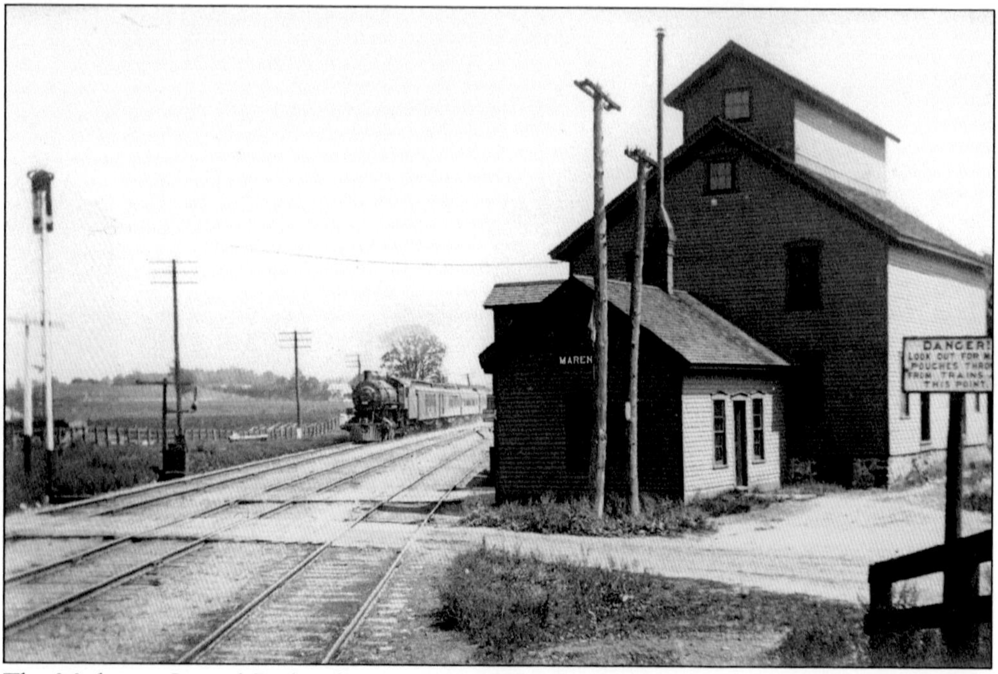

The Michigan Central Railroad passenger and freight depot along State Street in Marengo was used by farmers in this little village, five miles west of Albion, to ship their produce to markets abroad. It also served as a drop-off point for daily mail delivery until mail service was ended on October 31, 1933. The sign on the right warns, "DANGER! LOOK OUT FOR MAIL POUCHES THROWN FROM TRAINS AT THIS POINT." This photo is c. 1915.

Employees of Union Steel Products received an Award of Merit from the U.S. War Department for their production of vital equipment during World War I. The Award consisted of a certificate, and a bronze "War Worker" badge illustrated here. During World War I, Union Steel manufactured such items as woven wire trench cloth, folding bread racks, and folding dough troughs.

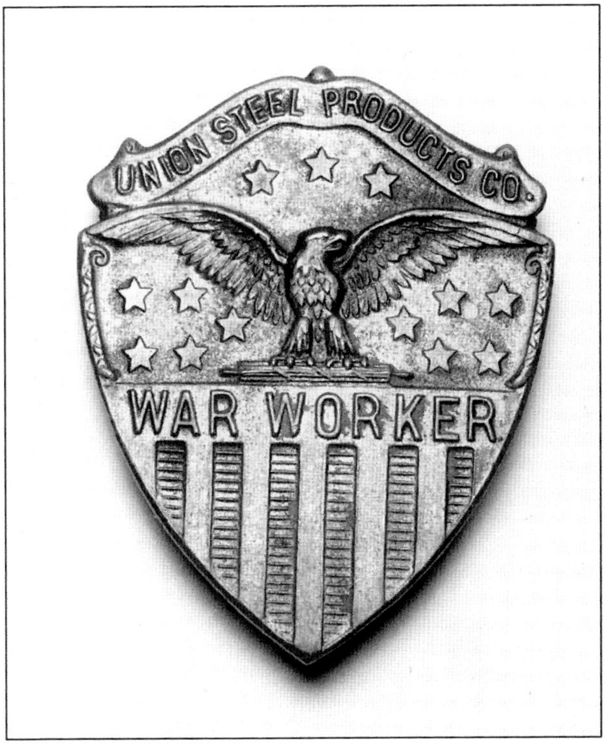


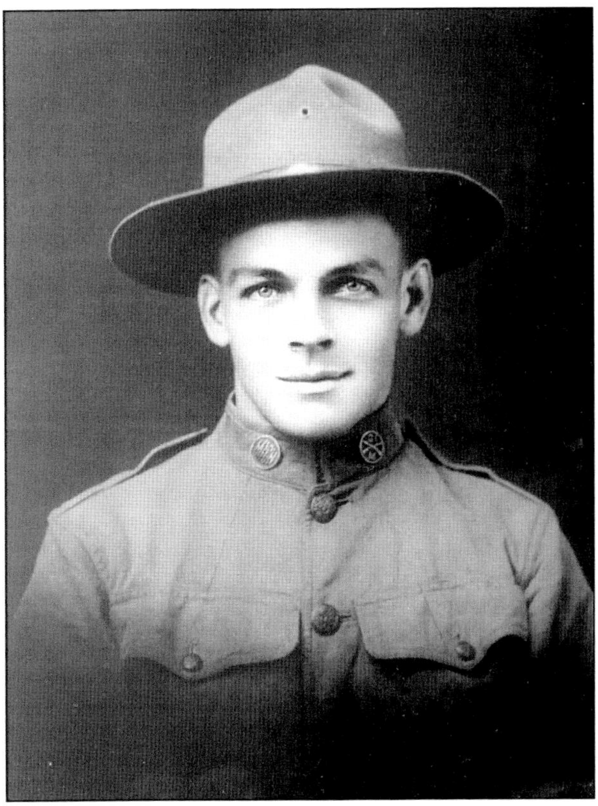

Patrick Leo Hanlon (1894–1918) was the first Albion soldier killed in World War I. A 1913 graduate of Albion High School, Hanlon enlisted in the National Guard in 1917, and was subsequently activated and placed in Company G of the 126th Infantry, 32nd Division. Corporal Hanlon was killed in action in France on August 18, 1918, and is buried there. The local American Legion Post No. 55 was named in honor of Hanlon when it was organized in 1919.

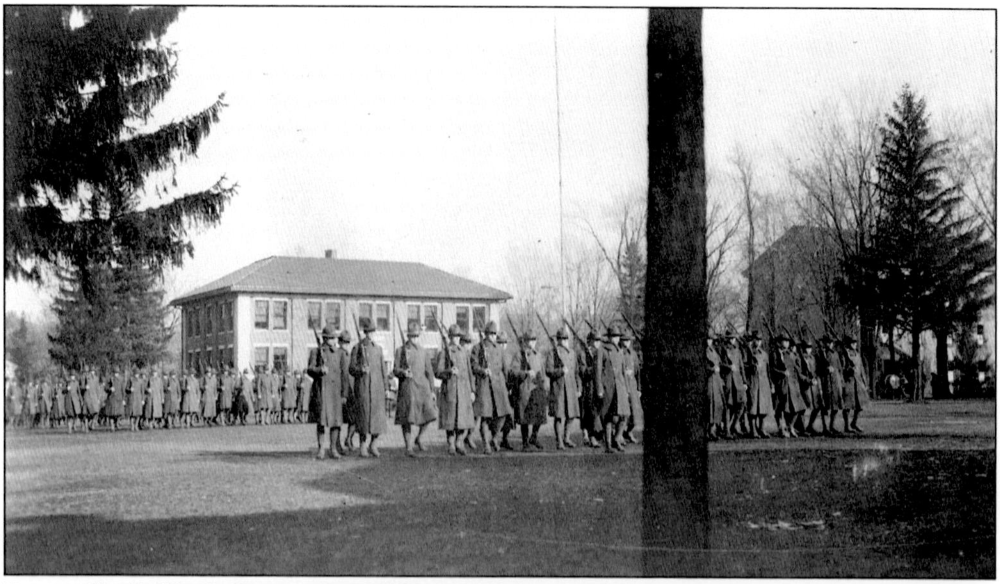

During World War I, the campus of Albion College was transformed into an army military base. The Student Army Training Corps was formed in 1917 to prepare Albion College students for military service. Student soldiers are shown marching on the college campus in this 1918 photograph, with the Epworth Building in the background. (Photo courtesy of Nancy Held.)

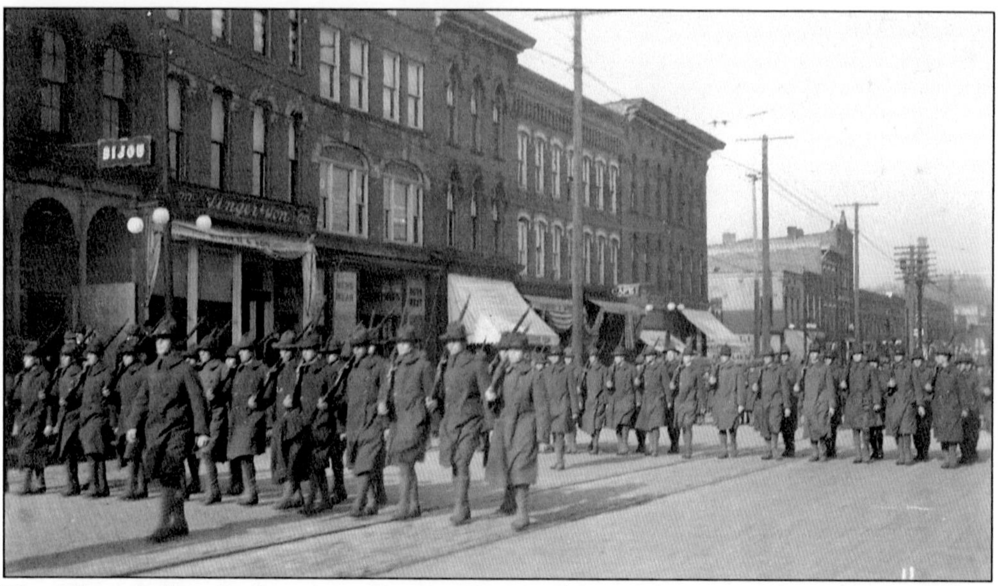


The Albion College Student Army Training Corps celebrates the supposed end of World War I by leading an impromptu parade in downtown Albion on November 9, 1918. The celebration was premature however, as the Armistice was not officially signed until November 11. November 9, 1918, has been dubbed by historians as the "False Armistice Day."

# *Two*

# The 1920s through the Great Depression

## 1920–1939

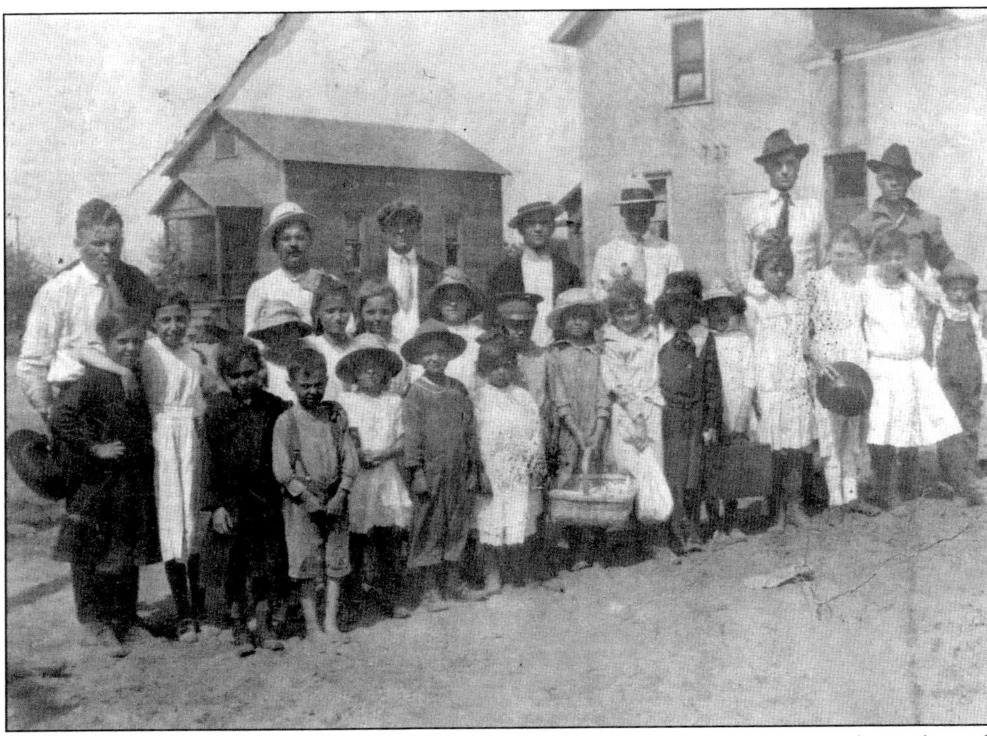

Numerous families from Russia and Eastern Europe came to live in Albion in the early 20th century. This photograph from the early 1920s was taken at the side of the Tom Slavoff home, 624 Austin Avenue. It shows a group of several fathers standing with their children. The last man on the right is Paul Zatalokin (1882–1962) with his daughter Mary (1909–1983) holding the hat, and son John on the end. In back on the left is the Leggett Chapel AME Zion Church, 806 North Albion Street. (Photo courtesy of Nina Nesselroad.)

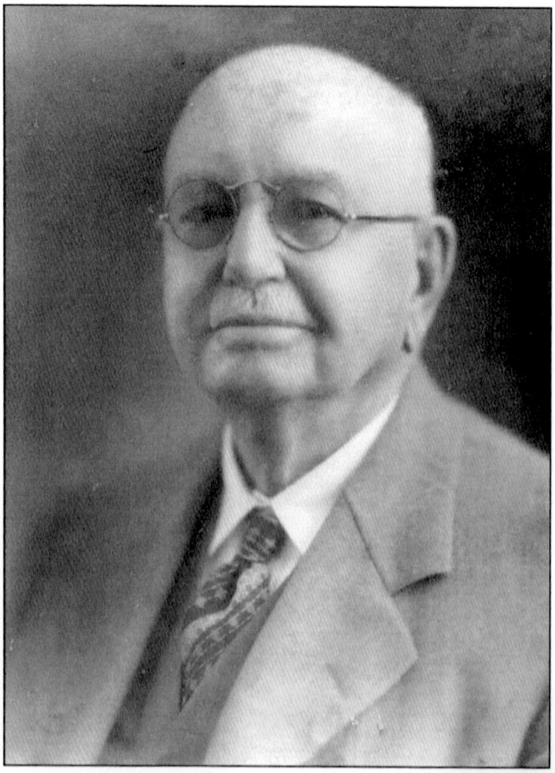

One industrialist who had a major impact upon Albion was Warren S. Kessler (1845–1933). Kessler was the founder and president of the Albion Malleable Iron Company, Albion's major employer of the early 20th century. The Malleable recruited large numbers of workers in the early 20th century, which significantly contributed to Albion's ethnic diversity. The company existed from 1888 until a merger in 1967, and today is known as Harvard Industries. Kessler was also one of the founders of the Albion State Bank and served as its vice president for many years.

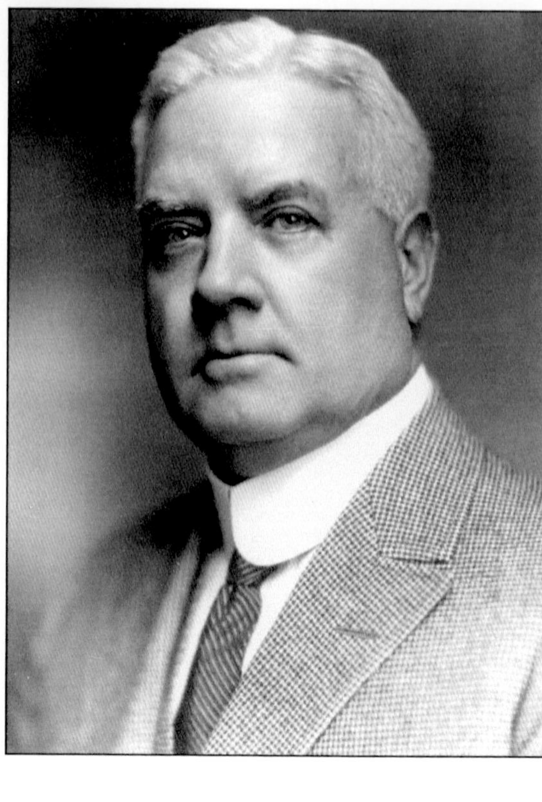

Warren S. Kessler's step-son Harry B. Parker (1871–1936) served as vice president and general manager of the Malleable for many years and became its president upon the death of Kessler in 1933. Under the duo's leadership, the Malleable grew substantially in size until it was one of the largest such concerns in the country.

Parker was philanthropically involved in the civic life of Albion. He provided funds for the erection of several Albion churches, gave the land for a new City Hall on West Cass Street, was active on the Sheldon Memorial Hospital board of trustees, and was a member of several clubs and organizations.

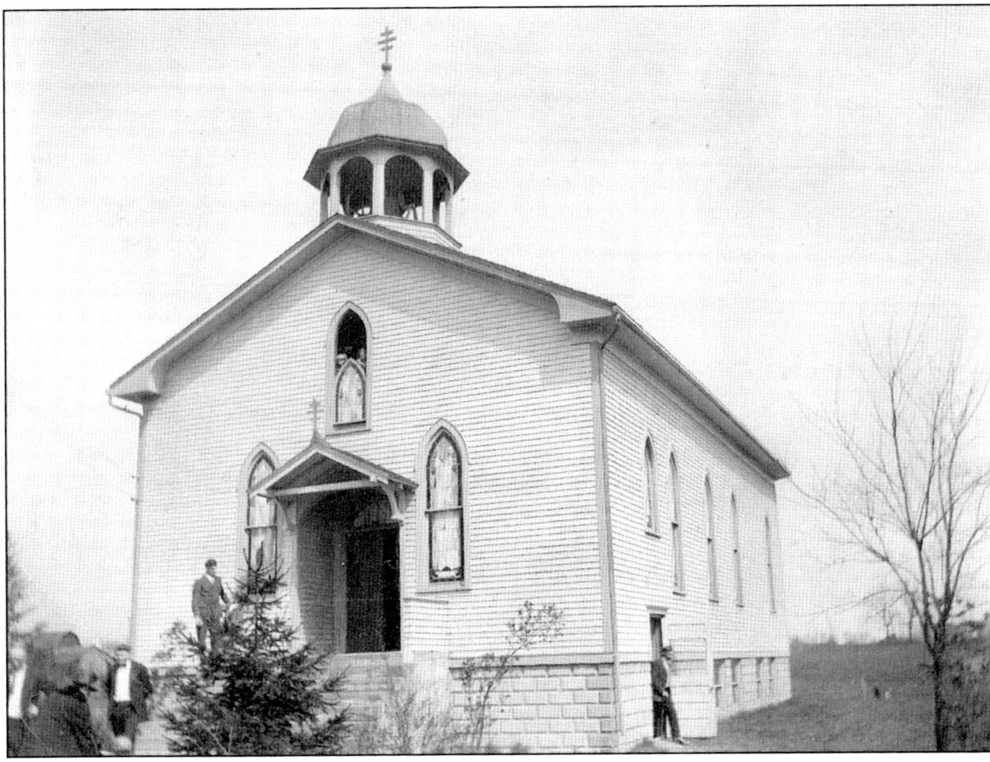

The Holy Ascension Orthodox Church at 810 Austin Avenue was erected in 1916 to serve the spiritual needs of the several hundred Eastern-European immigrants who had settled in Albion. Many were White Russians and Ukrainians who came here to work at the Albion Malleable Iron Company. The project was coordinated by Helen Egnatuk (1850–1946), the matriarch of the local Russian community. The church was named an official historic site by the State of Michigan in 1983, and still holds services today. Shown above is a 1928 view of the building. On the right is a 1927 snapshot of the church youth group standing on the front steps, proudly displaying the American flag. (Photos courtesy of Barbara Shaffer.)

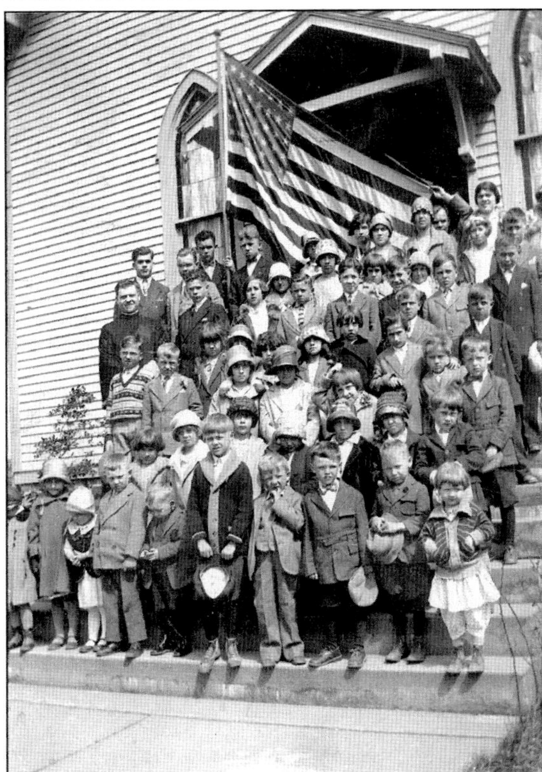

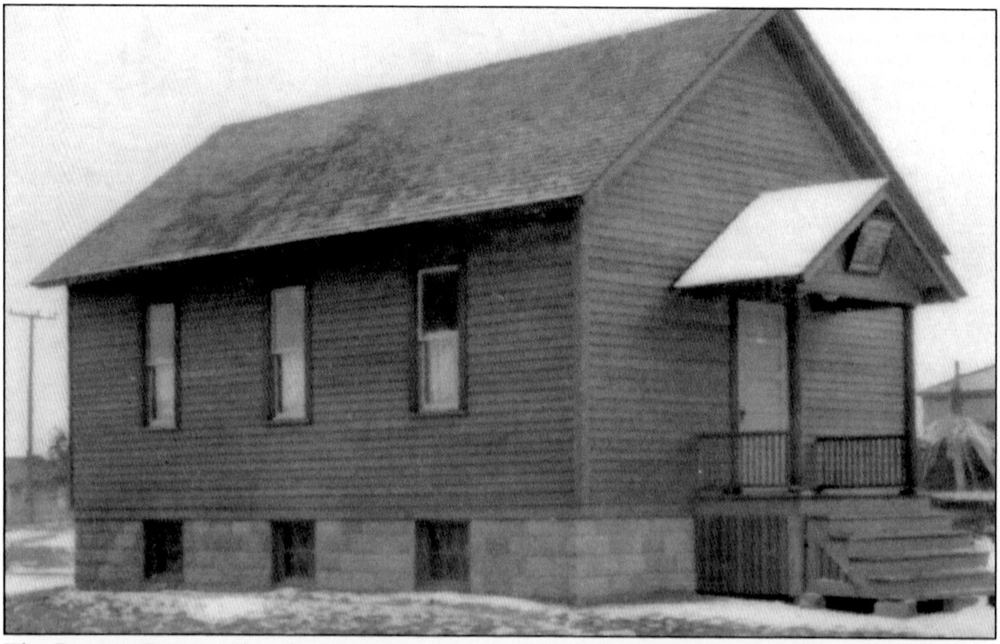

The Russian Baptist Church was organized in 1916 under the direction of Rev. Paul Truss, a native of Russia who came to Albion that year to work at the Albion Malleable Iron Company. Assisting him in the evangelical outreach work with the "foreign settlement" community in Albion was Konrad Felisky, who arrived in 1917. A church was built in 1918 at 614 Austin Avenue, on land donated by Harry Parker, vice president of the Albion Malleable Iron Company. Services were held here until a new church was erected on North Eaton Street in 1948. (Photo courtesy of Tim Felisky.)

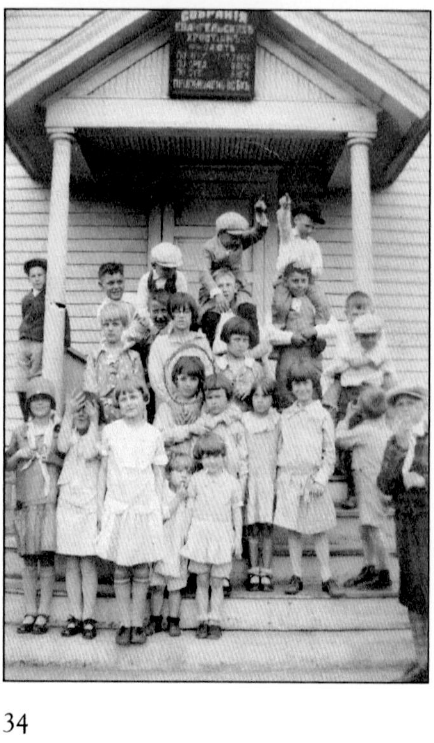

Many neighborhood youth were attracted to the ministry provided by the Russian Baptist Church, as this late-1920s photograph reveals. From left to right: (front row) Nada Lazarchuck, Frances Harry with hands up, Nina Bokovec, Leada Veramay with finger in mouth, Esther Veramay; then (up) Anne Veramay with a circle drawn around her head, Ruth Romanchuk, Dorothy Pasic, Esther Shifkey, unidentified youth with head turned, and John Harry on far right; (middle row) Helen Elushik, Peter Brankovich, Helen Kolodica, (down) and Estelle Elushik; (top row) Russell Krusik by pole, Frank Passic Sr., unidentified person with hat, Steve Veramay, with Victor Nesterenko on top of him, Peter Nesterenko, with Joseph Veramay on top of him, and Nick Kolodica with John Kolodica on top of him. (Photo courtesy Anne (Veramay) Thompson.)

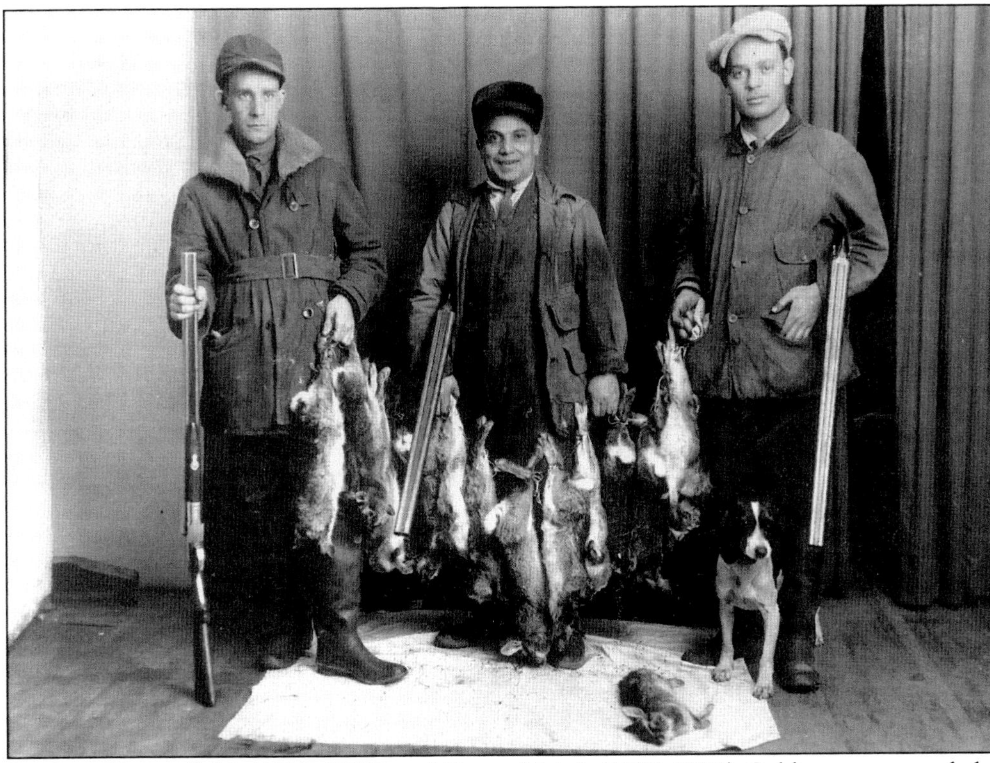

Brothers Victor (left) (1891–1979) and Santo (right) (1897–1972) Calderone operated the Albion Beverage Company from 1932 to 1966. Their cousin Sam Vitale (center) (1892–1982) is in the center. All were natives of Italy. Victor was one of Albion's most accomplished musicians and played clarinet in numerous bands and orchestras, including the professional Liberati band in Chicago. Santo served in the Italian "Bersaglieri" (sharpshooters) during World War I. The trio loved to hunt small game in the Albion area, and are shown in this 1930 photograph with their catch of rabbits. (Photo courtesy Guy Vitale.)

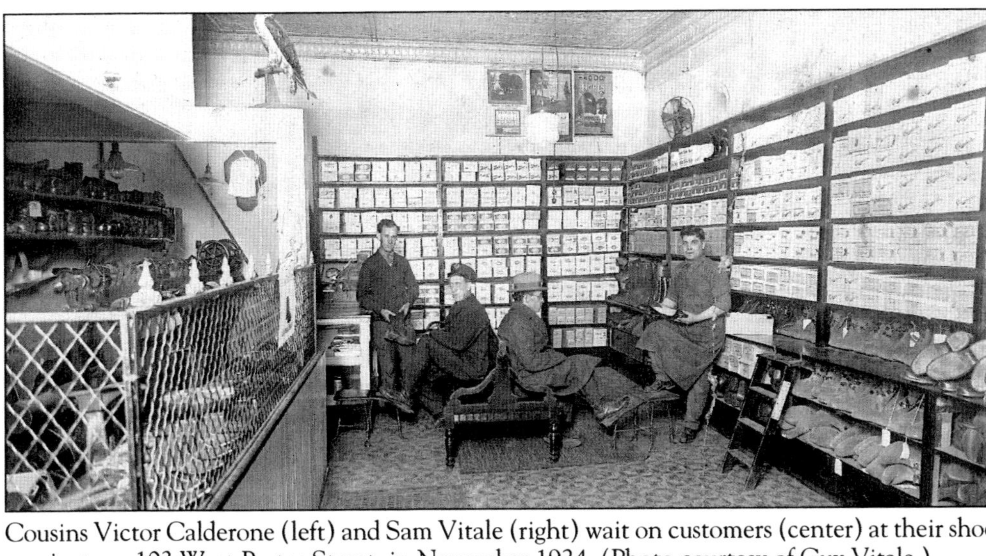

Cousins Victor Calderone (left) and Sam Vitale (right) wait on customers (center) at their shoe repair store, 103 West Porter Street, in November 1924. (Photo courtesy of Guy Vitale.)

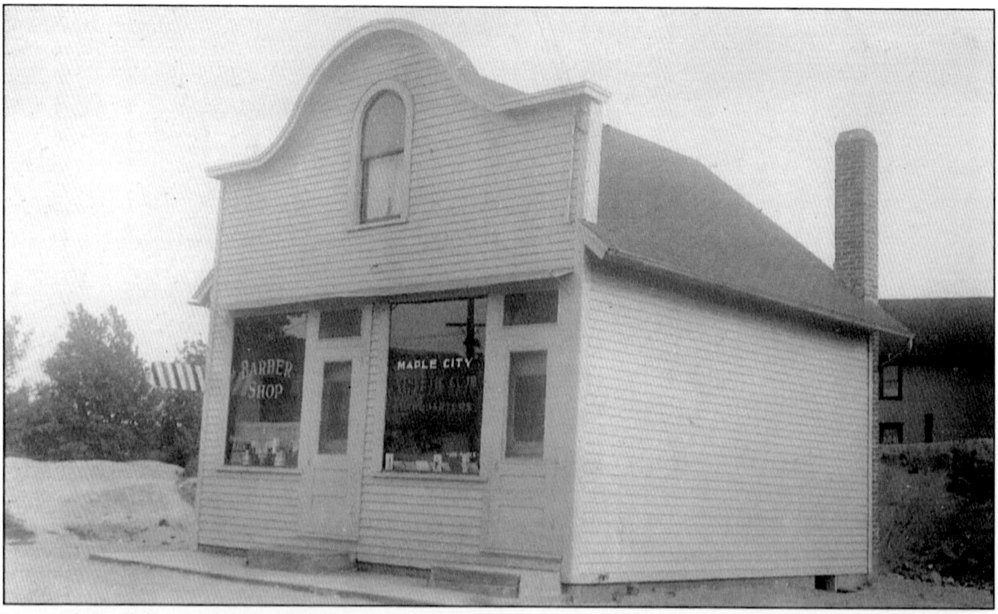


Konrad O. Felisky (1896–1981) was a well-known early 20th century Albion barber. A native of Russia, Konrad came to Albion in 1917 and was active in the local Russian Baptist Church. This 1929 photo depicts his barbershop at 611 Austin Avenue. The left window reads "BARBER SHOP." The right window states "MAPLE CITY ATHLETIC CLUB HEADQUARTERS, JOS. PASICK." The latter served as the business office for boxer Joseph B. Pasic (1907–1994) who trained Albion boxers in the 1920s and 1930s. (Photo courtesy of Tim Feliksy.)

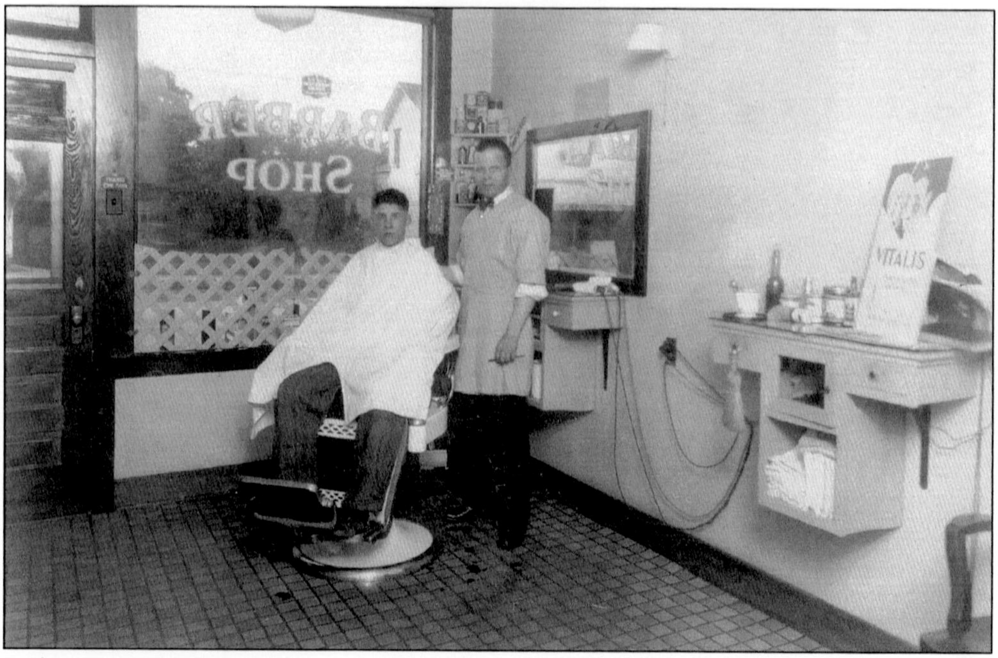


Barber Konrad Felisky waits on a customer in his barbershop. The photo is from c. 1929. (Courtesy of Tim Felisky.)

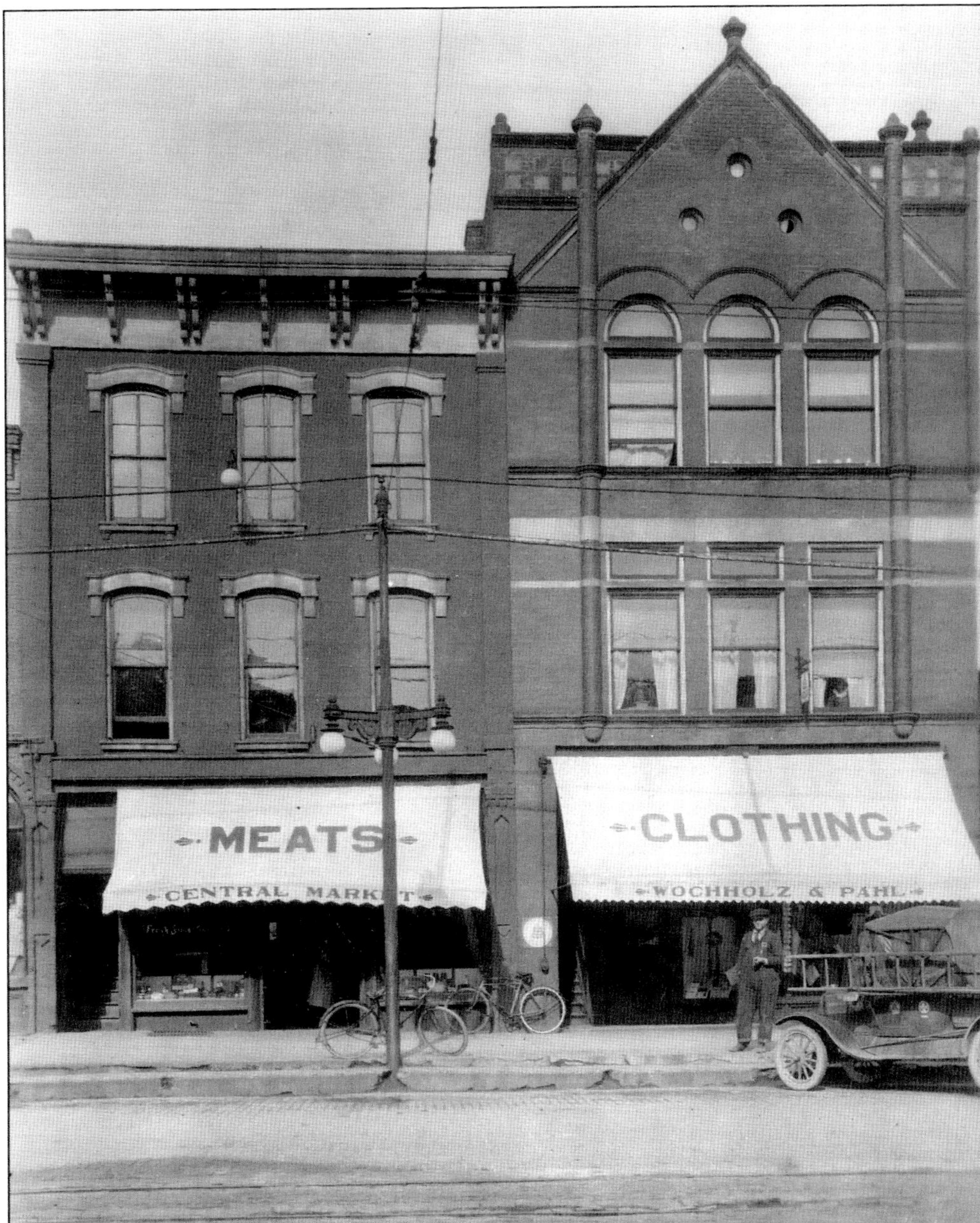

The Wochholz & Pahl Clothing Store (right) was owned by Frank A. Wochholz (1871–1940) and Frederick G. Pahl (1871–1935). It operated from 1910 to 1937 at 110 South Superior Street, and was subsequently sold to Ralph Seelye. The Michigan Bell Telephone Company was located upstairs on the second floor from 1900 to 1949. Whenever operators received distress calls for police, they would flash a red light on and off for the officers downtown to see, indicating trouble. R.V. Loomis operated his Central Meat Market at 112 South Superior Street (left) during the 1920s and 1930s.

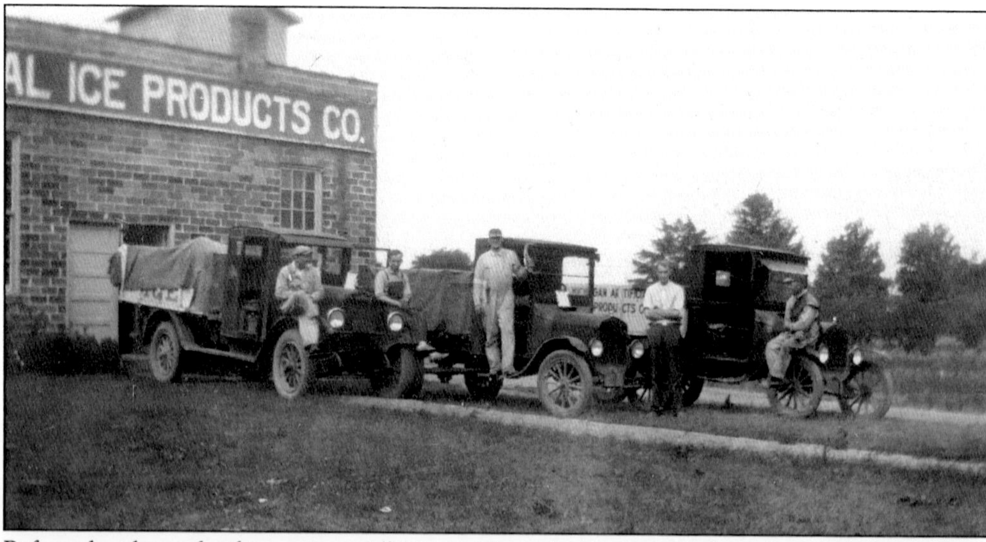


Before the days of refrigeration, Albion residents kept their food cool in iceboxes. People purchased chunks of ice that had been cut from the frozen lakes and rivers. In the early 1920s, the Michigan Artificial Ice Product Company was built on Barnes Street. It manufactured ice, which was delivered to residents in 25 lb. blocks. In the early 1930s, home refrigerators came on the market and the icebox became obsolete. The ice plant was closed around 1936. This late 1920s photograph shows the three delivery trucks and drivers, from left to right: Dave Coomer, unidentified, Elijah Marshall, Elwin Ruff, and William Dean. (Photo courtesy of Lena Ruff.)

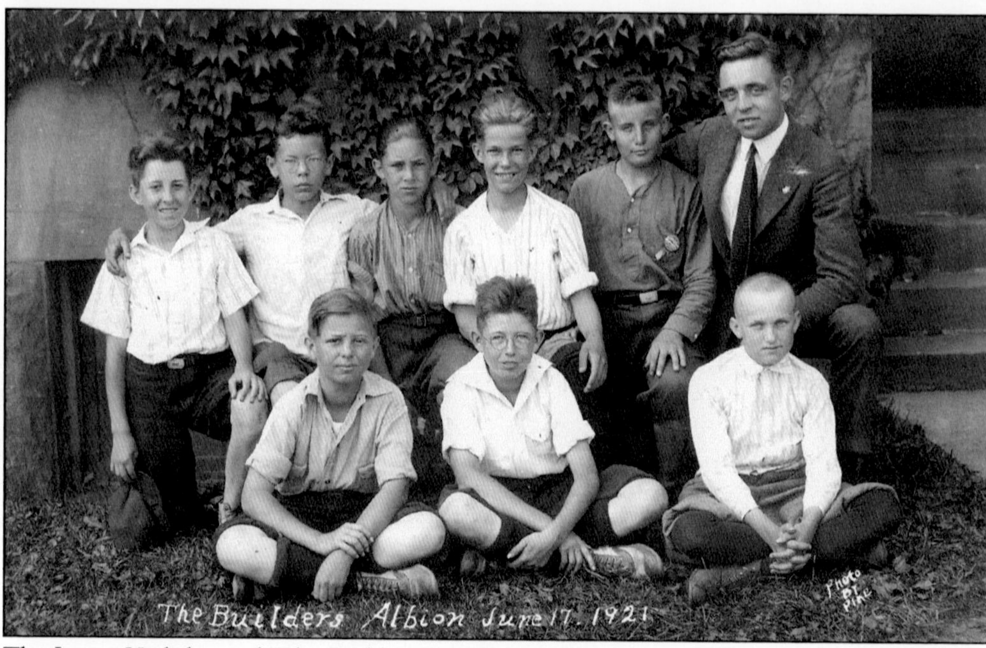


The Junior High boys of "The Builders" Sunday School class at the Methodist Church pause for this photograph on June 17, 1921. From left to right: (front row) Harry Morse, Phillips V. Hembdt, and John Fillmore; (back row) Myron Ellis, Stanley Penzotti, Clifford S. Ott, Edward Henderson, Dean Herriff, and teacher Sidney N. Geal, who was a student at Albion College. (Photo courtesy of Clifford C. Ott.)

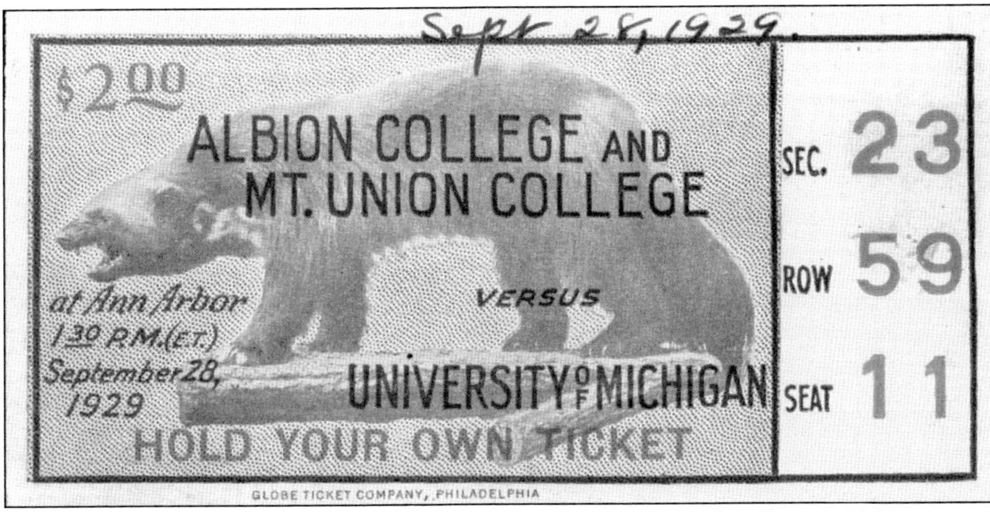


The Albion College football team even played the University of Michigan Wolverines, as attested by this admission ticket dated September 28, 1929. It was the final time these two teams met. The score: Michigan-39, Albion-0. Albion defeated the maize and blue only once, in 1891, by a score of ten to four.

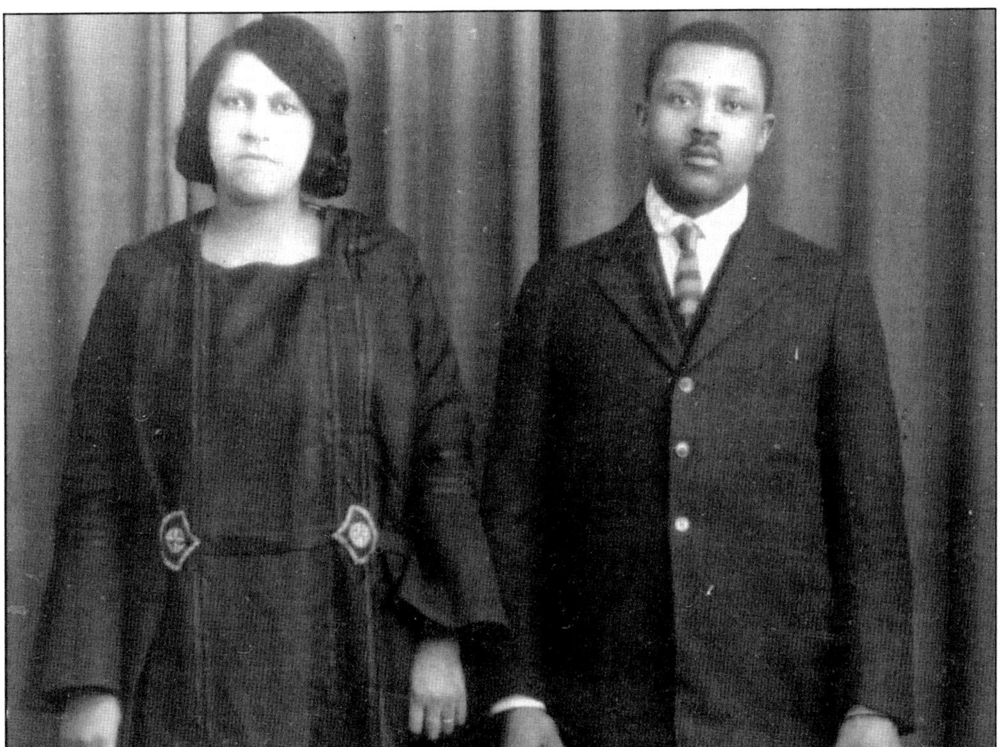

The Will Curtis Post No. 144 of the American Legion was organized in 1930 by local African-American veterans of World War I. The Post was named after Will Curtis (1896–1930) who was the first member of the group to die (of pneumonia). The Legion purchased lots in Riverside Cemetery where the majority of its members were subsequently interred. Mr. Curtis is pictured here standing with his wife Frances (Hall) (1890–1984). (Photo courtesy Dr. James L. Curtis M.D.)

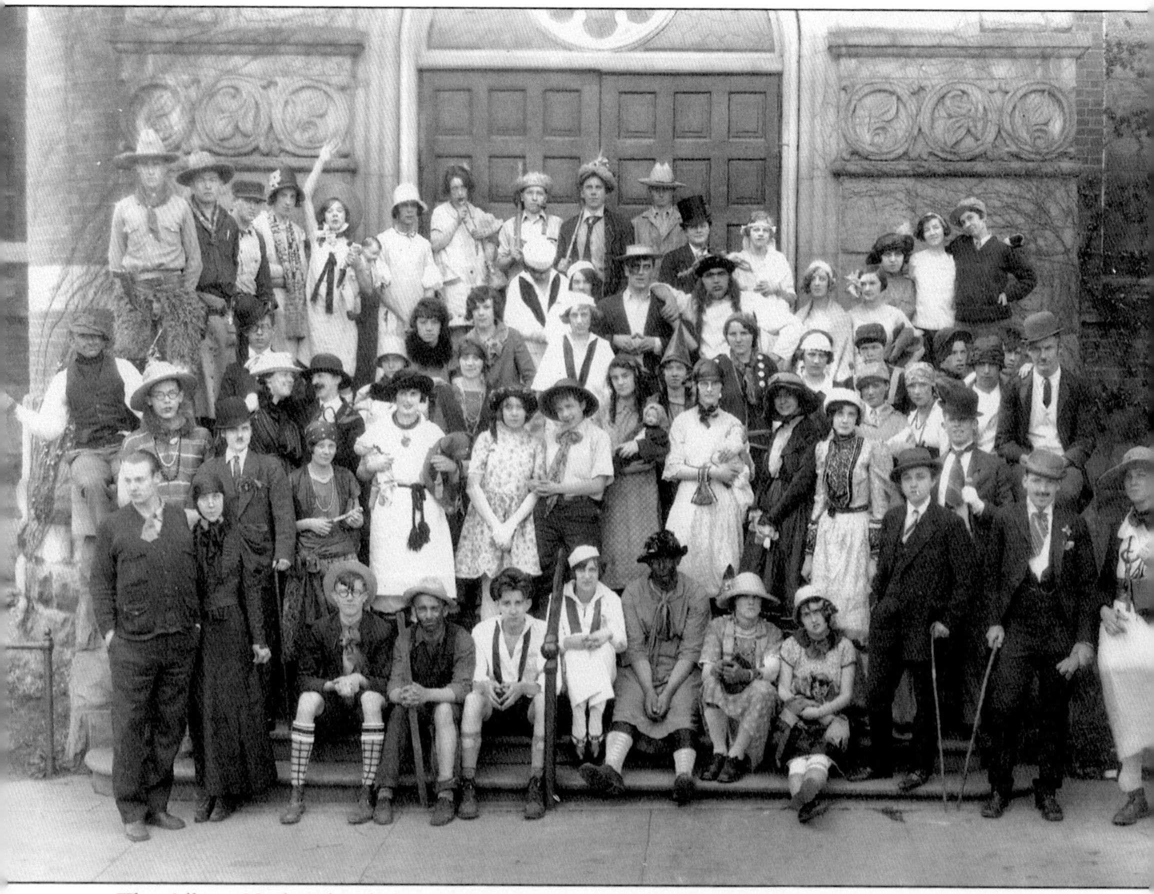

The Albion High School class of 1926 poses on the steps of the Methodist Church for "costume dress-up day." They are, from left to right: (standing) Floyd Dutton, Hazel Curl, (seated) Dan Dewey, Fred Nass, unidentified, Josephine Greenman, Dean Herriff, John Fillmore as a woman, E. Lauraine Brownell, Margareta Radtke as a man with a cane, Lester Dunn, and Glen Sebastian as a woman with a purse; (second row) unidentified man with brick, Stanley Penzotti, Mary Seaton as a man with hat, Beulah Davenport, Ila Thuma with dolls, Stella Oderkirk, Maxine Teller as a boy, Jessie Minkler with doll, Gladys Jeffers with dunce cap on, (down) Bernice White, (up) Lena Kaiser, (down) Josephine Groby, (up) Elvira Parsons, (down) Lucy Hicks, (up) Irene Osmun, (up) Margaret Wilson with Civil War cap, (down) unidentified, Louie Frederick with derby, (up) Harry Hoaglin, Clarence Hammond, unidentified, and Keith Allen; (third row) boy with tilted hat and glasses is Harry Morse, (down) unidentified woman with white hat, Clara Rogers with moustache, unidentified, L. Feroda Butzer with fur collar, (down) unidentified, (up) Virginia Sheldon, (up) unidentified with "V" collar, (down) Alberta Wochholz with "V" collar, (up) unidentified, Winfield Cole with black eye, and Floyd Densmore as a girl with long braids; (top row) Dick Hardt, Harold Bussing, William Wilson, Dick Nowlin as a girl, Elaine Nagle with hand raised, Marvin Pahl as a girl, Esther Hoaglin, Norman Ludlow with pipe, Allen Scherer, Emmett Gordon, Helen Lines with black top hat, Wilma Lewis, Jewell Morgan, Julia McKim, Josephine Gale, and last two unidentified.

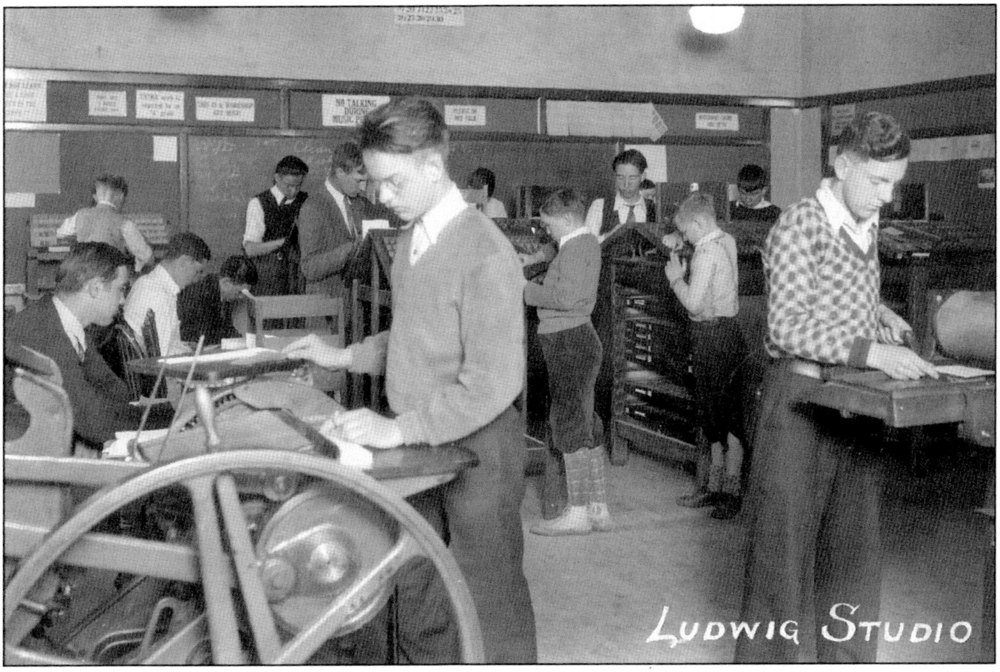

Student Richard Morgan (1915–1998) (center left) adjusts his printing plate in the Washington Gardner High School print-shop class in this April 1931 photo.

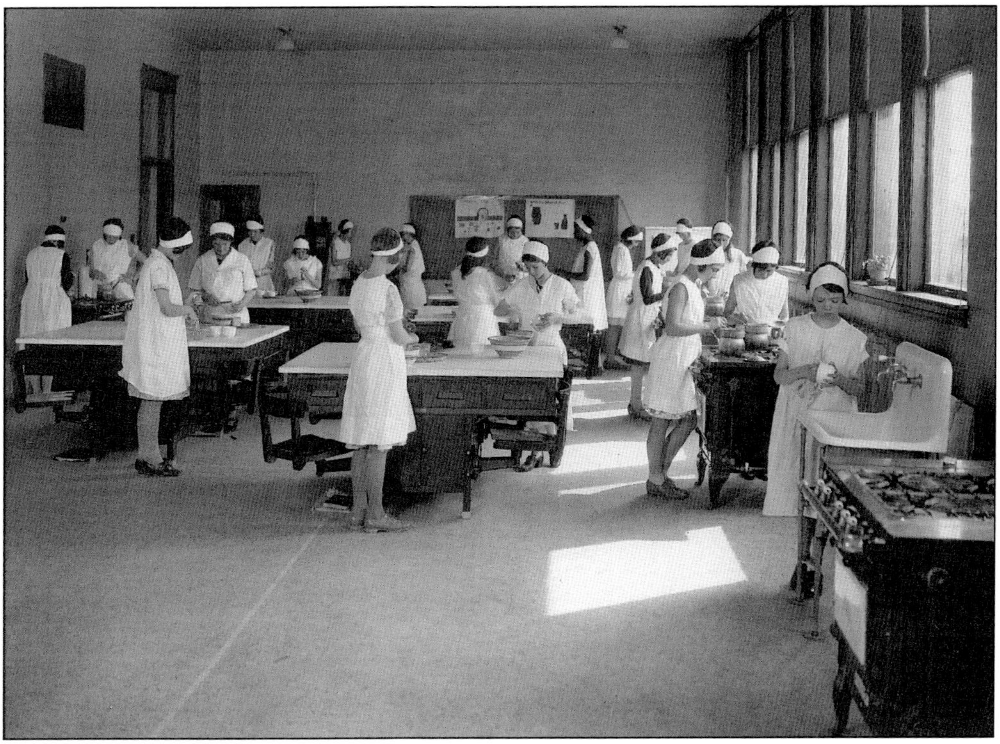
The girls in the Washington Gardner High School cooking class prepare food in their white uniforms in this in April 1931 photo.

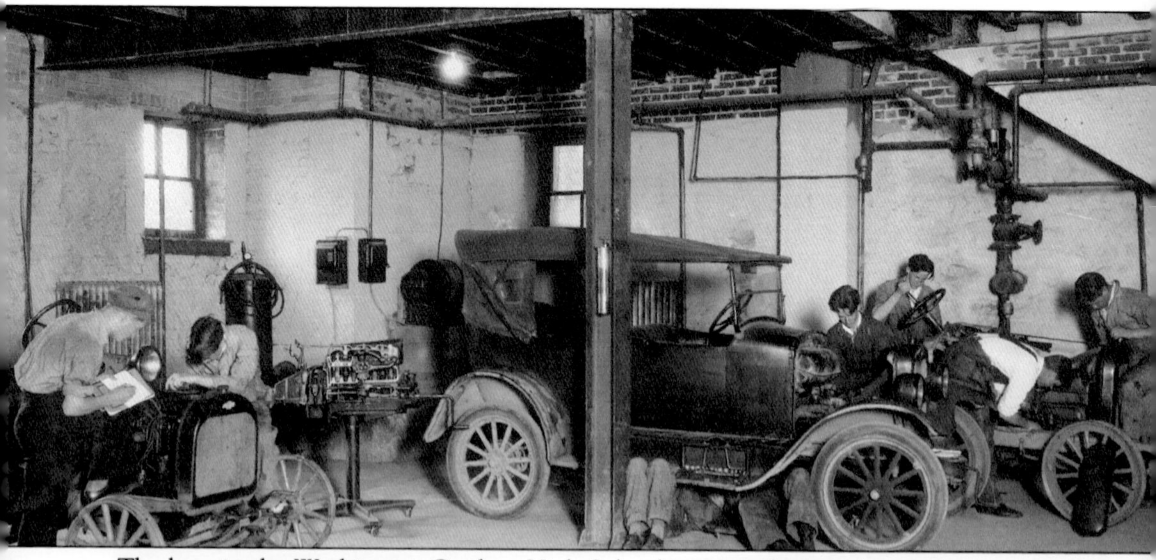

The boys in the Washington Gardner High School auto mechanics class work on a model-T Ford in this April 1931 photograph.

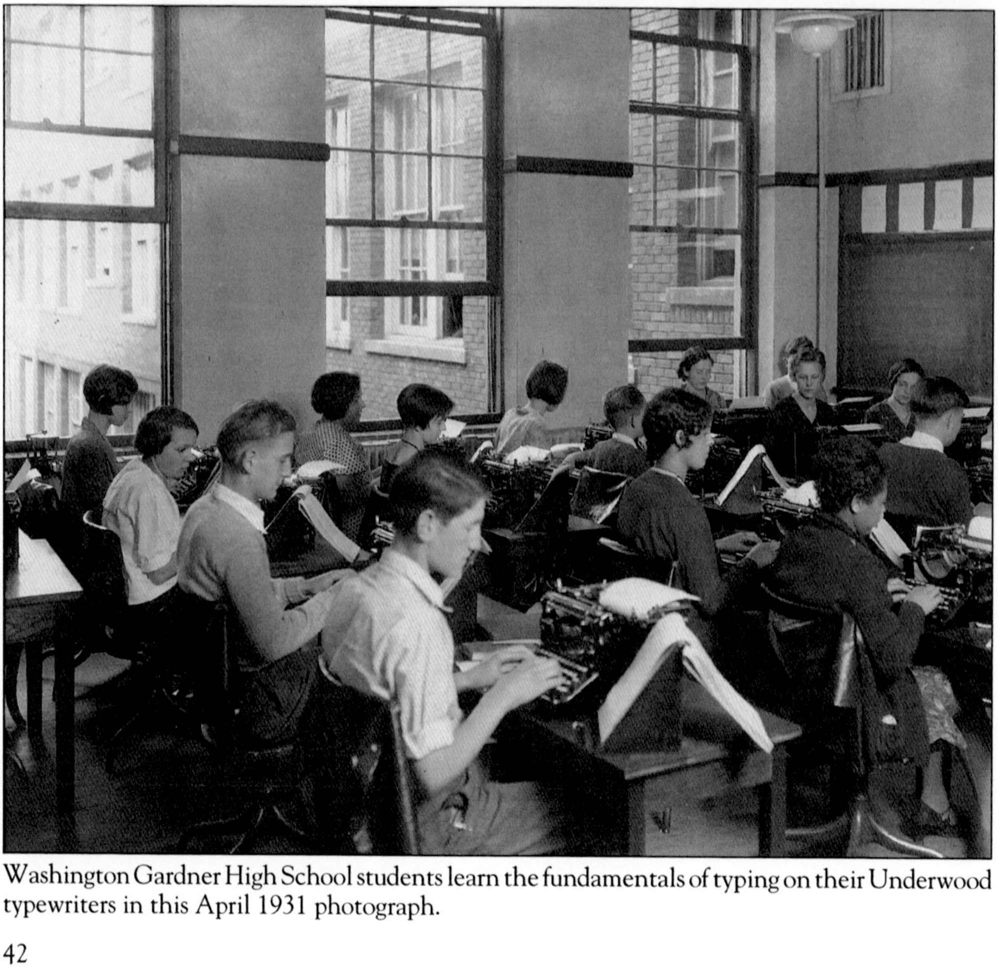

Washington Gardner High School students learn the fundamentals of typing on their Underwood typewriters in this April 1931 photograph.

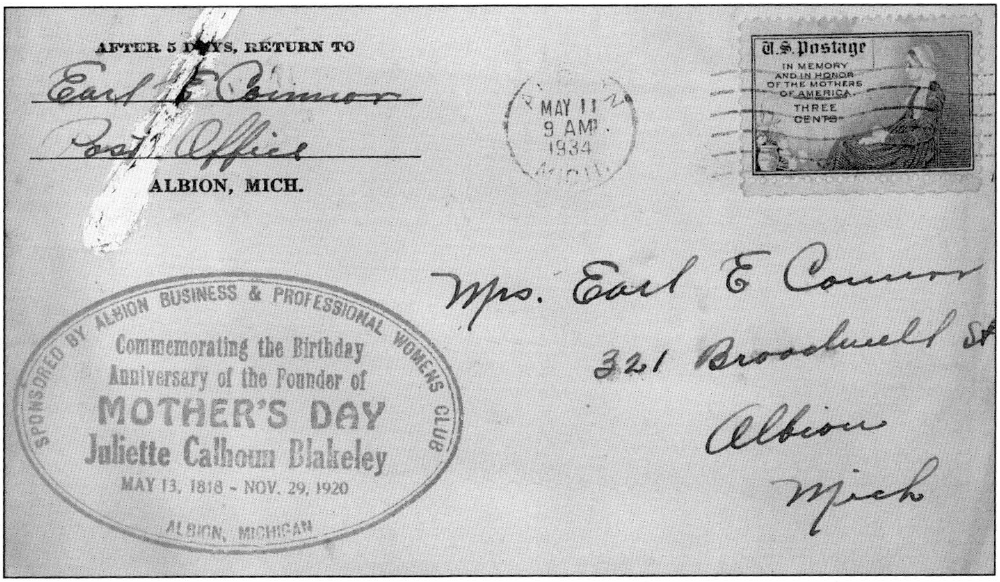


The Albion Business & Professional Women's Club issued this souvenir envelope in 1934 to commemorate Mother's Day, and Albion's "Original Mother of Mother's Day," Mrs. Juliette Calhoun Blakeley (1818–1920). (Envelope courtesy of the Connor family.)

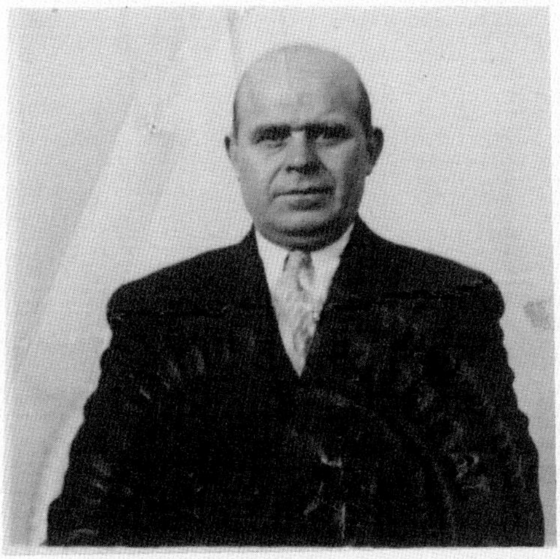

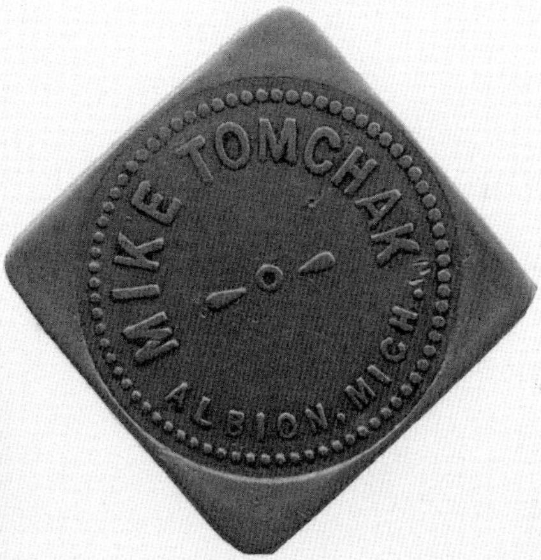


Mike Tomchak (left) (1892–1947) operated a popular pool hall and grocery store at 612 Austin Avenue from the 1920s through the 1940s. A native of Leskova, Russia, Mike came to Albion during World War I and originally worked at the Albion Malleable Iron Company prior to becoming a "west end" merchant. His establishment eventually became known as Tomchak's Tavern and was continued by his widow Catherine (1911–2002) through the 1960s. This aluminum token (right) was good for 5¢ in trade and was used in conjunction with pool games throughout the 1930s.

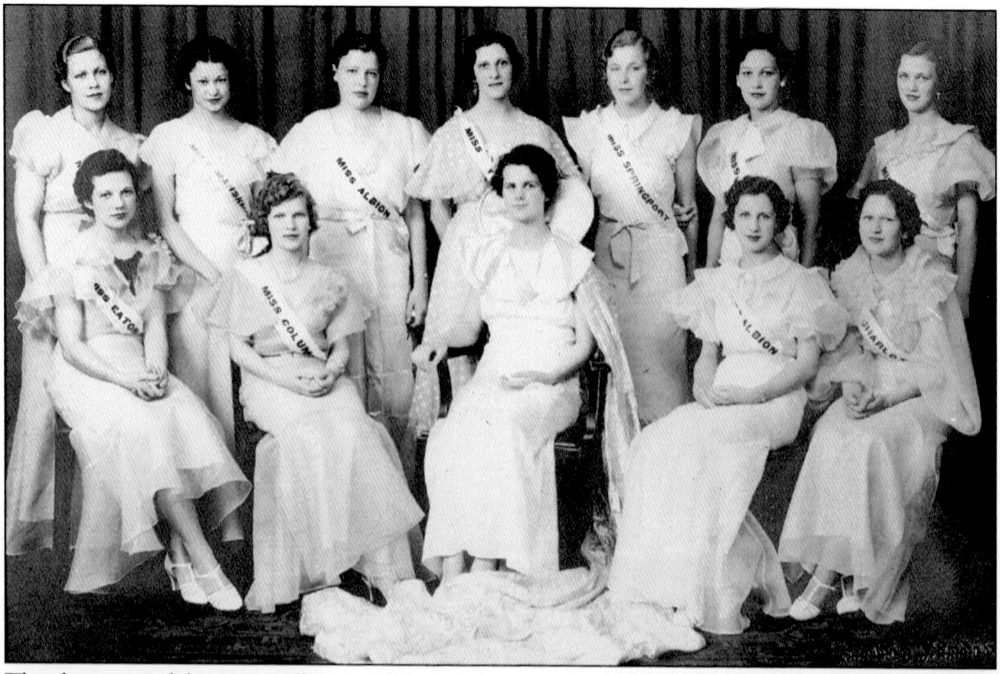


The biggest celebration Albion ever staged was the massive centennial celebration held July 1–7, 1935. Part of the festivities included the crowning of a centennial queen, and a centennial court. They are, from left to right: (front row) Miss Eaton Rapids, Agatha Miller; Miss Columbia (Albion runner-up), Cecile Weeks; Centennial Queen Lucille Biggs (1916–2002); Miss Albion, Inez Smith; and Miss Charlotte, Thelma Burns; (back row) Miss Concord, Barbara Butters; Miss Marshall, Helen Kraushaar; Miss Albion, Mary Bastian; Miss Litchfield, Eleanor Norris; Miss Springport, Treva Mitchell; Miss Parma, Lucille Krugman; and Miss Homer, Geraldine Luke.

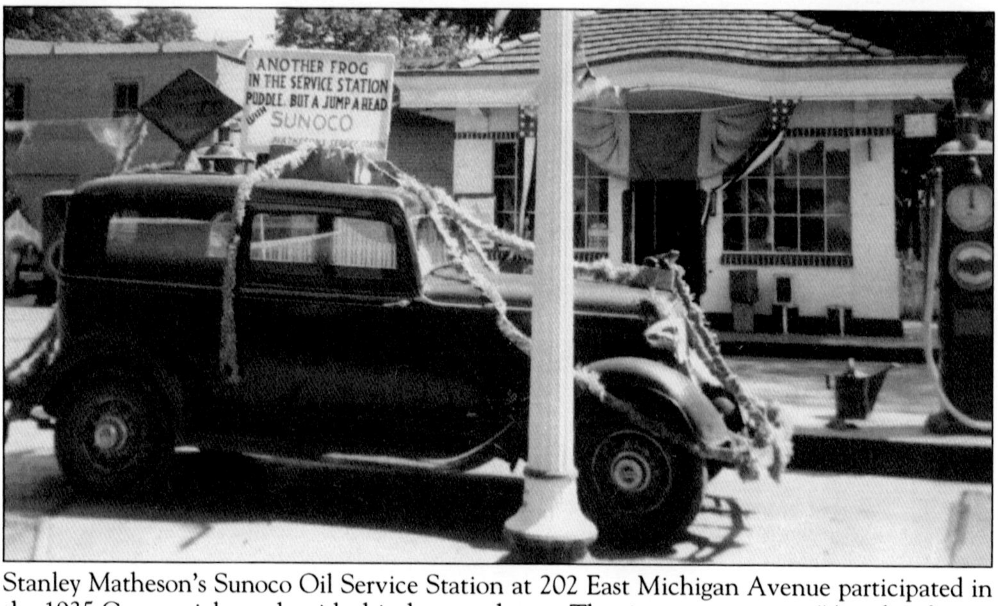


Stanley Matheson's Sunoco Oil Service Station at 202 East Michigan Avenue participated in the 1935 Centennial parade with this decorated auto. The sign on top states, "Another frog in the service station puddle, but a jump ahead with Sunoco. Matheson's Service Station."

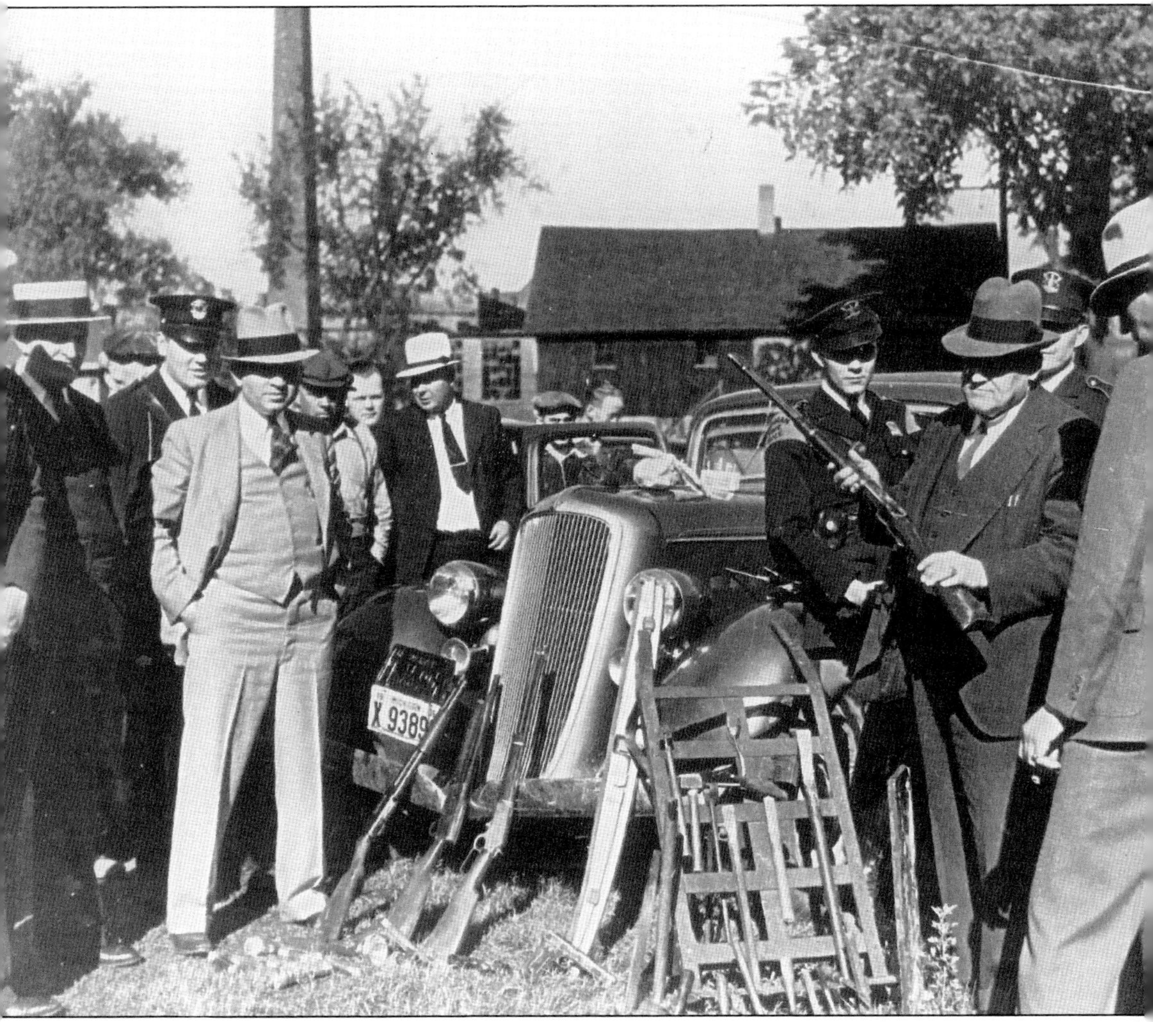

Law enforcement officials arrested members of the Purple Gang and seized their custom-equipped armored Graham-Paige sedan on June 3, 1936. The raid followed a spree of at least 15 safe robberies and burglaries in southern Michigan in the previous three months. Gang members operated a junk yard in the Market Place as a "front," where the raid took place.

The vehicle featured revolving license plates, bulletproof glass, and removable doors and seats so a large safe could be inserted. Various tools of the gangster trade and weapons were also confiscated, and are shown laying next to the car, including: various rifles and shotguns, hammers, chisels, tongs and crowbars, a two-wheeled safe-hauling cart, and bomb-making equipment on the hood, including nitroglycerine and a cake of Fels-Naptha soap. Michigan State Police Trooper Custer T. Carland (1913–2002) was one of 25 law enforcement officers from out of town that assisted in the raid, and is pictured in uniform behind the shotgun held by the man on the right. (Photo courtesy of the late Mr. Carland of Frankfort, and his niece, Polly S. Moore of Albion.)

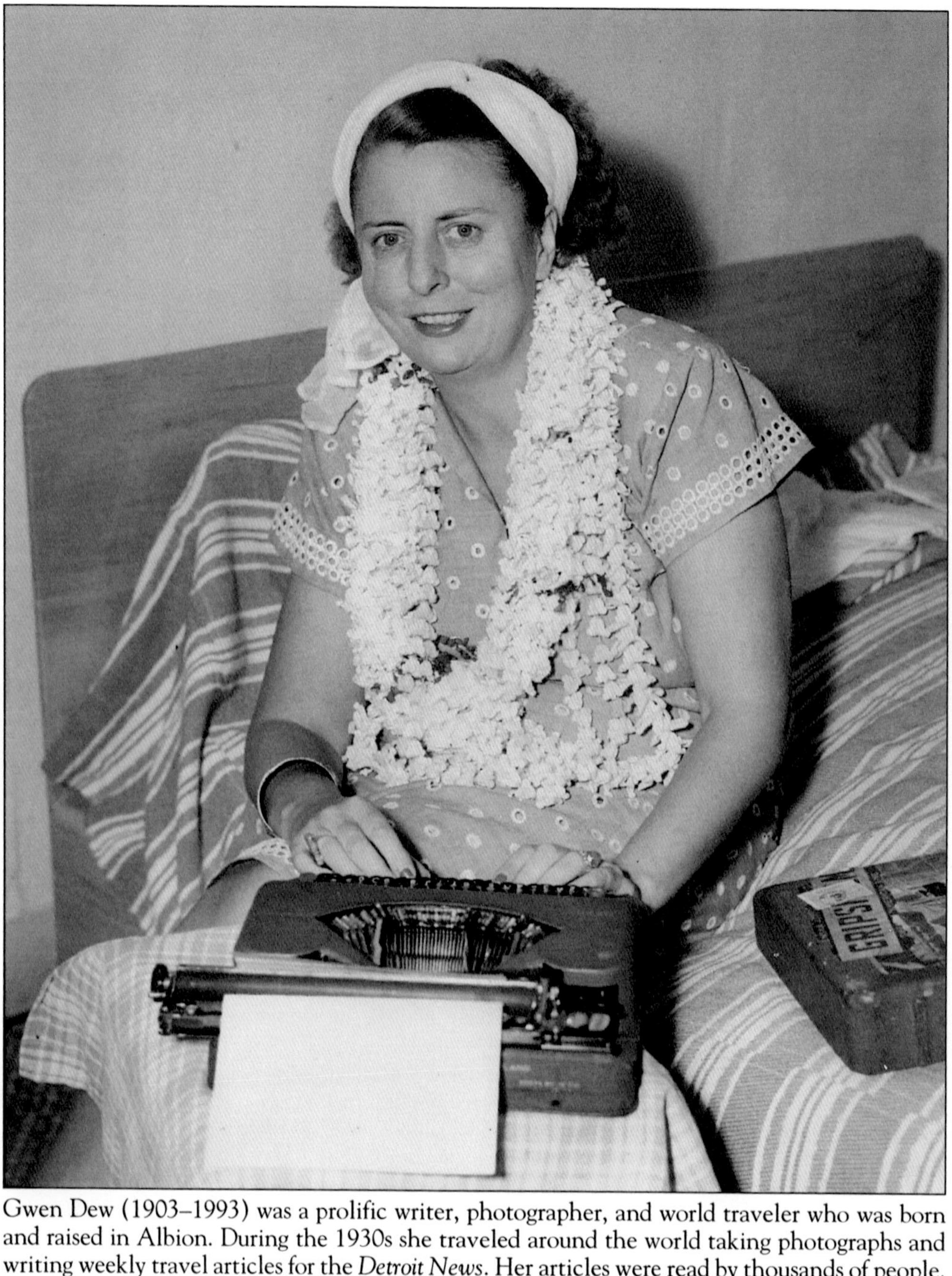

Gwen Dew (1903–1993) was a prolific writer, photographer, and world traveler who was born and raised in Albion. During the 1930s she traveled around the world taking photographs and writing weekly travel articles for the *Detroit News*. Her articles were read by thousands of people. She was captured in Hong Kong at the start of World War II and spent several months in a Japanese concentration camp before her release at the end of June 1942. She subsequently wrote a series of thrilling eyewitness accounts of her ordeal for the *News*, which received top billing in front-page installments. Her book *Prisoner of the Japs* was published in 1943. During the rest of the War, she toured the country for the U.S. Office of Strategic Services, lecturing about her experiences and raising more than $2 million in War bonds. This 1936 photo is from Honolulu, Hawaii, and she is seen with her typewriter "Tappy."

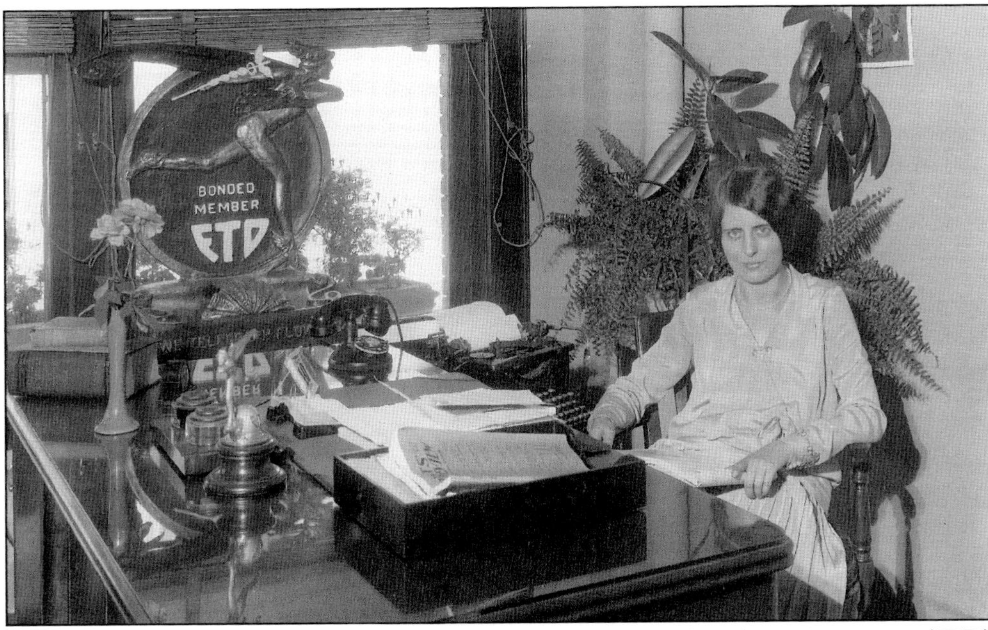


Gwen Dew started the publicity department of the Florists Telegraph Delivery Association (FTD). She designed the FTD Running Mercury logo and is shown here at her office in Detroit in 1928.

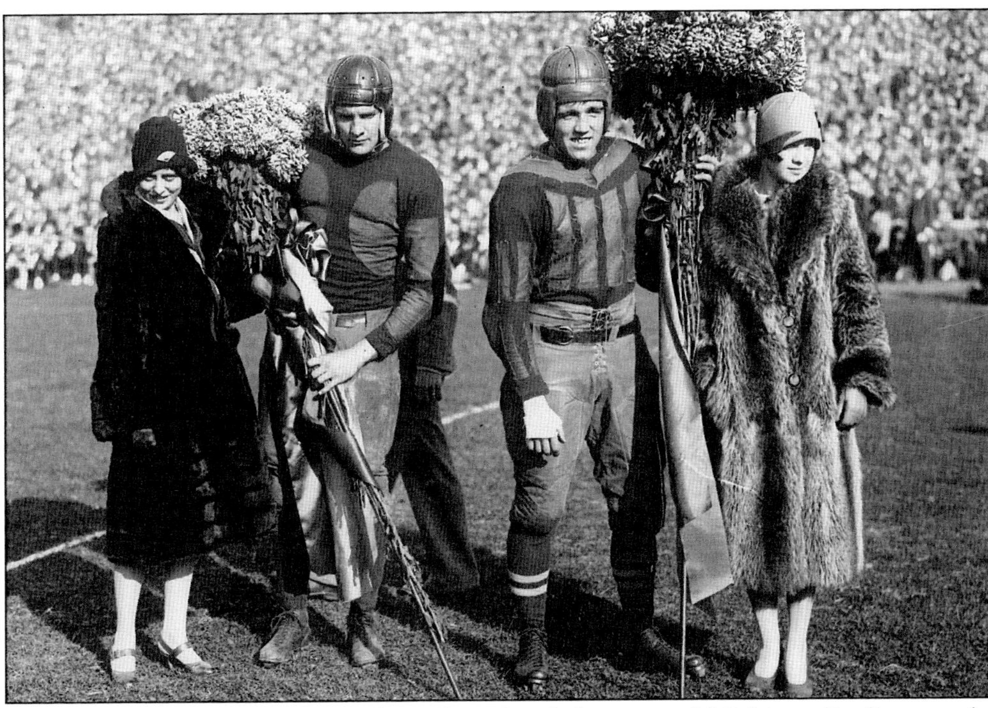

Gwen Dew served as "Miss Michigan" at the dedication of Michigan Stadium at the University of Michigan on October 23, 1927. She is shown here on the right with Michigan football captain Bennie Oosterbaan, who is holding a large bouquet of FTD flowers. On the left is the Ohio State captain and queen.

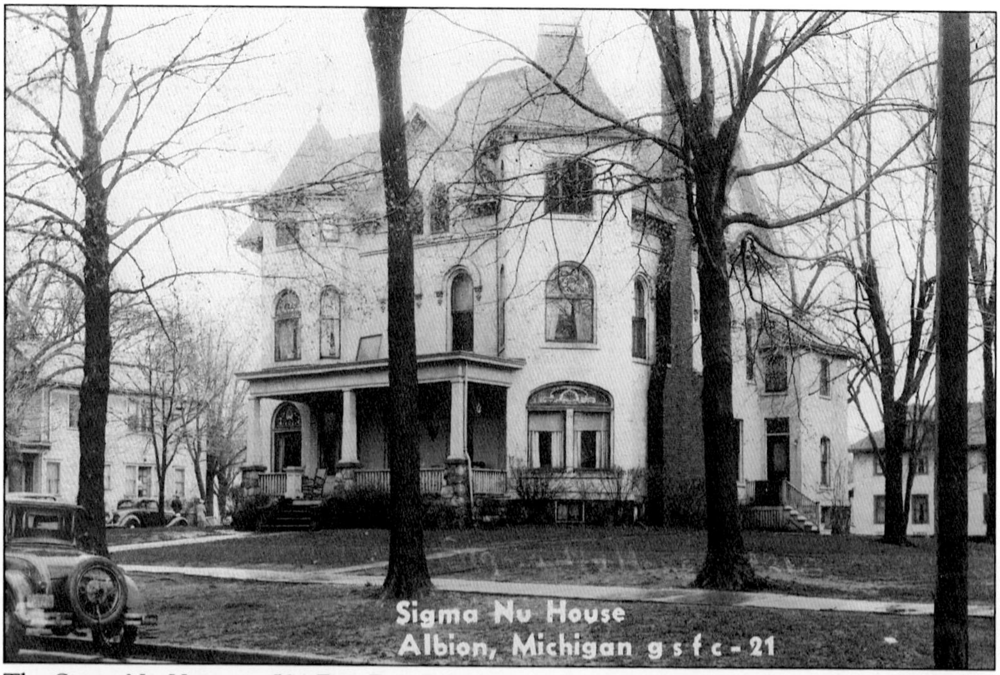


The Sigma Nu House at 504 East Erie Street was one of several large and majestic fraternity houses on the campus of Albion College that were landmarks for many years. Nicknamed "the castle," the house had originally been the home of Sylvester Allen, vice president of the Commercial & Savings Bank. Replacement fraternity houses were built by Albion College in 1966, and the Sigma Nu House, as well as others, were thereby demolished.

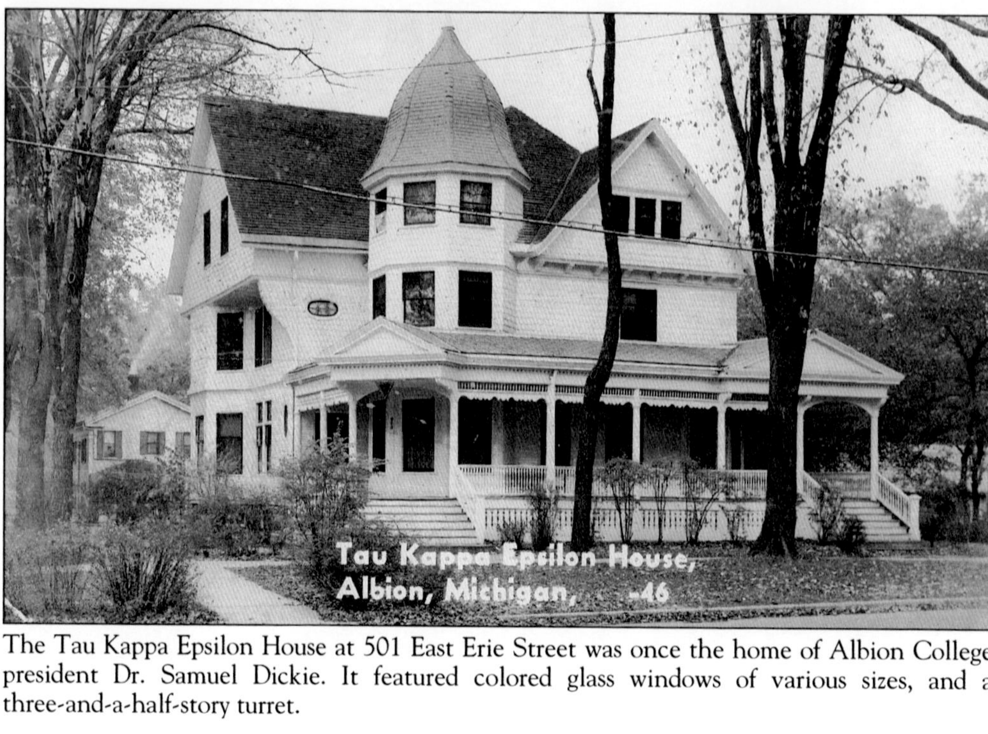


The Tau Kappa Epsilon House at 501 East Erie Street was once the home of Albion College president Dr. Samuel Dickie. It featured colored glass windows of various sizes, and a three-and-a-half-story turret.

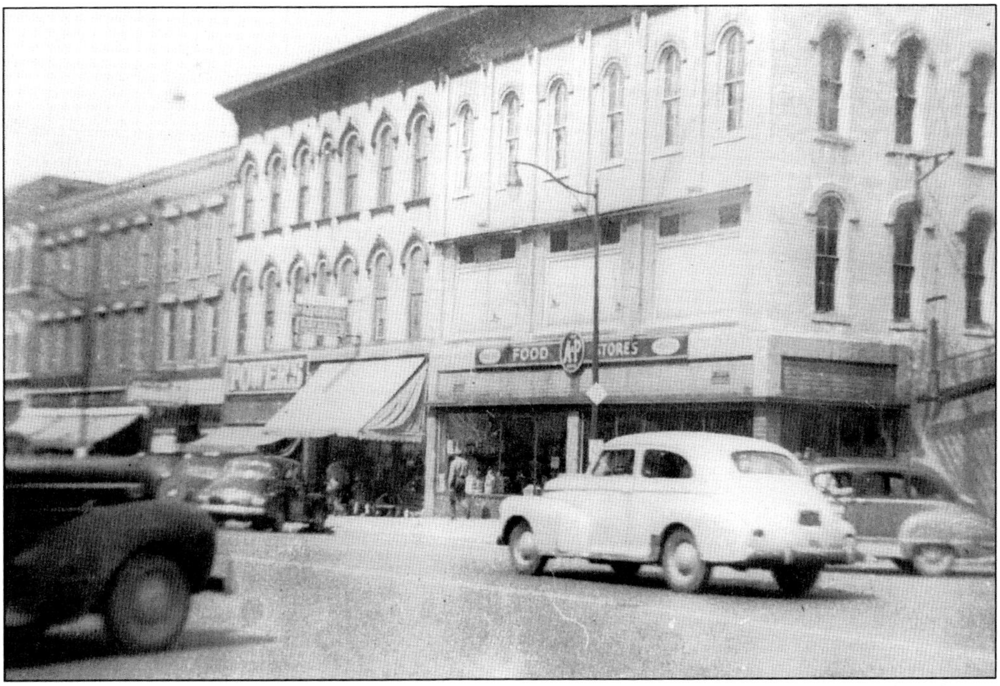


The Atlantic & Pacific Tea Company came to Albion in 1921. In 1934 it moved to larger quarters at 315 South Superior Street, as shown in this late 1930s photo. It remained here until the A&P Supermarket opened on South Eaton Street in 1954. Here we see automobiles competing for crossing rights at the busy intersection in front of the store.

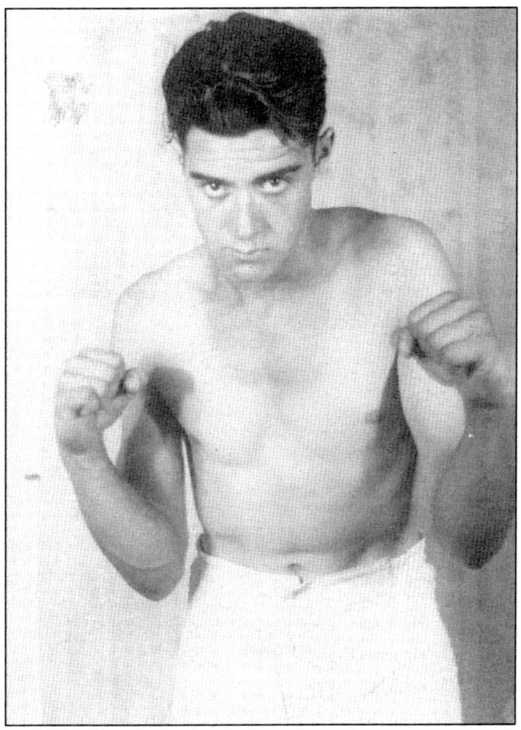

Ralph Locke began his amateur boxing career in 1931, and promoted his first amateur boxing show in Albion in 1937. Locke has coached numerous local, state, and national Golden Glove tournaments. A legend in the boxing community, he is shown in this 1937 photograph as a welterweight. Locke was inducted into the Michigan Amateur Sports Hall of Fame in 1976, and was named the 1985 Michigan Golden Gloves Outstanding Coach of the Year. (Photo courtesy of David Locke.)

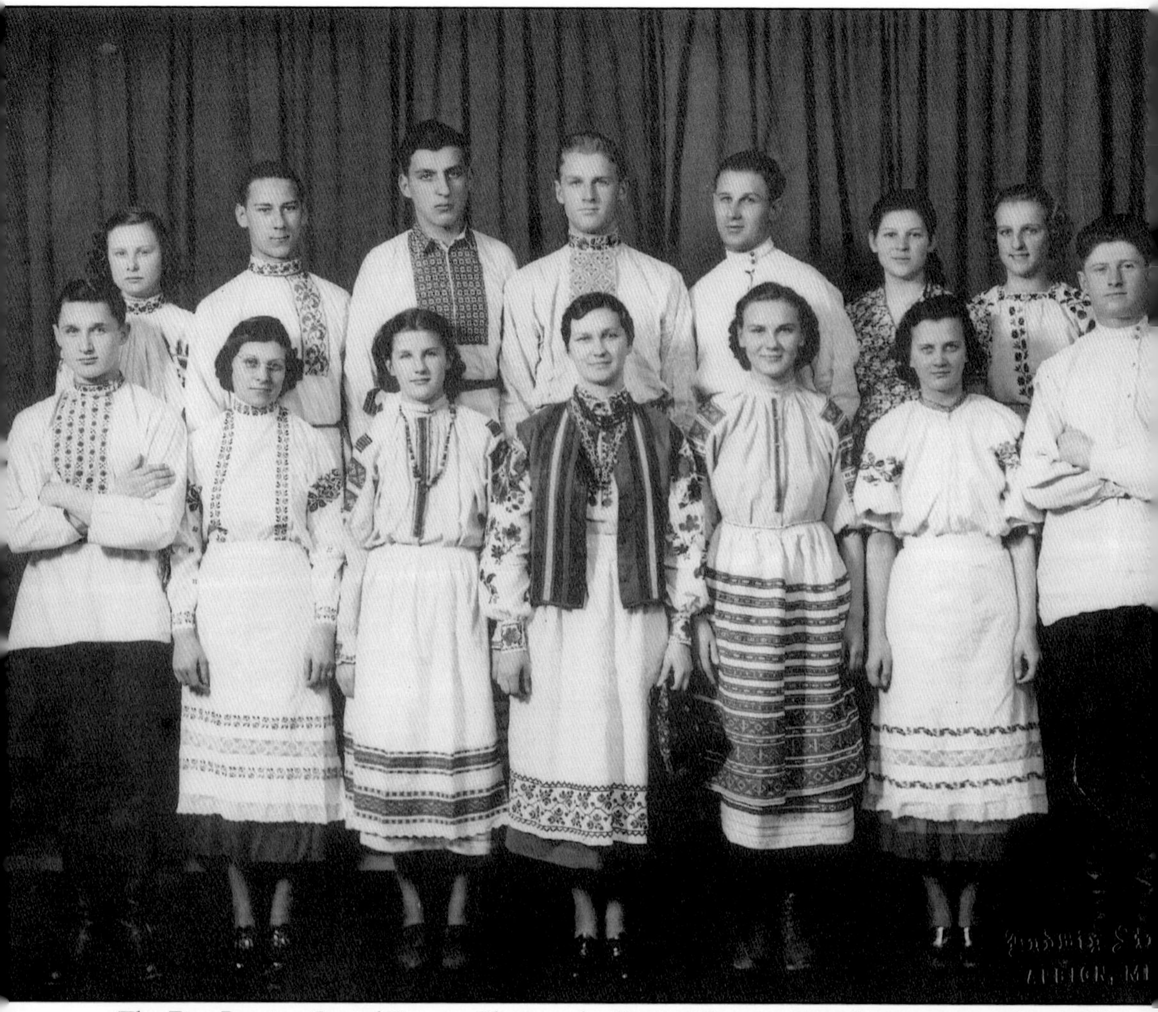

The First Russian Gospel Singers Choir at the Russian Baptist Church was organized in 1935 under the direction of Mary (Prigodich) Felisky. The costumes were made by the parents of the choir members. This choir made recordings for short-wave radio stations, which transmitted behind the Iron Curtain during the era of Communism. The choir was in existence until 1959. This was the choir lineup in 1938, from left to right: (front row) Joseph Veramay, Stella Elushik, Esther Veramay, Mary Felisky, Naida Lazarchuk, Leada Brankovich, and John Harry; (back row) Sophie Grenevitch, Victor Nesterenko, Russell Elushik (who was killed during World War II), John Veramay, Steve Veramay, Katherine Veramay, and Helen Elushik. (Photo courtesy of Tim Felisky.)

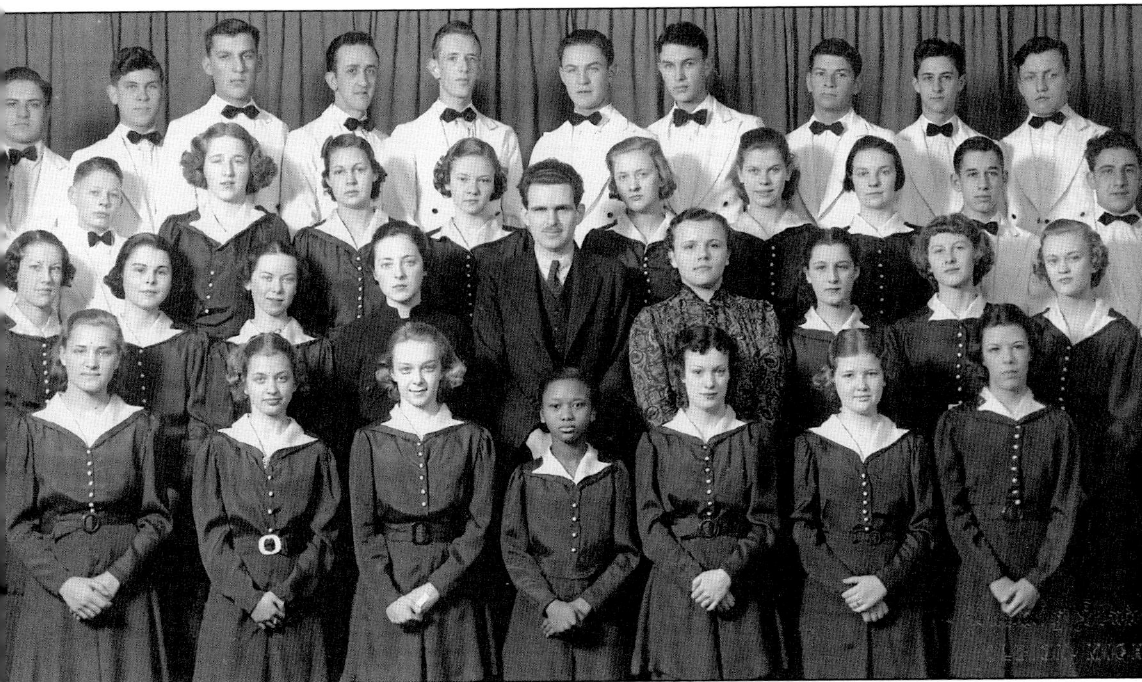

The Albion High School Glee Club, 1936-37 year is captured for posterity, from left to right: (front row) Olga Podayko, Jean Comfort, Norma Esling, Ruth Carr, Virginia Bohm, Jean Hart, and Viva O'Dell; (second row) Hazel Simmers, Wilta Behling, Evelyn Dolberg, Mary Jarvis, Mr. Hardin Van Deursen, instructor, Elizabeth Birdsall, Geraldine Bradford, Helen Randall, and Esther Caines; (third row) James Curtis, Bud Davis, Virginia Payne, Lucille Kreger, Priscilla Gale, Mary Caines, Alfreda Sweeney, Mary E. Davis, Frank Stetler, and Guy Vitale; (back row) Richard Nass, Alfred Sweeney, Russell Elushik, John Johnson, David Billings, K. Bruce Maier, H. Bruce Ragan, David Shifkey, Stephen Hathaway, and Wayne Fitch. (Photo courtesy of Guy Vitale.)

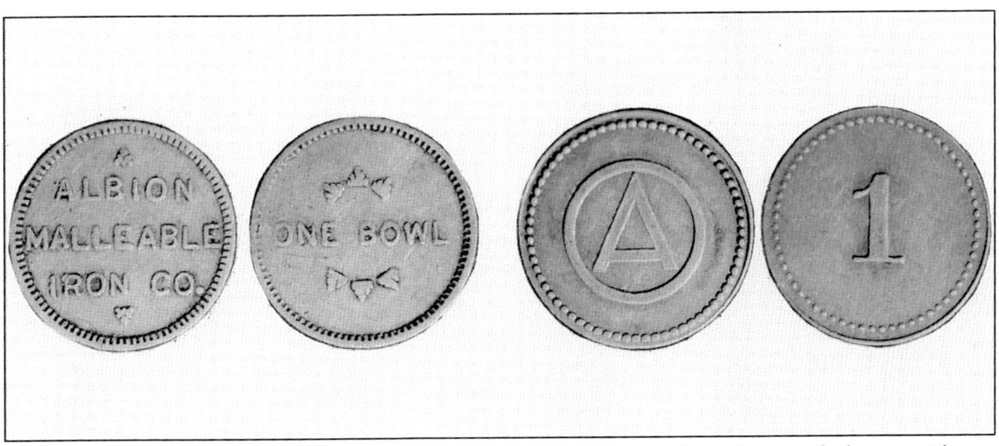


Workers at the Albion Malleable Iron Company received these token chips each day as evidence of their piece-rate during the 1930s through 1937. "Bowl pushers" collected the hot molten iron in buckets from the furnace and poured it into ladles. "Pourers" poured the ladles of iron into molds to form castings. Tokens were given for each bucket or ladle poured, and workers turned them in at the end of the workday in order to get properly paid.

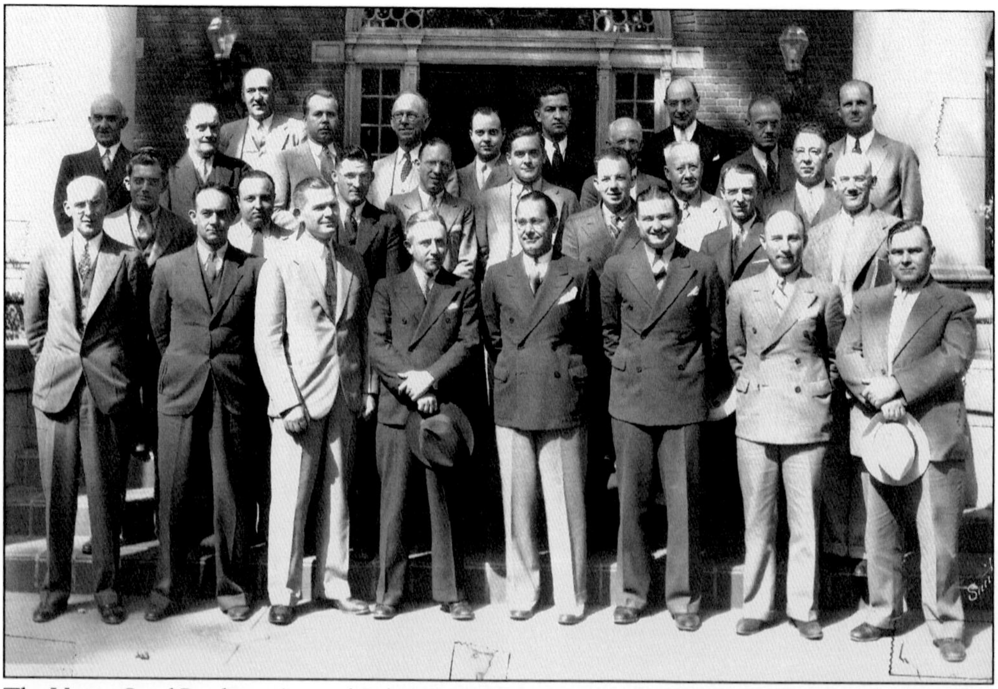

The Union Steel Products Annual Sales Meeting in 1935 was held at the Parker Inn. Participants were, from left to right: (front row) I.A. Marshall, Fredd Barr, Dewey Bitney, Brockway Dickey, Oliver Otting, Miles Decker, A.N. Cohen, and Charles Hughes; (second row) Lloyd Bacon, O. Blankenbaker, Clarence Hagerman, Norman Gibbings, Harley Transue, Ed Griffin, W.J. MacBeth, T.M. Smith, Walter Evans, and Reginald Smith; (back row) Robert Thompson, Walter Peak, Charles Gaffney, Stuart Carver, A.T. Bruffee, Bernard Chesebrough, Wayne Stevens, Phil Steinmiller, Carl T. Hatch, Herbert Johnson, and W. Clark Dean.

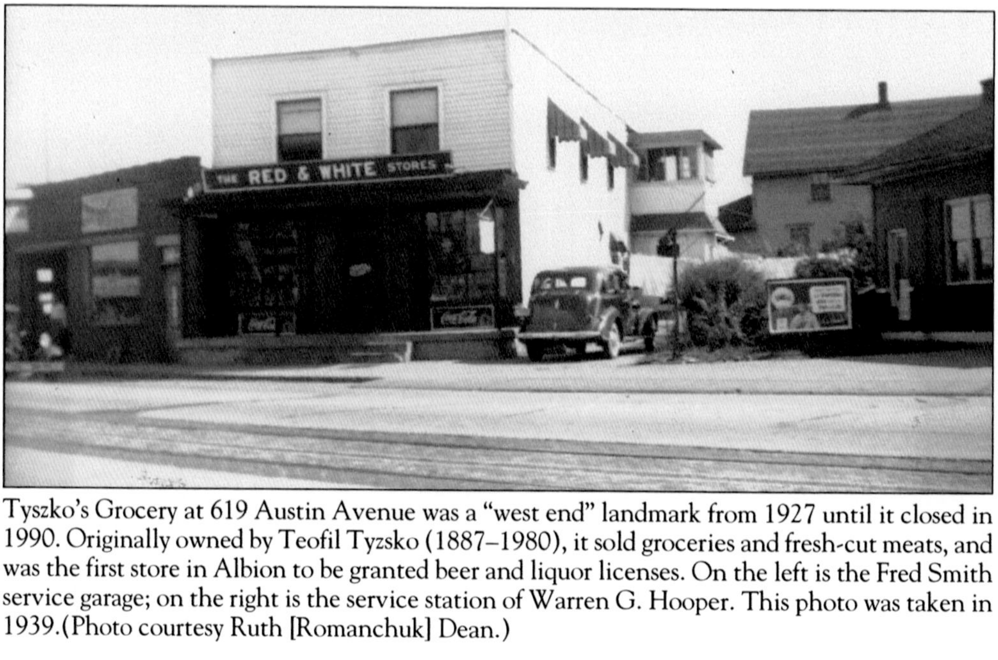


Tyszko's Grocery at 619 Austin Avenue was a "west end" landmark from 1927 until it closed in 1990. Originally owned by Teofil Tyzsko (1887–1980), it sold groceries and fresh-cut meats, and was the first store in Albion to be granted beer and liquor licenses. On the left is the Fred Smith service garage; on the right is the service station of Warren G. Hooper. This photo was taken in 1939.(Photo courtesy Ruth [Romanchuk] Dean.)

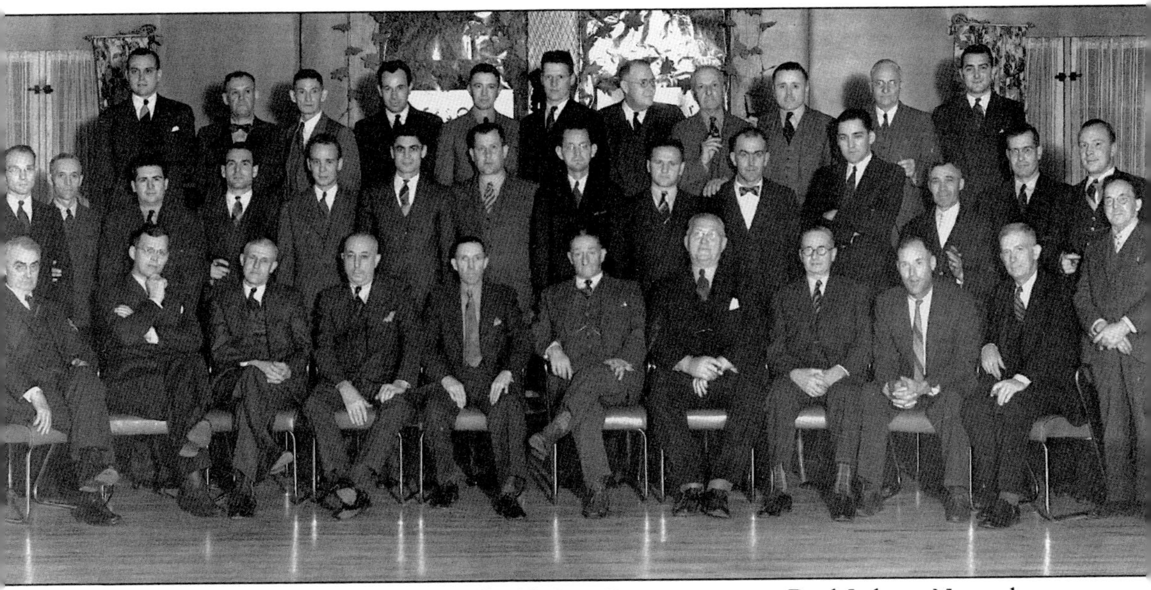

Officials and supervisors of the Albion Malleable Iron Company meet at Duck Lake on November 18, 1938. They are, from left to right: (front row) August Lohrke, George Schumacher, Emil Holtz, Ed Kotz, Ross Greene, Harry Greene, Carl Schumacher, George Overy, Dr. Alf Hafford, Lee Boyd, and Billy Banks; (center row) Darwood Coddington, Charles Kopp, unidentified, Al Smith, Gardner Lloyd, Steve Pasick, Paul Knopp, Bert Lambert, Paul Sawchuk, Harry Kline, Don Edwards, Fred Kopp, Harold Ford, and Collins Carter; (top row) Thomas T. Lloyd, Ernest Cable, Leo Wheeler, Al Stone, Waldo Murray, Jack Burden, William Bellman, Fred Bell, Larry Morris, Alvin Dice, and Don Dice.

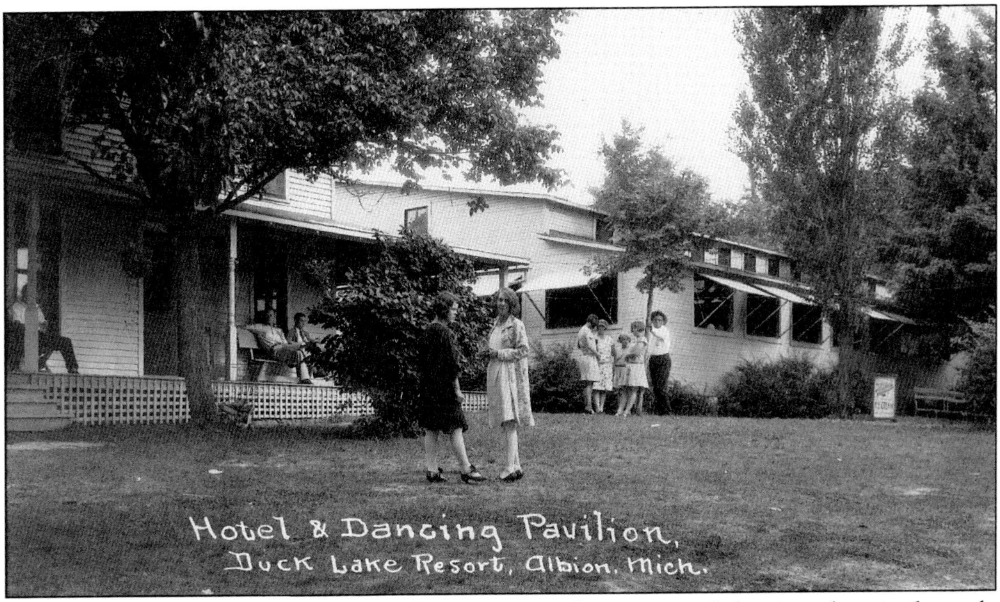


The Duck Lake Hotel and Dance Pavilion was a popular eating and dancing place in the early 20th century. A general store and a dining room operated in the hotel portion shown here on the left, while orchestras played in the 1920-built pavilion addition on the right. The complex burned on May 31, 1936, and was replaced by the "Wells Dine, Drink and Dance."

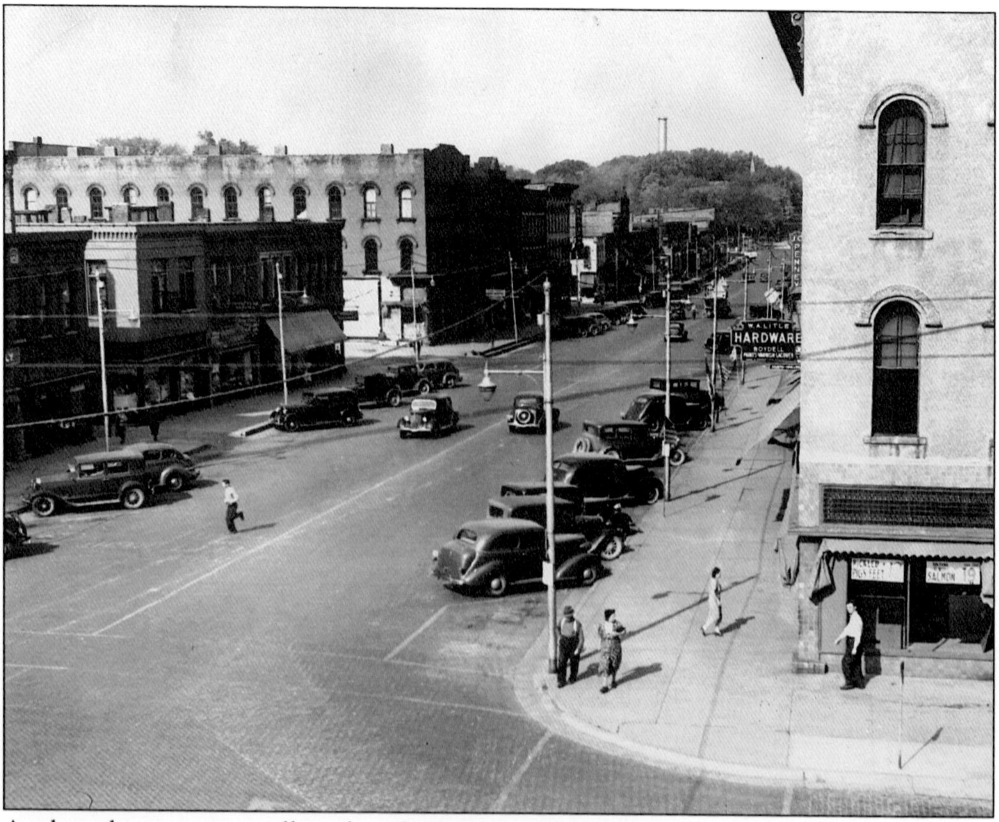

Angle parking was once allowed on Superior Street in downtown Albion, as shown in this 1939 photograph, looking north from Erie Street. The following year (1940) the street bricks were replaced with new ones, and parallel parking lines were laid. (Photo courtesy of the *Albion Recorder*.)

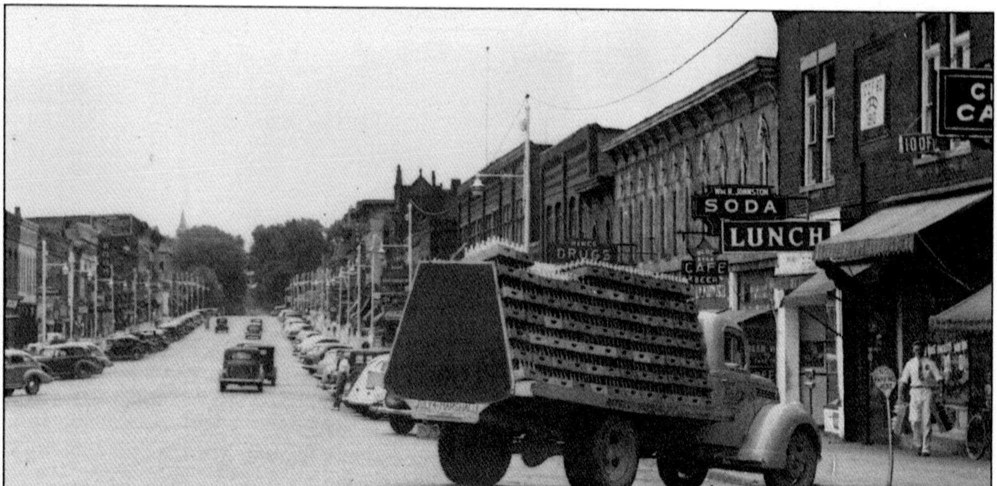

This beverage truck is angle-parked on the east side of the 200 block of North Superior Street in this 1939 photograph. (Photo courtesy of the *Albion Recorder*.)

*Three*

# A Time of War, A Time of Peace 1940–1959

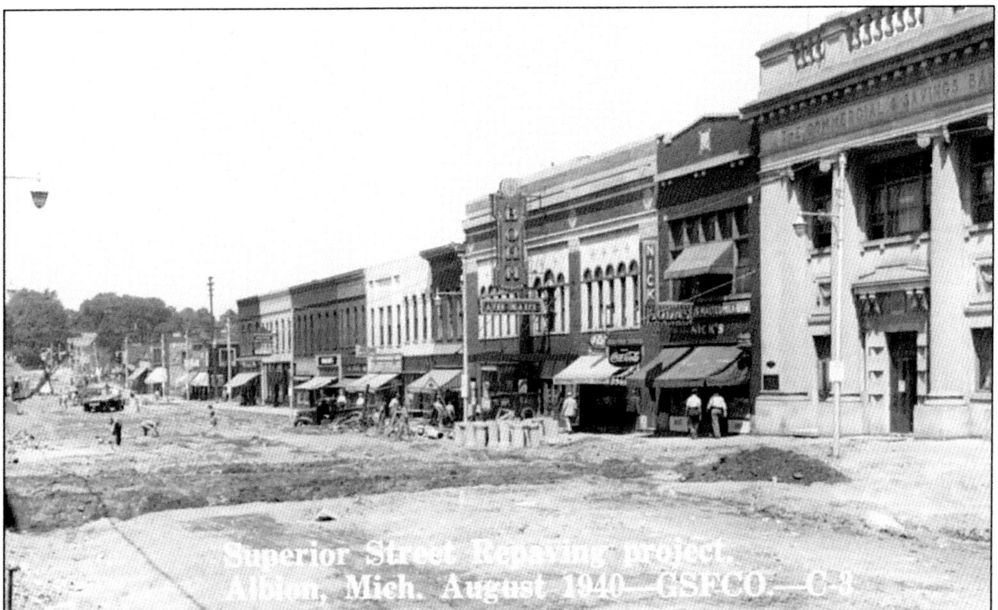


Superior Street in downtown Albion was repaved with new paving bricks in the summer of 1940 at a cost of $55,319. Here we see work being done in preparation for the laying of a new concrete base. The 1940 bricks were replaced with new ones in 1993.

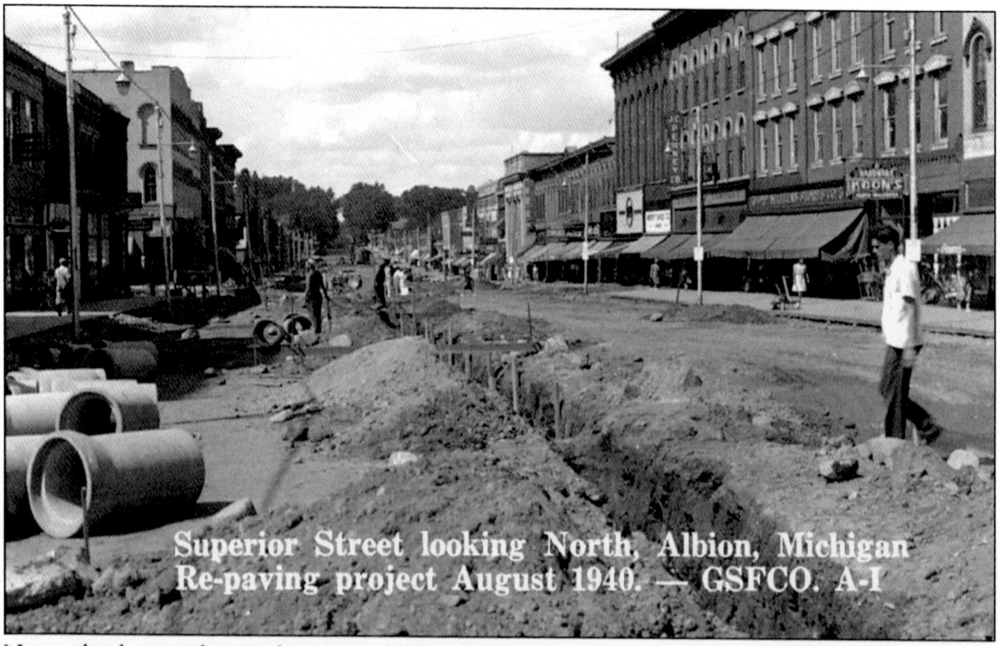


New utility lines and storm drains were laid under Superior Street as part of the 1940 repaving project. Steve Marvin (right) is shown walking across the street in this reconstruction photograph.

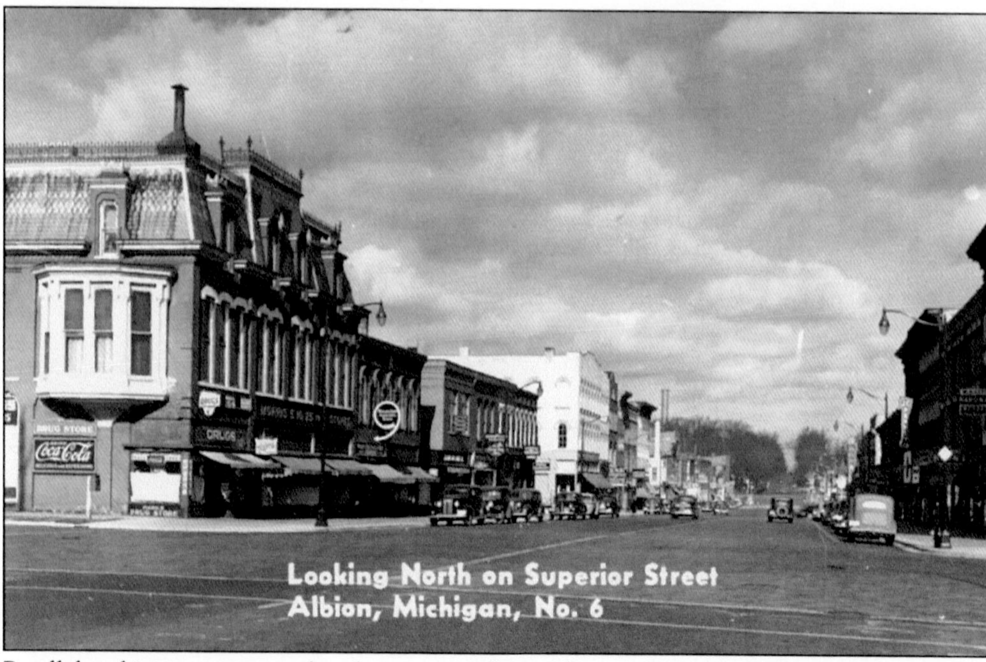


Parallel parking was instituted in downtown Albion following the laying of new street bricks in 1940. The pavement carried two lanes of traffic each way on busy M-99, as shown in this scene from the mid-1940s. On the left in the Sheldon Block is Parks Drug Store, a long-time Albion business, followed by the Morris Variety Store.

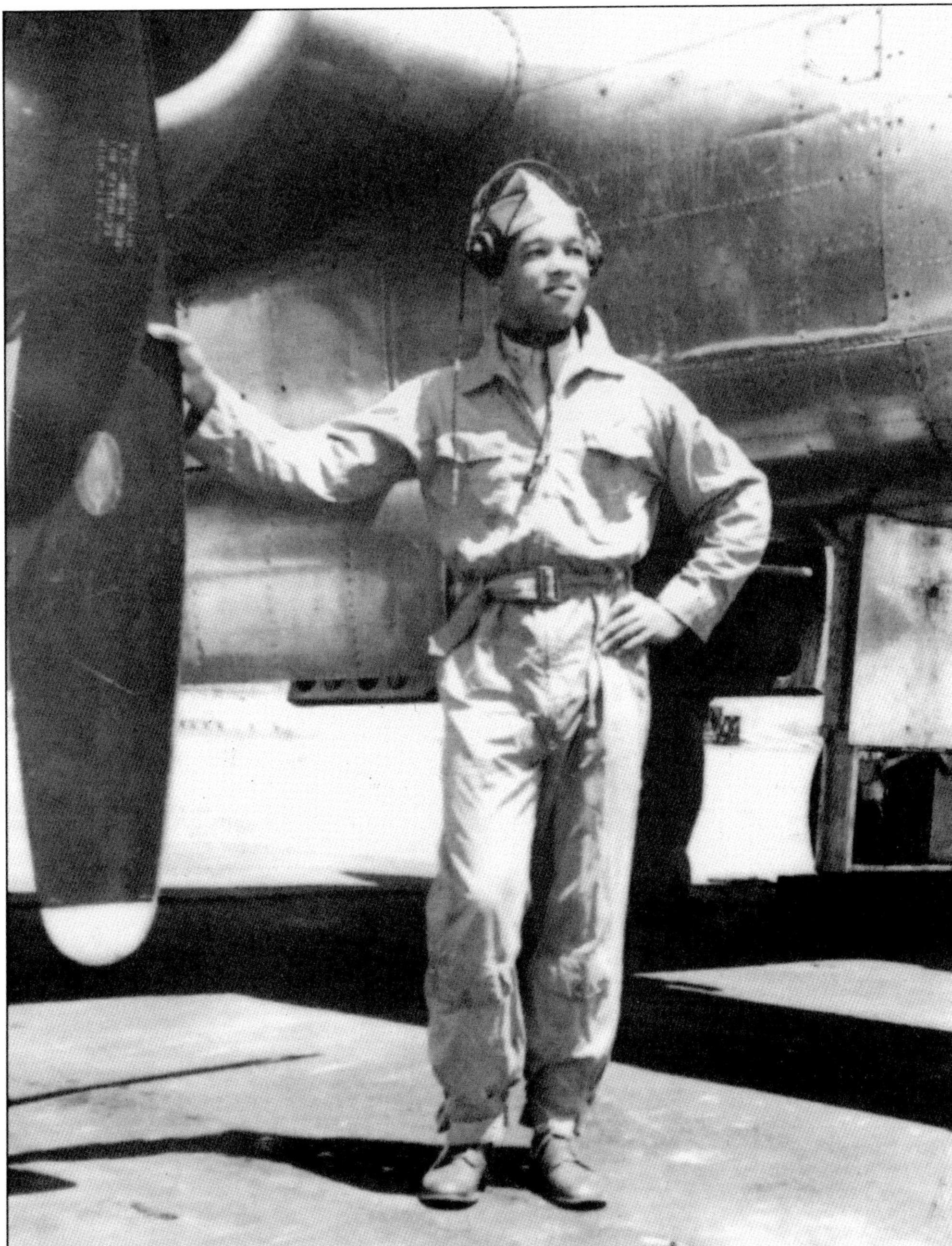

Four World War II soldiers who lived in Albion at various times served as Tuskegee Airmen during World War II: Robert Chandler, Grover Crumbsy, Finis Holt, and Richard Weatherford. The Tuskegee Airmen consisted of nearly 1,000 black soldiers who were trained at the Tuskegee Institute in Alabama to become pilots in the U.S. Army Air Corps. The Airmen unit served valiantly in Europe and North Africa, flying over 1,500 missions. Albion's former Airmen were recognized at a special reception held in their honor on February 22, 1998 at Starr Commonwealth. ABOVE: Pilot Richard Weatherford poses next to his B-52 Mitchell bomber in this 1943 photograph.

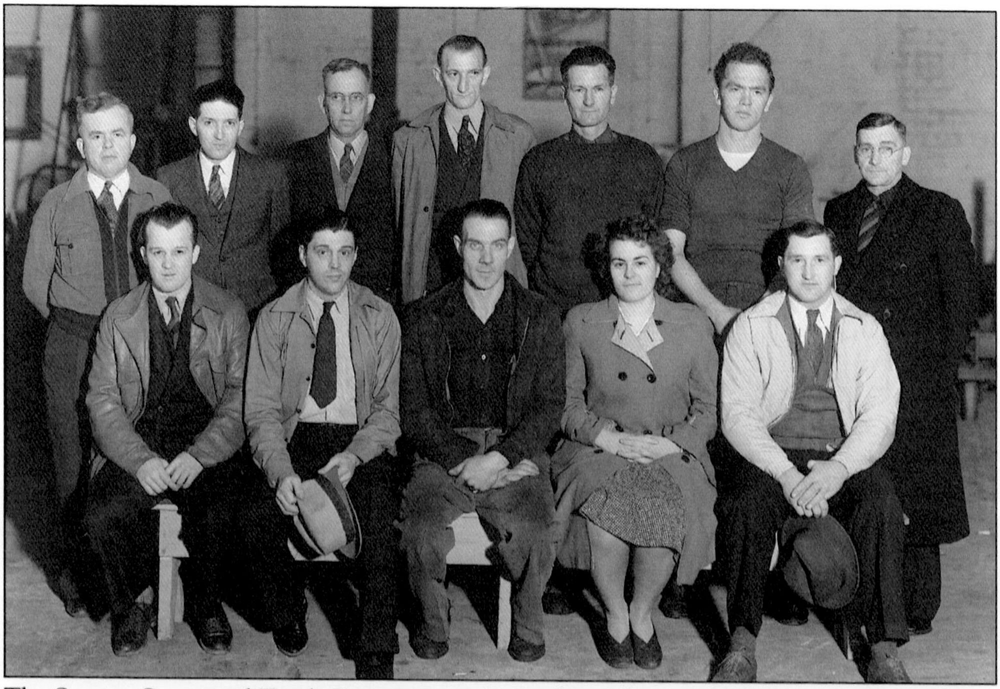

The Service Caster and Truck Company was located in Albion from 1923 to 1954, and was a major producer of casters, industrial trucks, trailers, and fork lift trucks. Pictured here are union officials, *c.* 1940, from left to right: (front row) Gilbert Sharrar, Robert Woods, Ken Matson, Helen Ellerby, and Harley Guy; (back row) Frank Radtke, Gerald Davis, Carl Franklin, Don Stockton, unidentified, John Marzic, and Ray Stahl.

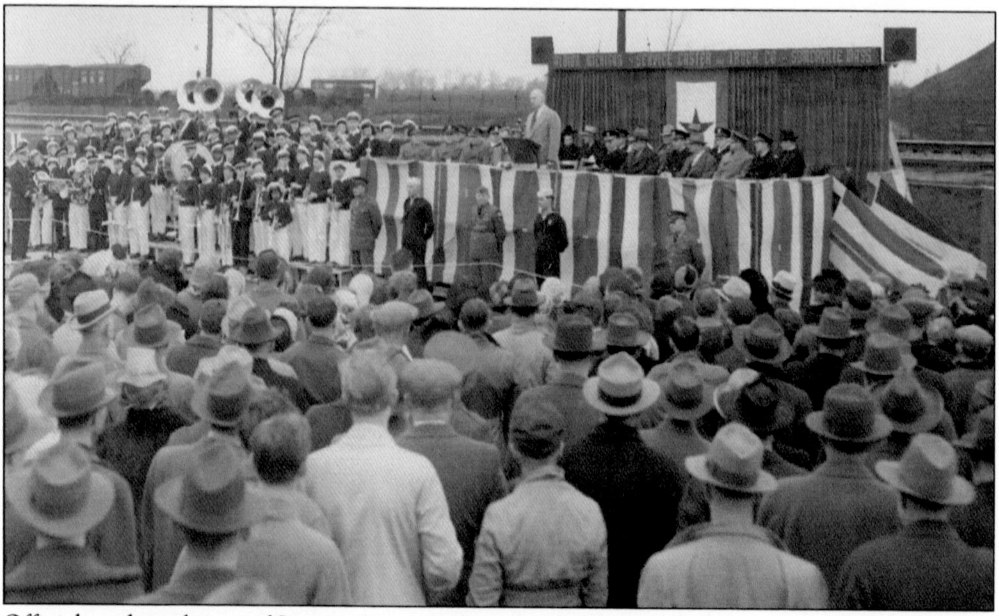

Officials and employees of Service Caster gathered on March 24, 1943, to receive the prestigious Army-Navy Production "E" Award for high achievement in the production of War equipment. Master of ceremonies was State Senator Joseph A. Baldwin.

Colonel Joseph Duckworth (1902–1964) was the first person to purposely fly through the eye of a hurricane (July 27, 1943). Colonel Duckworth was an experienced U.S. Air Force pilot, and is considered the "father" of modern-day instrument flying. His training manuals were used by the Air Force for many years and were a major contribution to World War II, and the 1948 Berlin airlift. He was in command of Hickman Air Force Base in Hawaii when he retired in 1955. Duckworth spent his retirement years in Albion where his wife Mildred (1899–1976) taught elementary school. He is buried in Riverside Cemetery.

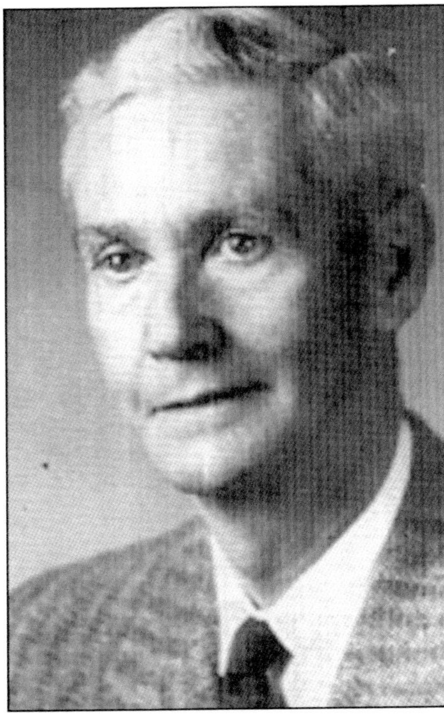

Albion native Audrey K. Wilder (1896–1979) served as dean of women at Albion College from 1949 to 1962, and was active in numerous local, state, and national organizations. During World War II, Audrey was one of 191 teachers enrolled in a work-study program in Detroit stores and factories to help with the War effort. She is pictured here operating a lathe at the Dodge automotive plant in Detroit in 1944.

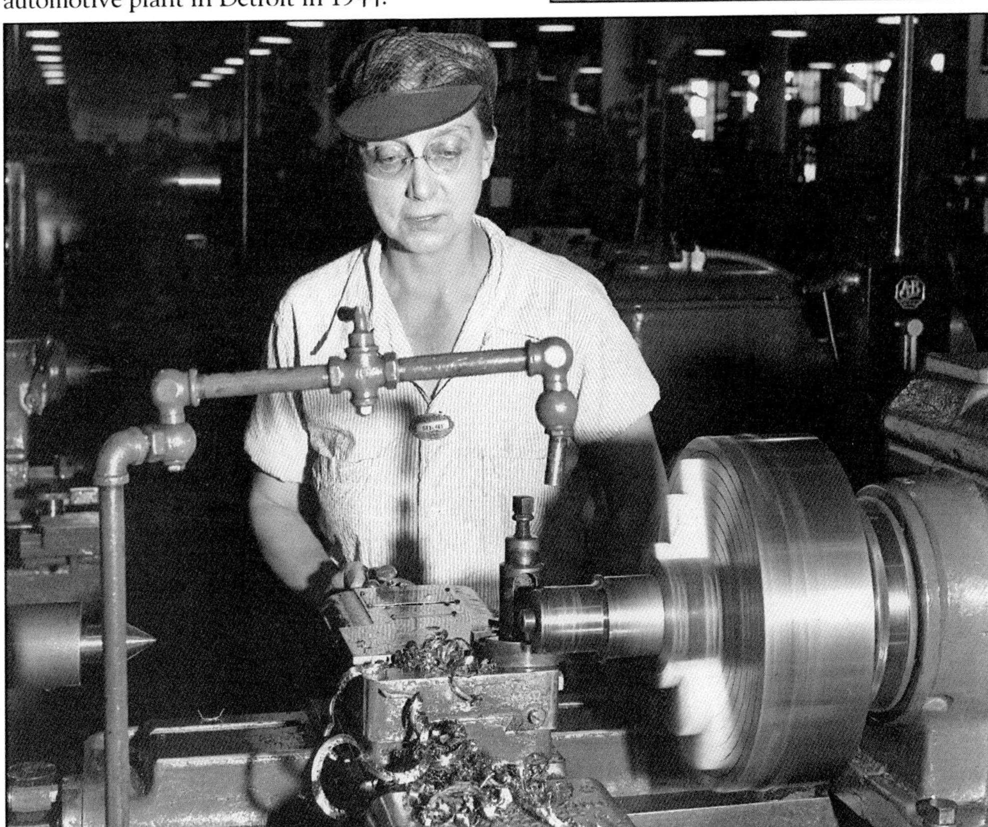

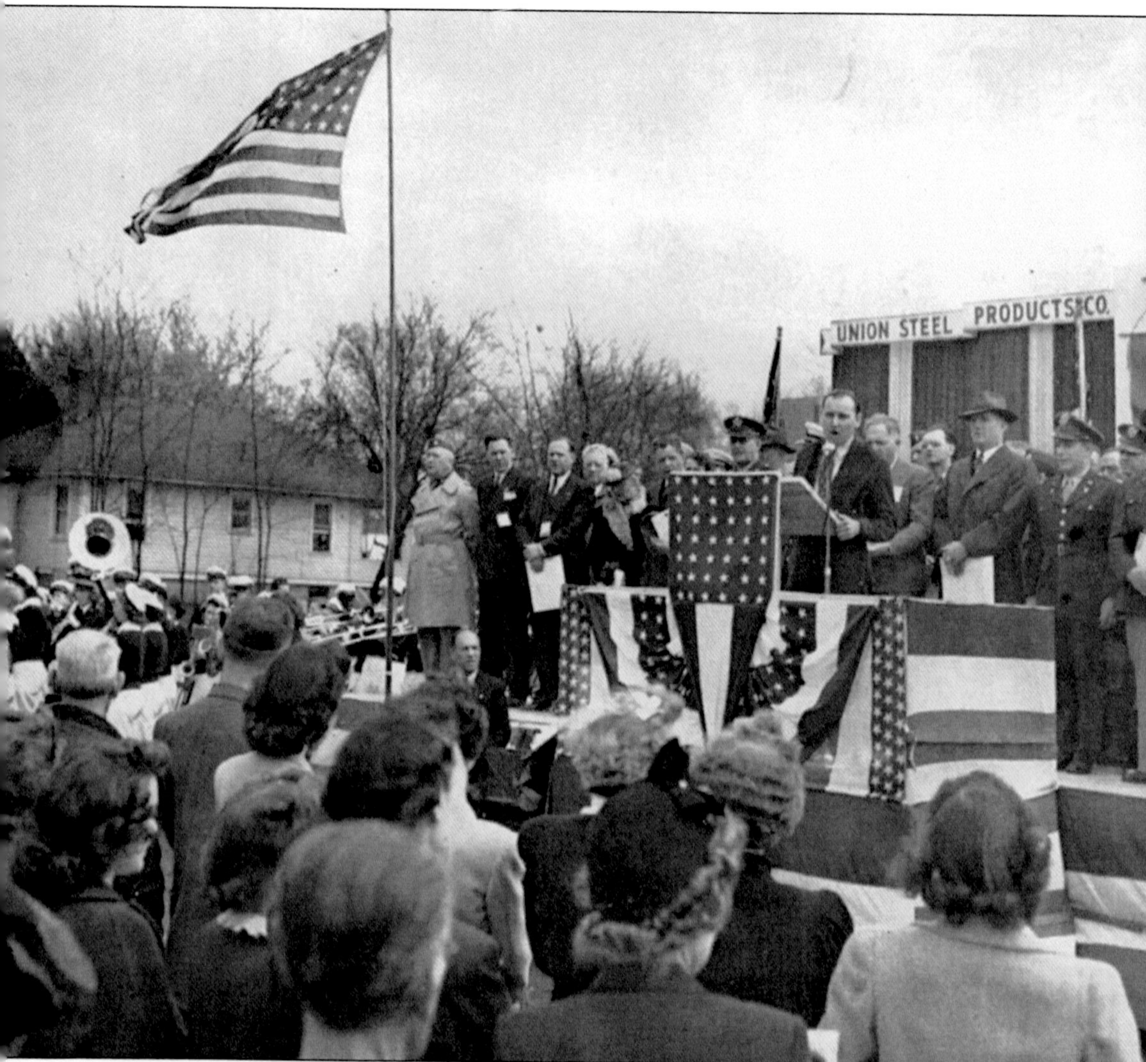


Mike Nester (1910–1999) leads the crowd of over 1,500 persons at Union Steel Products in the singing of "America" on May 5, 1943. On that day Union Steel Products received the Army-Navy "E" Award, the nation's highest tribute for excellence in war production. During World War II, Union Steel manufactured numerous items for military use, including: hydrostatic bombs used against enemy submarines, submarine parts, torpedo components, bakery shelves, bakery and field ovens, racks, airplane landing mats, airplane shell ejector chutes, and handling baskets for ammunition, motor parts, shells, and casings. Around-the-clock production kept war materials rolling out in record quantities.

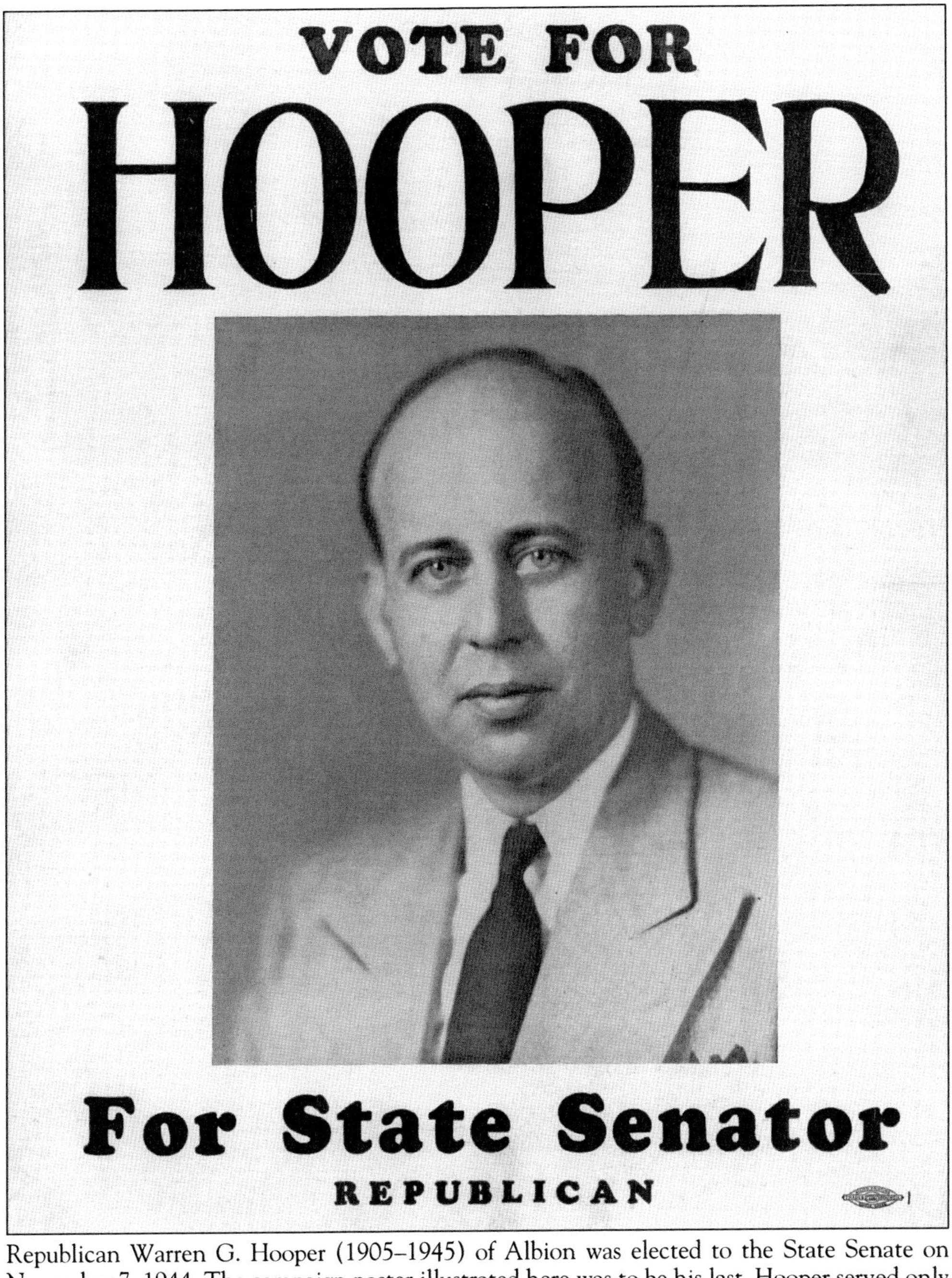


Republican Warren G. Hooper (1905–1945) of Albion was elected to the State Senate on November 7, 1944. The campaign poster illustrated here was to be his last. Hooper served only two weeks in office beginning in January 1945. He was scheduled to testify to a grand jury about corruption and bribery that existed in the Michigan Legislature, of which Hooper had been member of (House of Representatives) since 1938. Senator Hooper was shot to death in his car gangland style coming back from Lansing along a lonely stretch of M-99 north of Springport on January 16, 1945. Members of the notorious Purple Gang were suspected of carrying out the dastardly deed at the direction of political bosses. Four Gang members were subsequently convicted of conspiracy to murder Senator Hooper.

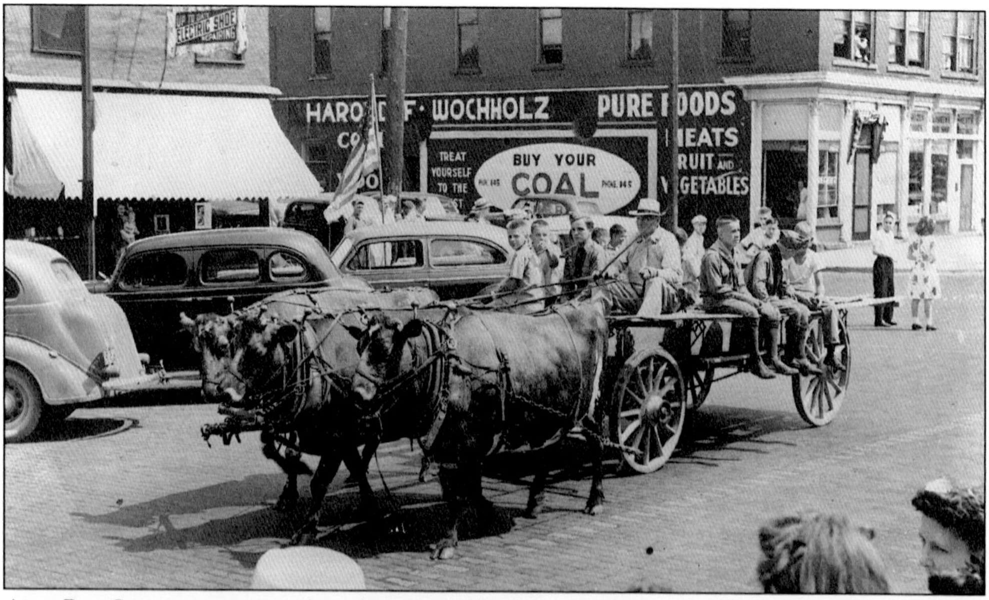


Area Boy Scouts participated in the 1943 4th of July parade with this wagon float pulled by oxen, from left to right: Ralph Butler Jr., David Mills (pointing), Don Crandall, unidentified driver, Wayne Crandall, Larry Crandall, and unidentified. The Bournelis Shoe Repair is on the left, with the Wochholz Fuel & Grocery on the right. (Photo courtesy of Steve Mills.)

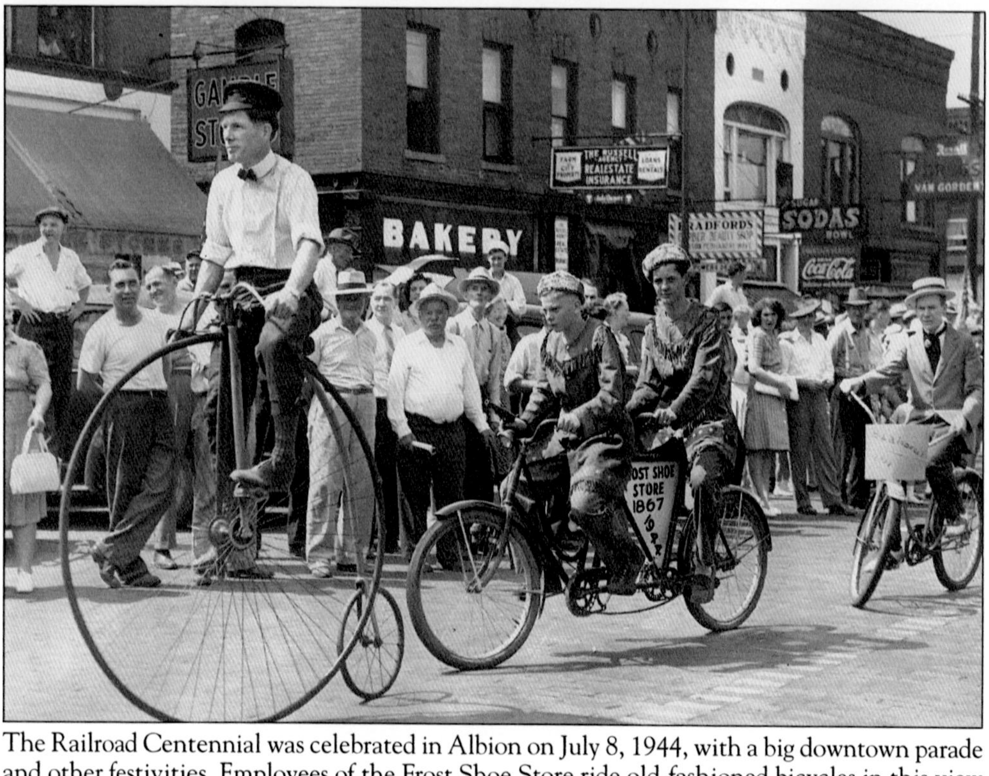


The Railroad Centennial was celebrated in Albion on July 8, 1944, with a big downtown parade and other festivities. Employees of the Frost Shoe Store ride old-fashioned bicycles in this view facing the west side of the 100 block of South Superior Street.

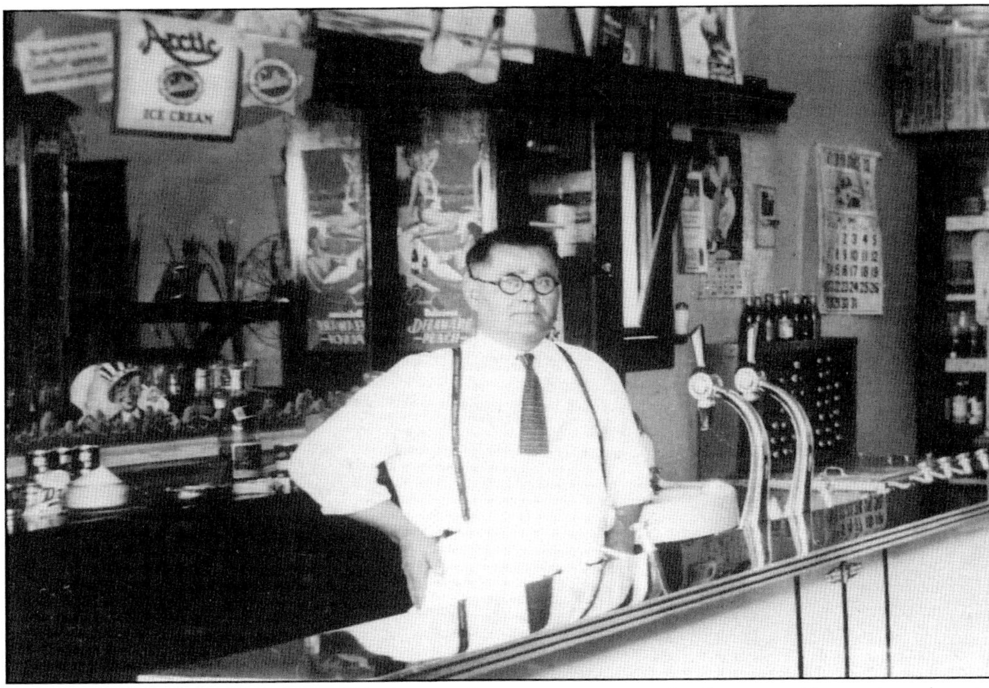


The Koroluk Confectionary at 610 Austin Avenue was a popular "west end" meeting place in the early 20th century. A native of White Russia, Paul Koroluk (1888–1967) came to Albion in 1927, and operated his candy-soda-ice cream establishment until 1948. He is shown standing in back of the counter in this May 1945 photograph.

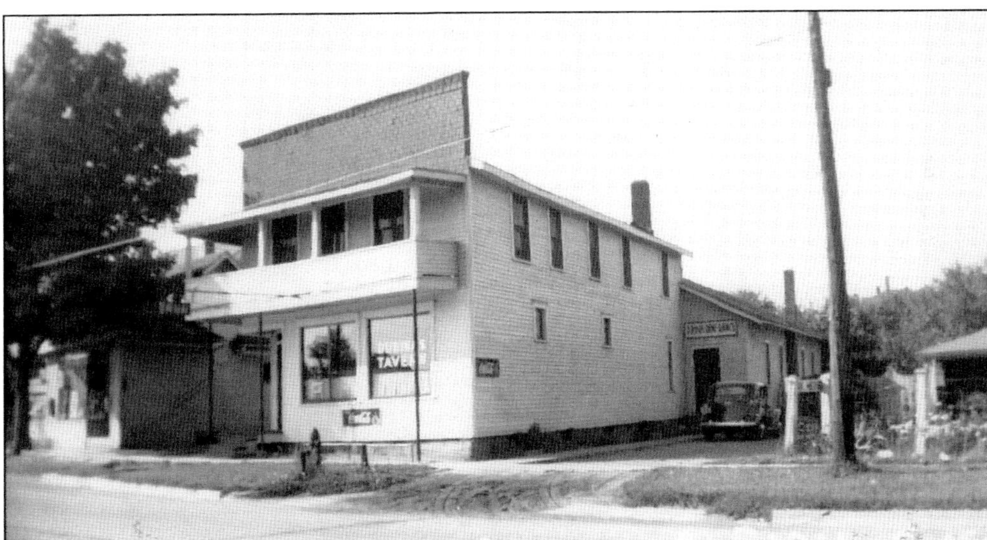

Polka parties were held on Saturday nights at Dubina's Tavern and Dance Hall at 604 Austin Avenue during the 1930s and 1940s. The Dance Hall sign in the back states "DINE, DRINK, DANCE." Mike (1886–1959) and Sophia (1878–1972) Dubina were the first immigrants to open a grocery store on the "west end," in 1916. They also operated a boarding house for Albion Malleable Iron Company workers. This photo was taken in 1939. (Photo courtesy Ruth [Romanchuk] Dean.)

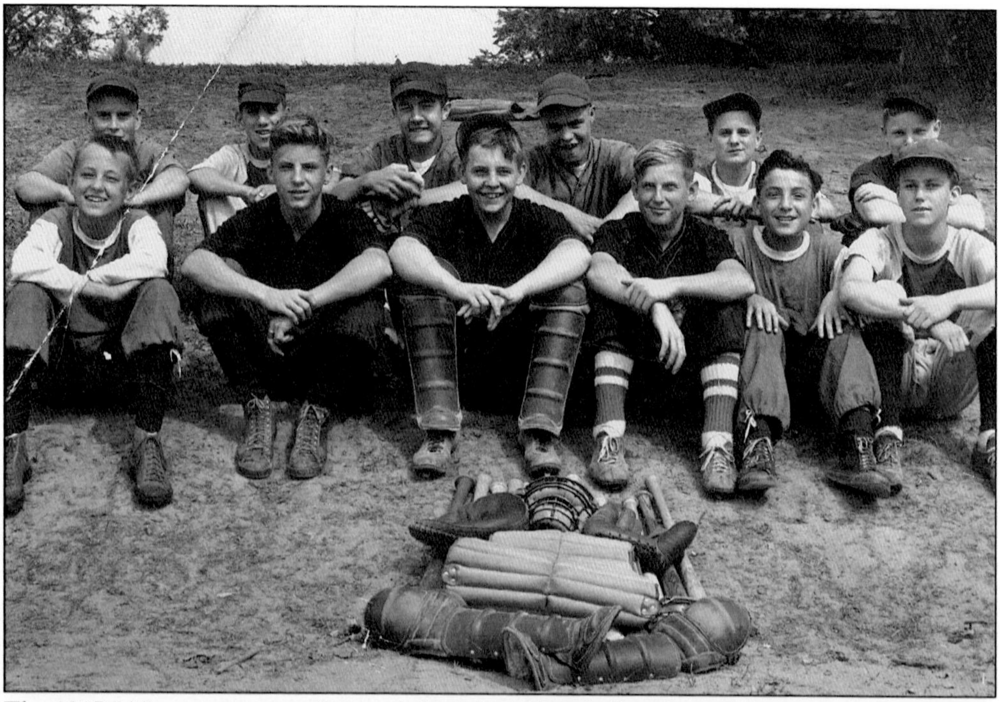

The 1947 "A" team was one of several that played baseball in the summer recreation program that year. The members, from left to right, are: (front row) Leonard Kracko, Harold "Jim" Sayles, David Mills, David Veramay, Frank Paniccia, and Tom Wallace; (back row) Frank Clark, Jim Bommarito, Phil Murran, Jim Shepherd, Ted Gibbs, and Clarence Torrey. (Photo courtesy of Steve Mills.)

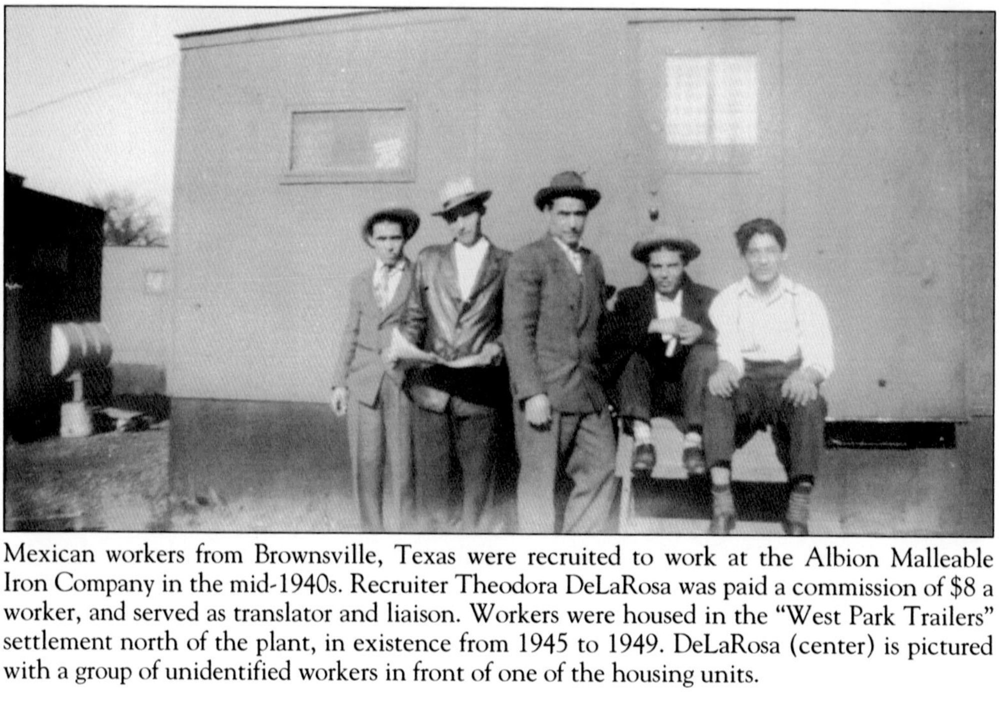

Mexican workers from Brownsville, Texas were recruited to work at the Albion Malleable Iron Company in the mid-1940s. Recruiter Theodora DeLaRosa was paid a commission of $8 a worker, and served as translator and liaison. Workers were housed in the "West Park Trailers" settlement north of the plant, in existence from 1945 to 1949. DeLaRosa (center) is pictured with a group of unidentified workers in front of one of the housing units.

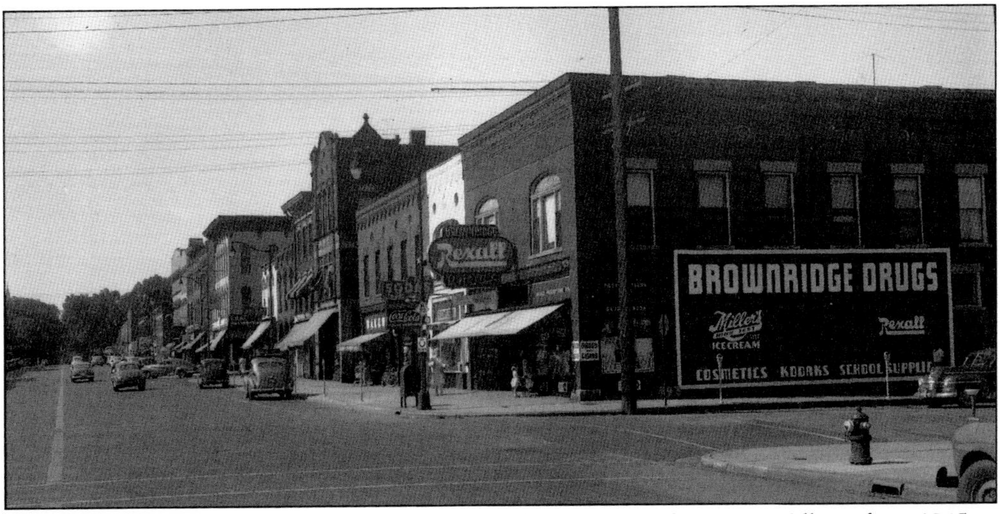


Brownridge Drugs was a well-known business establishment in downtown Albion from 1945 to 1965, as shown here in the late 1940s. It featured Rexall-brand drugs, and was operated by Joseph G. Brownridge. The store had formerly been known as Van Gorden Drugs from 1912 to 1945.

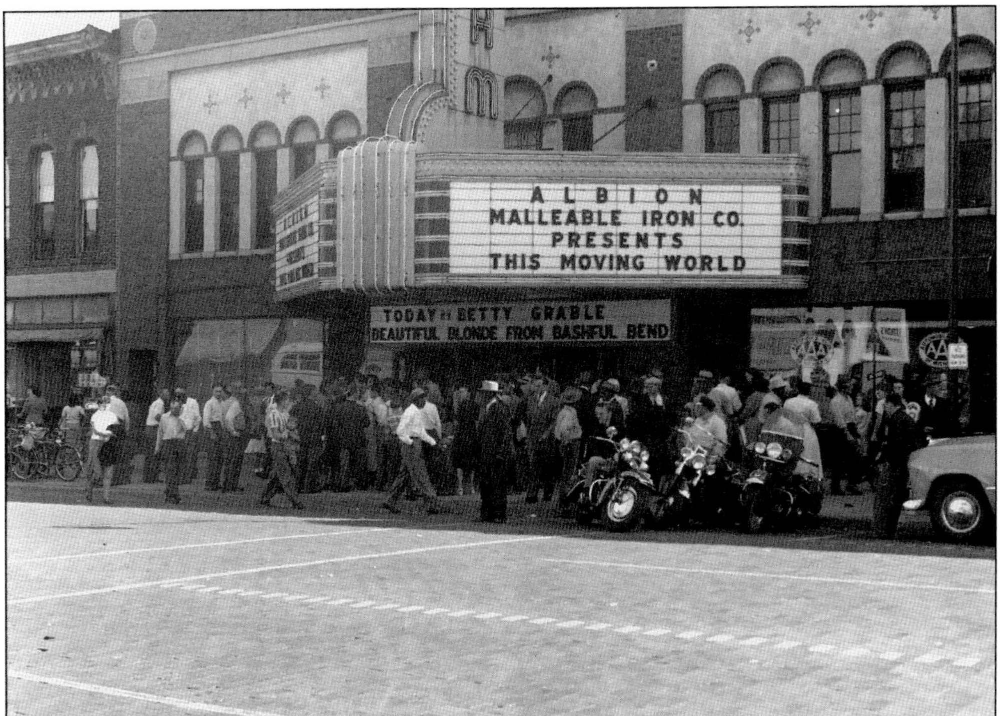


The Bohm Theatre marquee has been a landmark in downtown Albion ever since it was installed during World War II. This scene from October 8, 1949, shows a portion of the crowd of approximately 1,250 persons that attended the premier public showing of the industrial film *This Moving World*. The film dealt with the methods and processes used in producing malleable iron, and its direct application to the American economy. Produced for the Malleable Founders Society, several scenes of this technicolor film were shot locally at the Albion Malleable Iron Company.

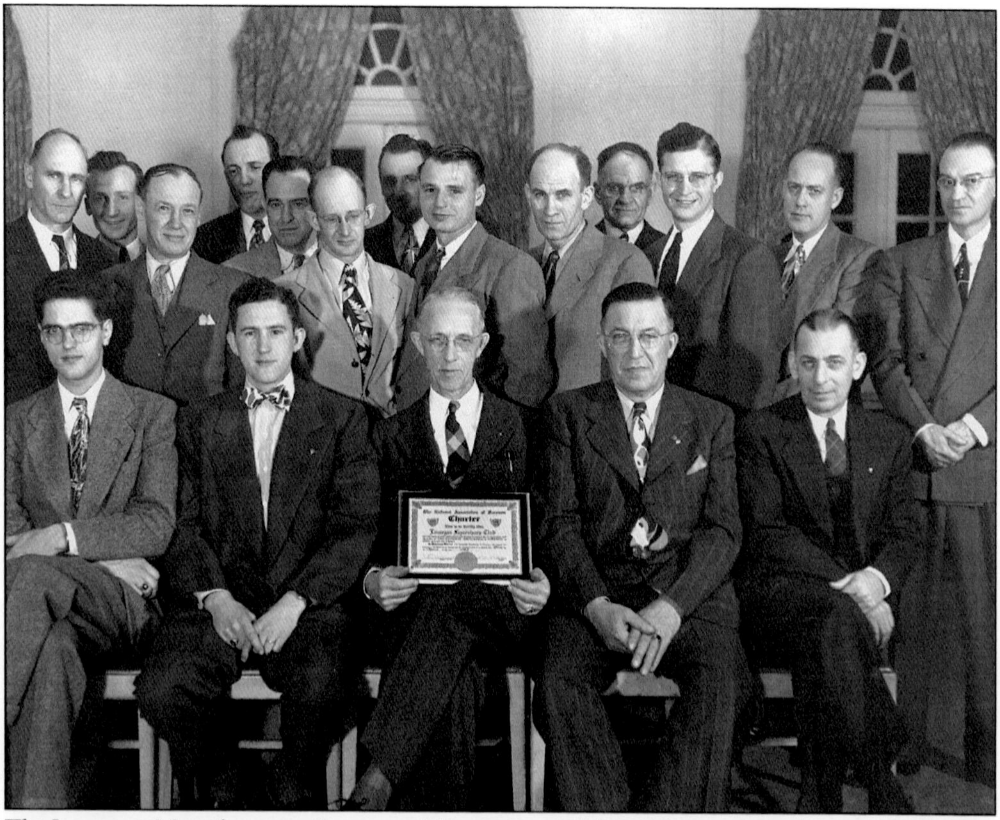

The Lonergan Manufacturing Company "Supervisors Club" celebrates their charter membership in the National Association of Foremen in this photo. From left to right: (front row) Jack Pahl, Vaud Pickens Jr., Clarence Messacar, Leon Jones, and Harry Payne; (middle row) Ivan Zeller, Albus Durham, Lynn Bushong, Clyde Ladd, Henry Quiter, Joseph Fitzgerald, Louis Lockwood, and Harold Hill; (top row) Erdman Newman, Harry Guyselman, Archie Taylor, Albert Smith, and Henry Ribbey.

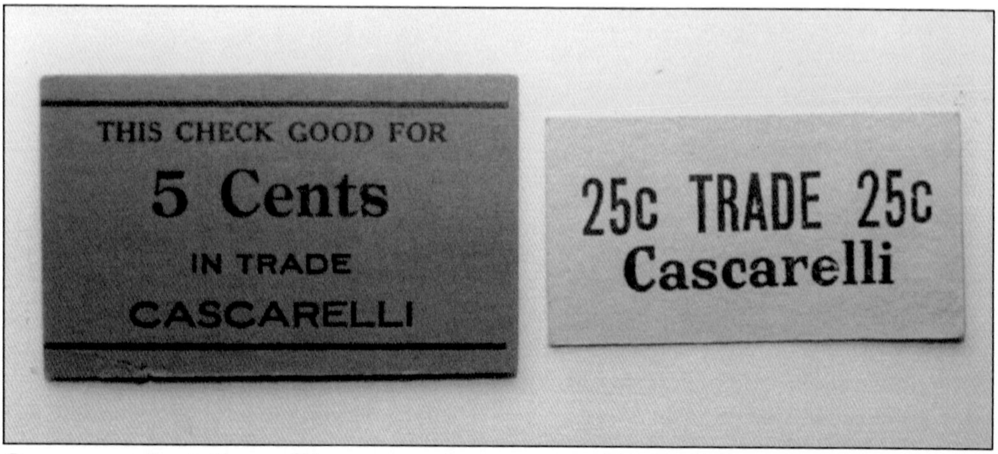


Customers at Louis Cascarelli's tavern and restaurant at 116 South Superior Street once used these cardboard "good for" trade checks in the 1940s. Cascarelli's was especially known for its fresh-roasted peanuts.

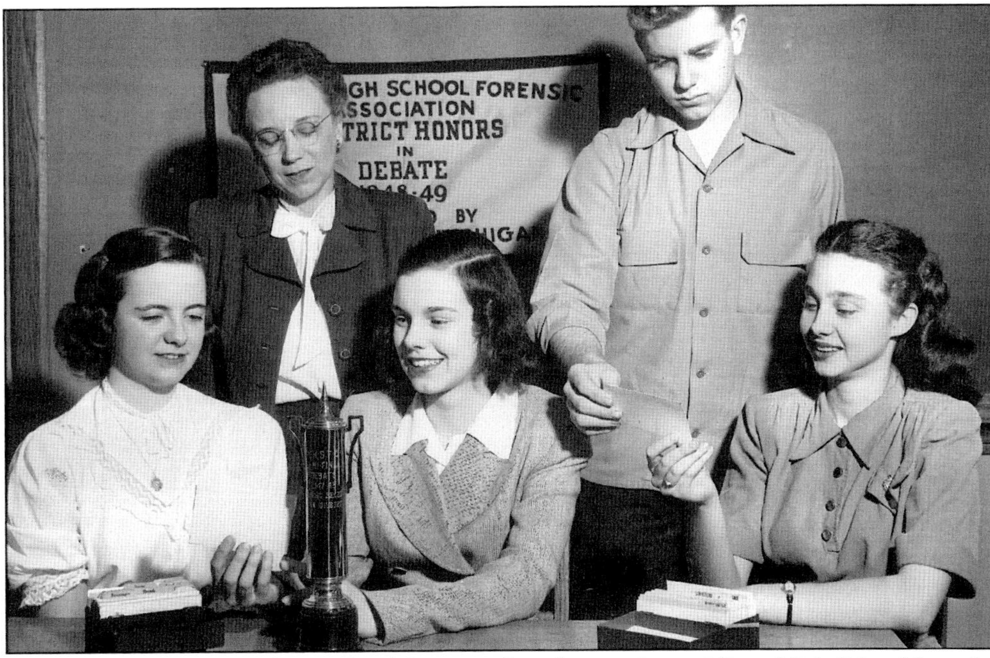


Ethel Fleenor (1905–2000) served as debate coach and counselor at Albion High School from the 1940s to the 1970s. Under her leadership, the Albion forensic teams won many regional and state awards during her career. The team members in this 1949 photo are, from left to right: (front row) Sallee Fox, Sue Carter, and Shirley Nice; (back row) Coach Fleenor and John Gilbert.

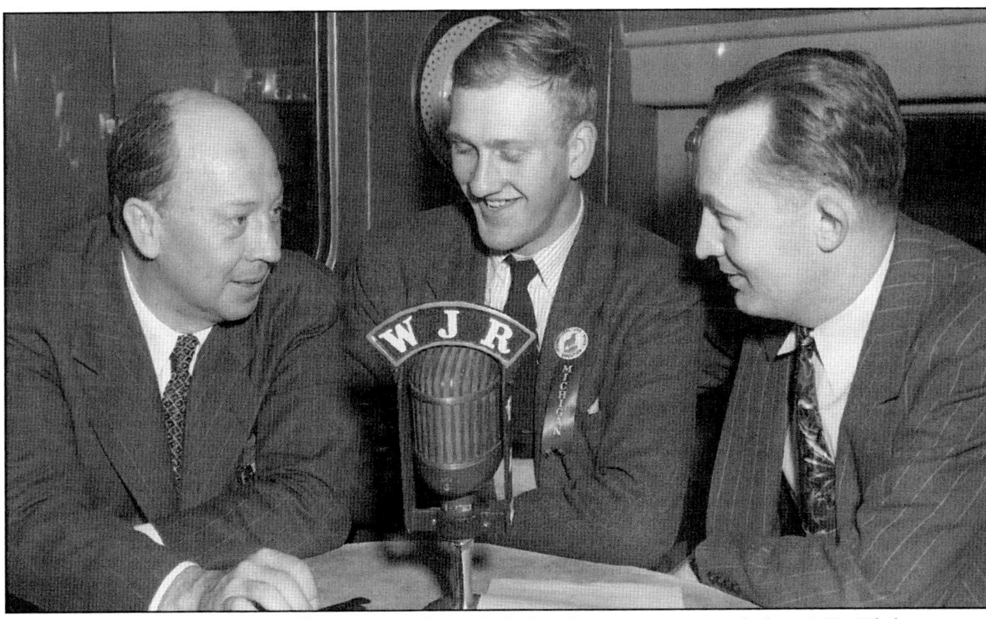


Eugene Boehlke of rural Albion was the 1948 Michigan winner of the 4-H Club tractor-maintenance program. He received an all-expense paid trip to the National 4-H Congress in Chicago. Eugene (center) is being interviewed by radio personality Marshall Wells (left) of Detroit radio station WJR. James M. Patterson, field representative for the Standard Oil Company, which sponsored the 4-H program, sits on the right.

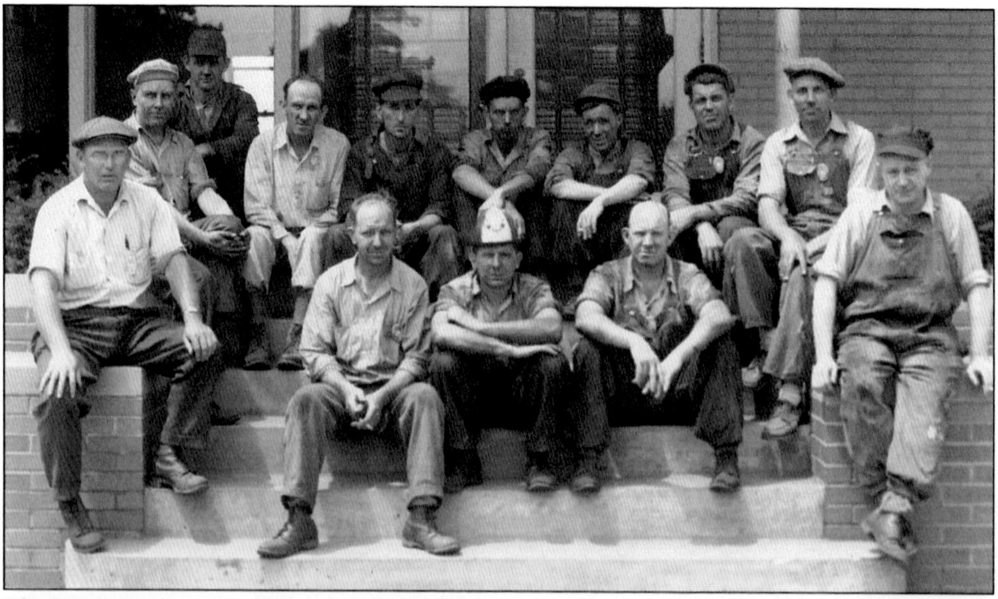

The Fire Brigade at the Albion Malleable Iron Company was organized in January 1948 to help provide adequate fire protection at the local plant. The members are, from left to right: (front row) Hardy Berry, Alvin Wood, and Myron Kingsbury; (back row) Lloyd Collins, Al Skinner, Ted Klinkelwicz, Herb Bailey, Art Sexton, Olen Huffman, Jimmy McCloud, Don Wright, Art Dailey, and Ben Knight.

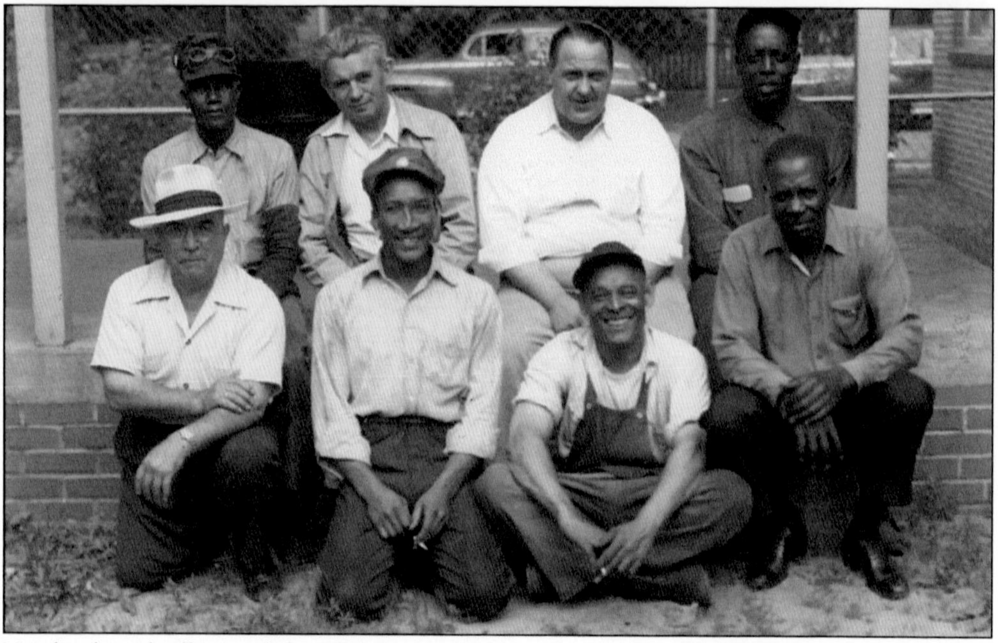

Newly elected officers of the Union Local 413 at the Albion Malleable Iron Company are shown in this June 1948 photograph, from left to right: (front row) Frank Domingo, sergeant at arms; M.C. Simmons, recording secretary and trustee; John Jefferson, president and treasurer; and Park Kelley, inductor; (back row) Henry Williams, vice-president; Joe Hummel, financial secretary; Clarence Greenman, corresponding representative; and Willie Harris, trustee.

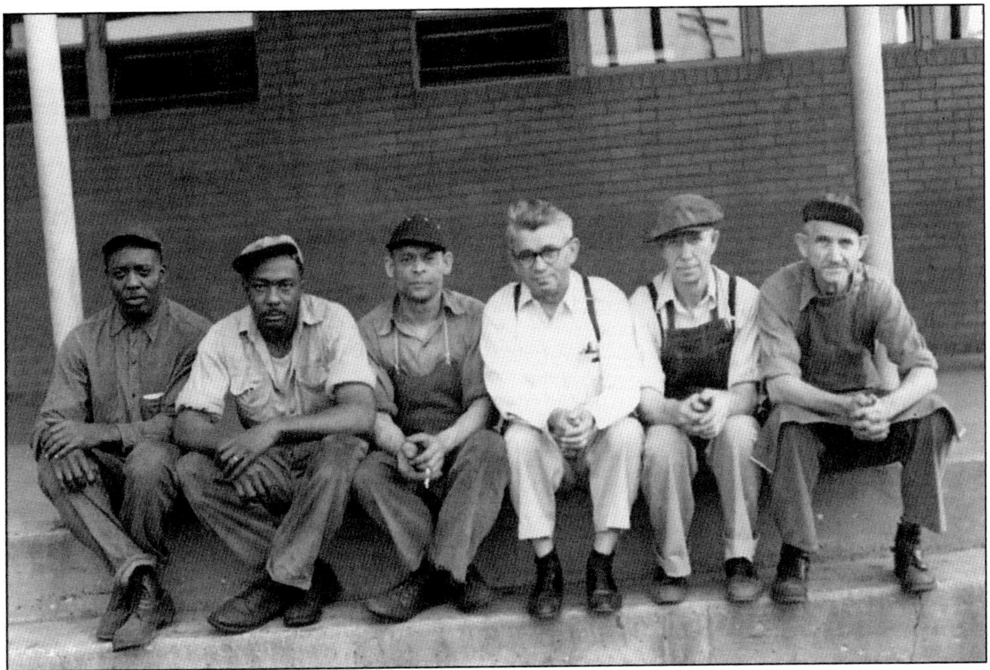

Officers (1949-50) of the Union Local 413 at the Albion Malleable Iron Company are shown, from left to right, in this June 1949 photo: Willie Harris, trustee; James Hawkins Jr., president; John Jefferson, vice-president; Joe Hummel, financial secretary; Errit Timmons, treasurer; and Avelt Nass, trustee.

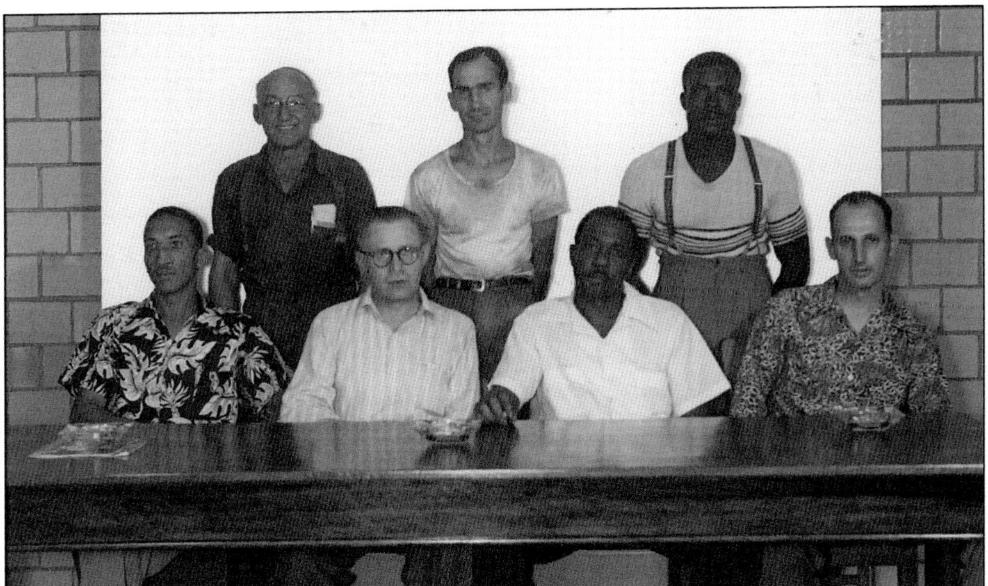

The 1952-53 senior committee of the Local 413 of the International Molders and Foundry Workers Union of North America at the Albion Malleable Iron Company are shown in this July 1952 photo, from left to right: (front row) M.C. Simmons, trustee; Ben J. Knight, president; James Hawkins, Jr., corresponding representative; Frank Klinkle, committeeman; (back row) committeemen Clarence Wheeler, Julius Kulikowski, and John Gamble.

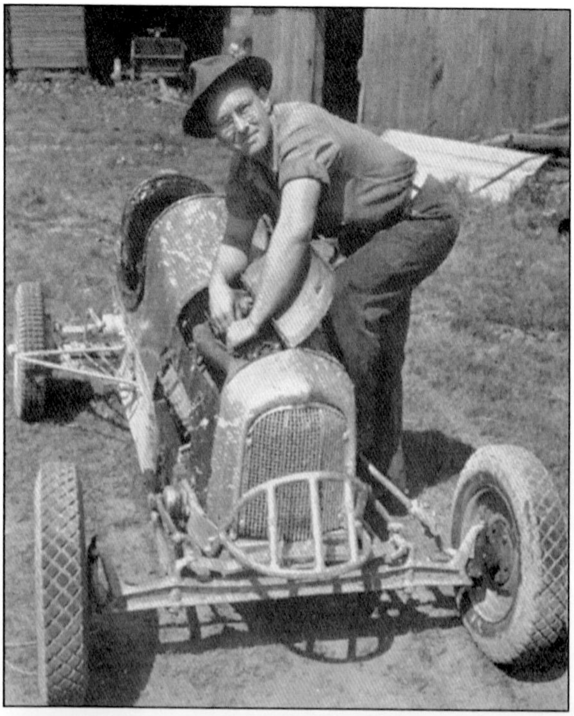

Midget auto racing was a popular sport during the 1940s and 1950s. George Luedtke (1915–1991) is shown in this 1946 photograph with his eight-foot length midget car containing a V-8 engine. George and his brother Lewis (1917–1989) would race on tracks in Michigan and Ohio, winning enough money to support their hobby. Lewis won the Class B midget championship in 1948. A race consisted of three trips around a quarter-mile track.

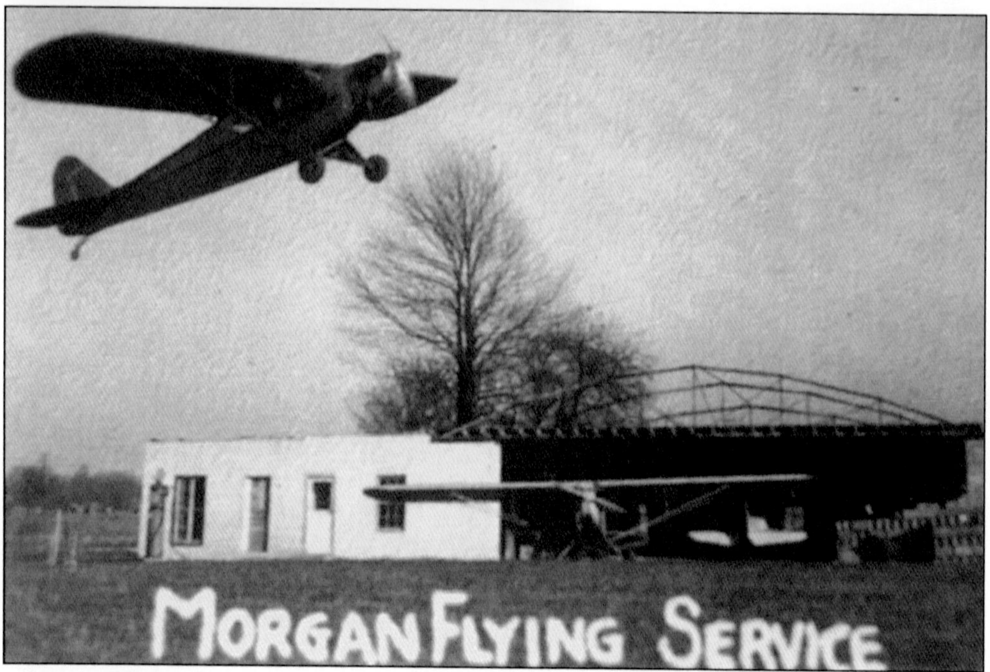


Albion's airfield Morgan Field was located on leased land east of town southwest of the M-99 and U.S. 12 intersection. It was opened in 1946 by Stanley Morgan, who gave flying lessons and promoted the sport in the Albion area. A local flying club called the Skyrangers was formed, consisting of 20 members. Eight planes were based at Morgan Field, including two owned by the Michigan National Guard. Morgan Field was closed in 1951, and the Amberton Village subdivision was subsequently erected on the site in the 1960s.

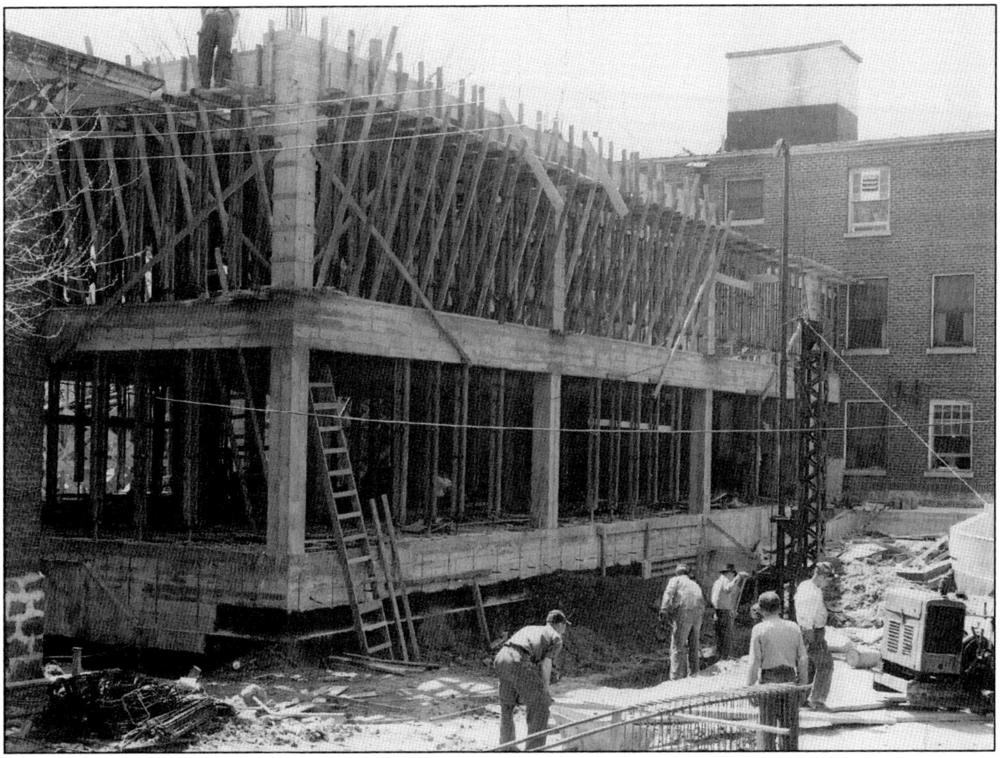

By the late 1940s, Sheldon Memorial Hospital was filled to capacity, and construction began in 1950 on a new half-million dollar east wing. It doubled the capacity of the hospital and opened in 1952. This 1951 photo shows construction in progress.

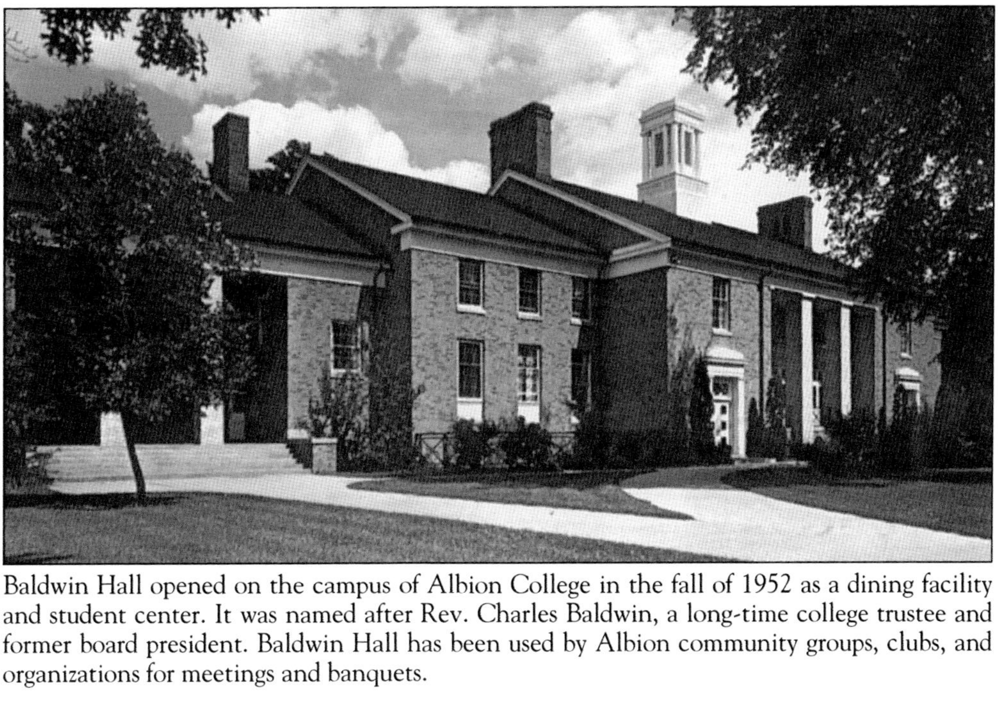

Baldwin Hall opened on the campus of Albion College in the fall of 1952 as a dining facility and student center. It was named after Rev. Charles Baldwin, a long-time college trustee and former board president. Baldwin Hall has been used by Albion community groups, clubs, and organizations for meetings and banquets.

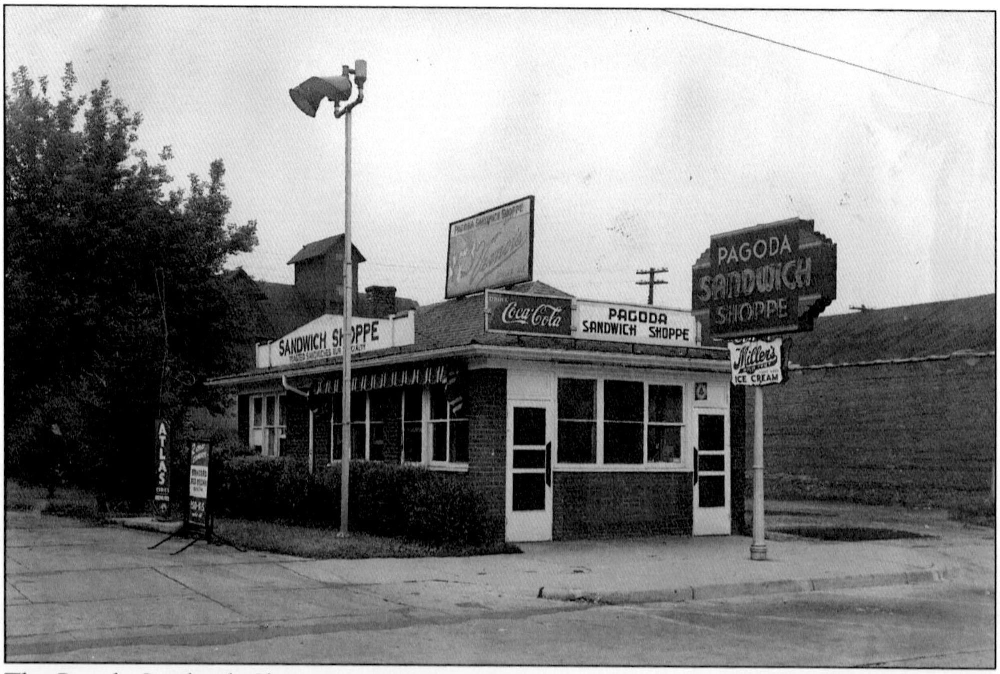


The Pagoda Sandwich Shoppe, at 113 East Michigan Avenue, opened in 1927 and became a popular eating place along busy U.S. 12 between Detroit and Chicago, before Interstate-94 opened in 1960. It still operates today. This photo is c. 1948.

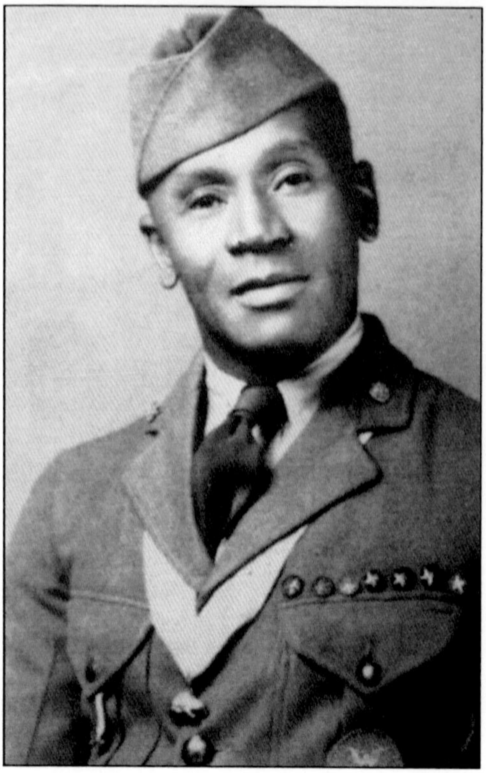

Boy Scout Troop #62 was organized in November 1928 and consisted of 30 African-American boys from the west end of town. First Scoutmaster was Edward "Doc" Anderson (1903–1977), who provided fatherly leadership and guidance for many years. He was assisted by several prominent adult leaders of the African-American community. For his years of unselfish and outstanding service, Anderson was awarded the silver beaver award by the Land-O-Lakes Council in 1953. A crane operator at the Albion Malleable Iron Company and a native of Pensacola, Florida, Anderson is pictured in this 1953 photograph wearing his silver beaver award.

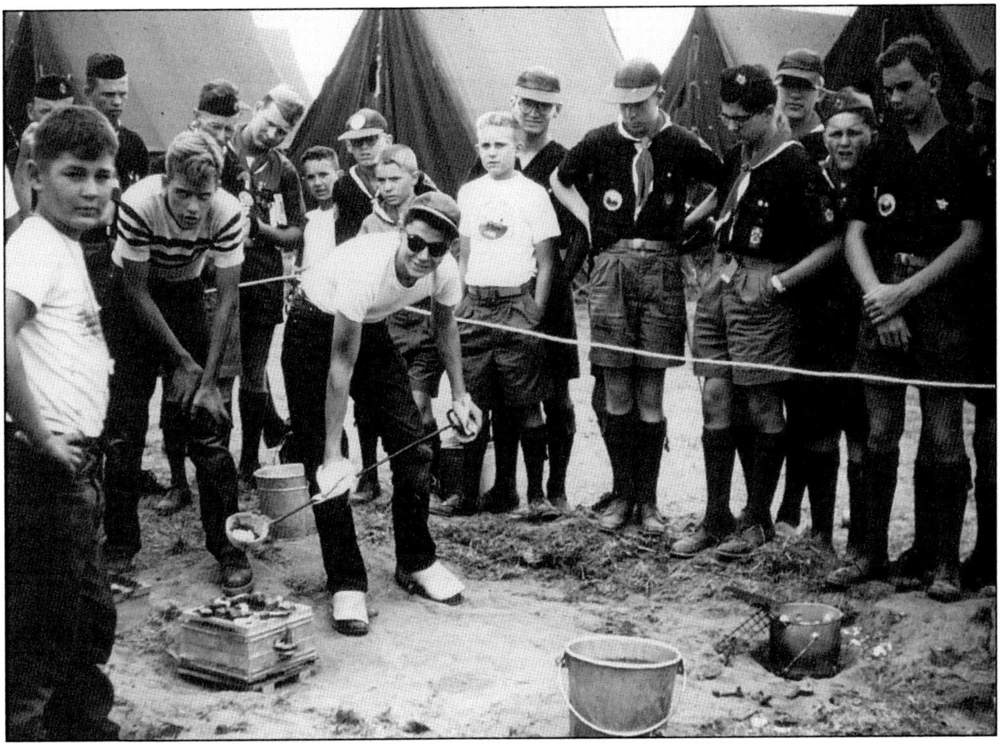

Twenty-three Albion area Boy Scouts participated in the 1953 National Jamboree held at Irvine Ranch, California. The Albion Malleable Iron Company provided the boys with a "miniature foundry" that was one of the most popular attractions at the event. The boys demonstrated pouring molten aluminum into molds and casting them as neckerchief slides in the shape of the seventh Scout region emblem. Above: Scouts from other troops watch as Dave Farley (center with sun glasses) pours the aluminum into the mold, assisted by Frank Rote (striped shirt) and Alden Hensel (far left).

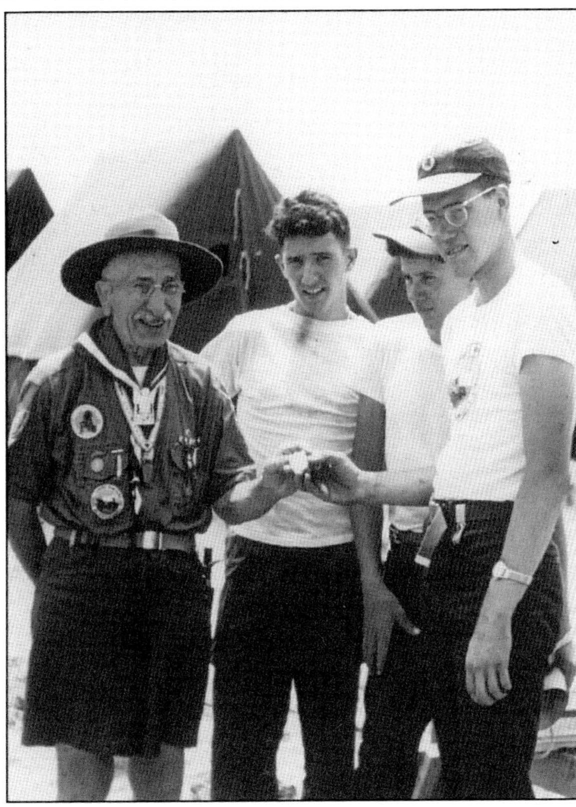

A finished neckerchief slide is presented to pioneer scout leader Dan Beard (left). Next are scouts Jim Pritchard of Homer, Dave Farley, and Don Henderson.

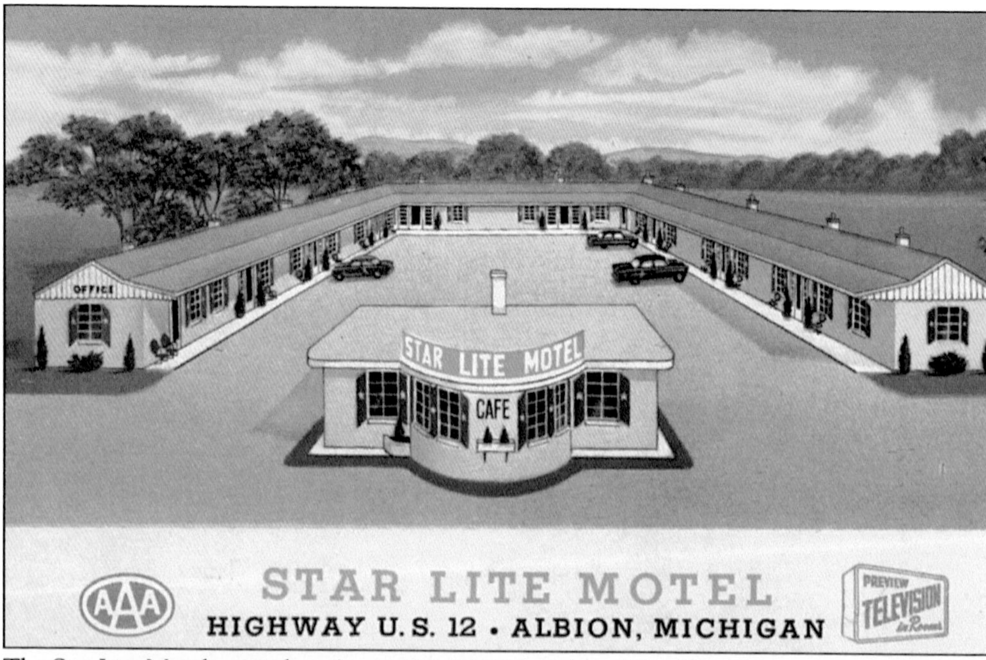


The Star Lite Motel opened on August 23, 1952 along busy U.S. 12 just east of town. Owned by Mike Nester (1910–1999), this 16-unit motel was the first in the Albion area to compete with the bulky and traditional Parker Inn a mile way. It was designed for busy travelers who wanted to easily move "in and out" and get on their way. This artist's conception from the 1950s even depicts non-existent mountains in the distance.

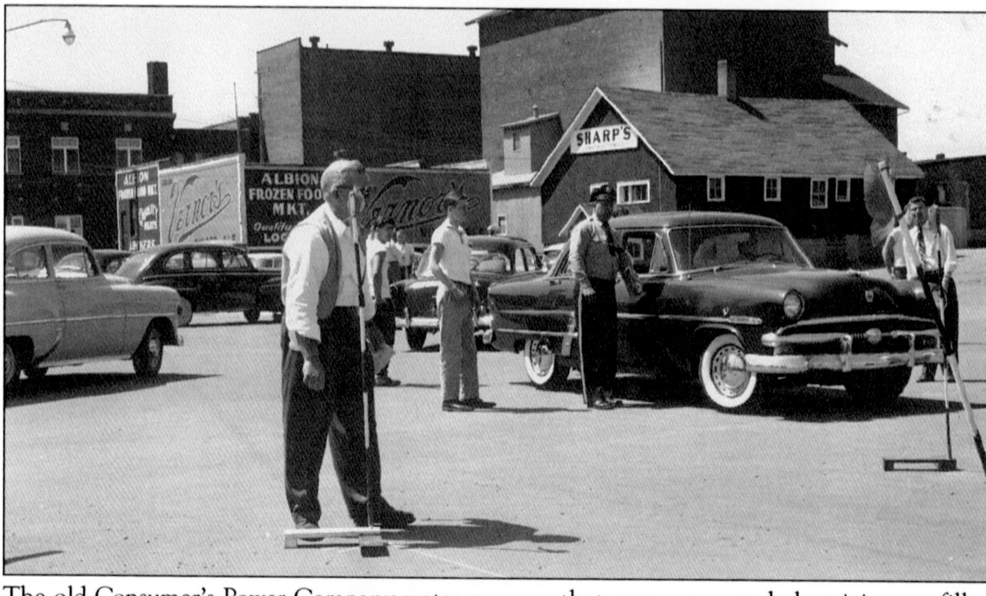


The old Consumer's Power Company water raceway that once generated electricity was filled during the summer of 1954. The Market Place area was subsequently transformed into a giant asphalt parking lot. Various events were held here in the late 1950s, such as this car rally depicted above. In the distance on the right is Sharp's Construction Company, and behind it the large Albion Elevator. On the left is the Albion Frozen Food Market.

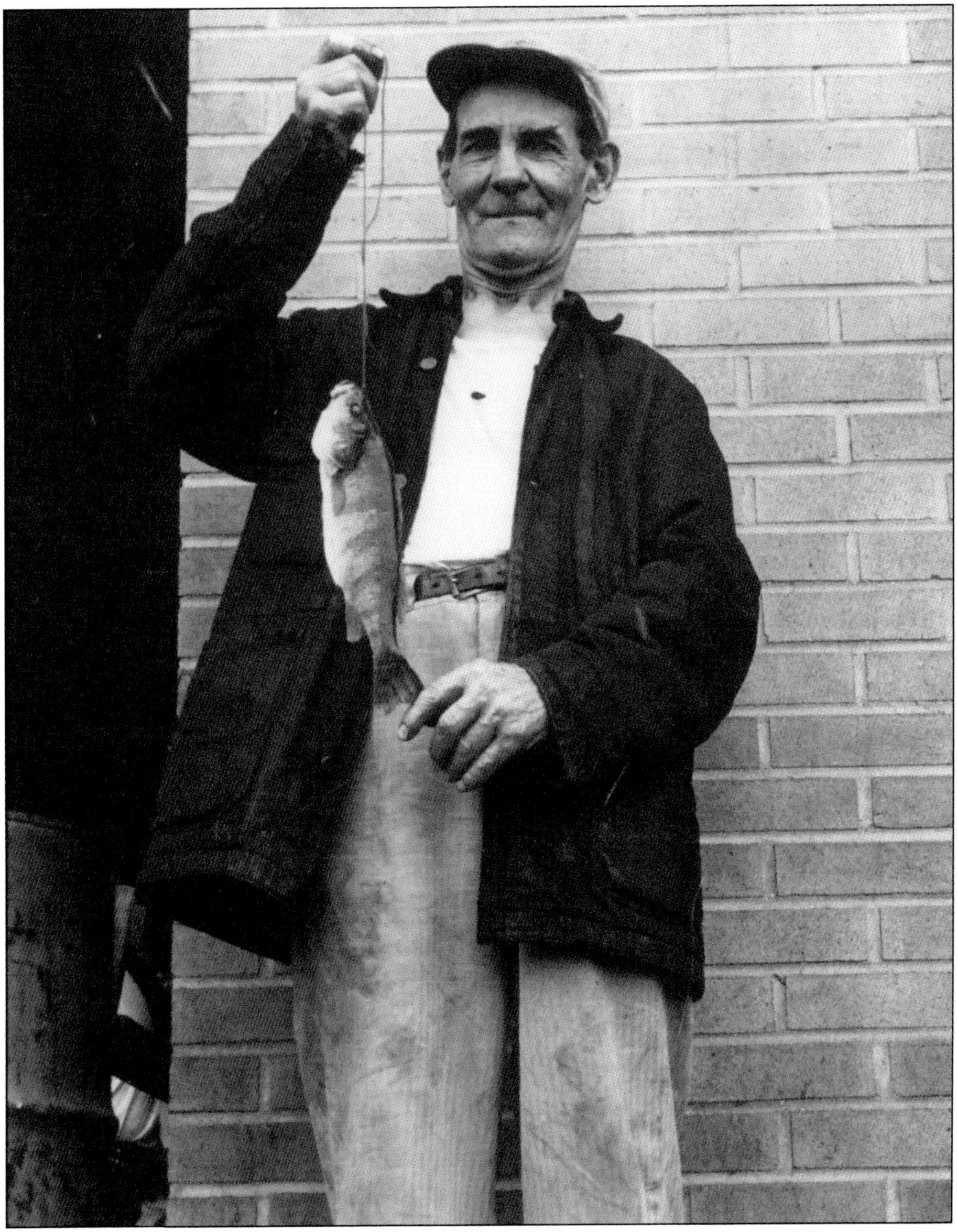

The Albion Malleable Iron Company sponsored several fishing contests for its workers during the 1950s. Pictured in this September 1955 photo is a smiling Mike Kulikowski (1890–1975) with his first prize 13-inch yellow perch, for which he was awarded $7.50 in prize money. Mike was representative of the many men who came from Eastern Europe to work at the Malleable. A native of Nevardenai (near Varniai), Lithuania, he came to America in 1911 as Nikodemas Kulikauskas, first settling in Chicago/Cicero, Illinois where he worked at a foundry there. He came to Albion to work at the Malleable in September 1918, and retired in 1958 after nearly 40 years of service. He raised a family of 14 children and there are numerous descendants living in the Albion area today.

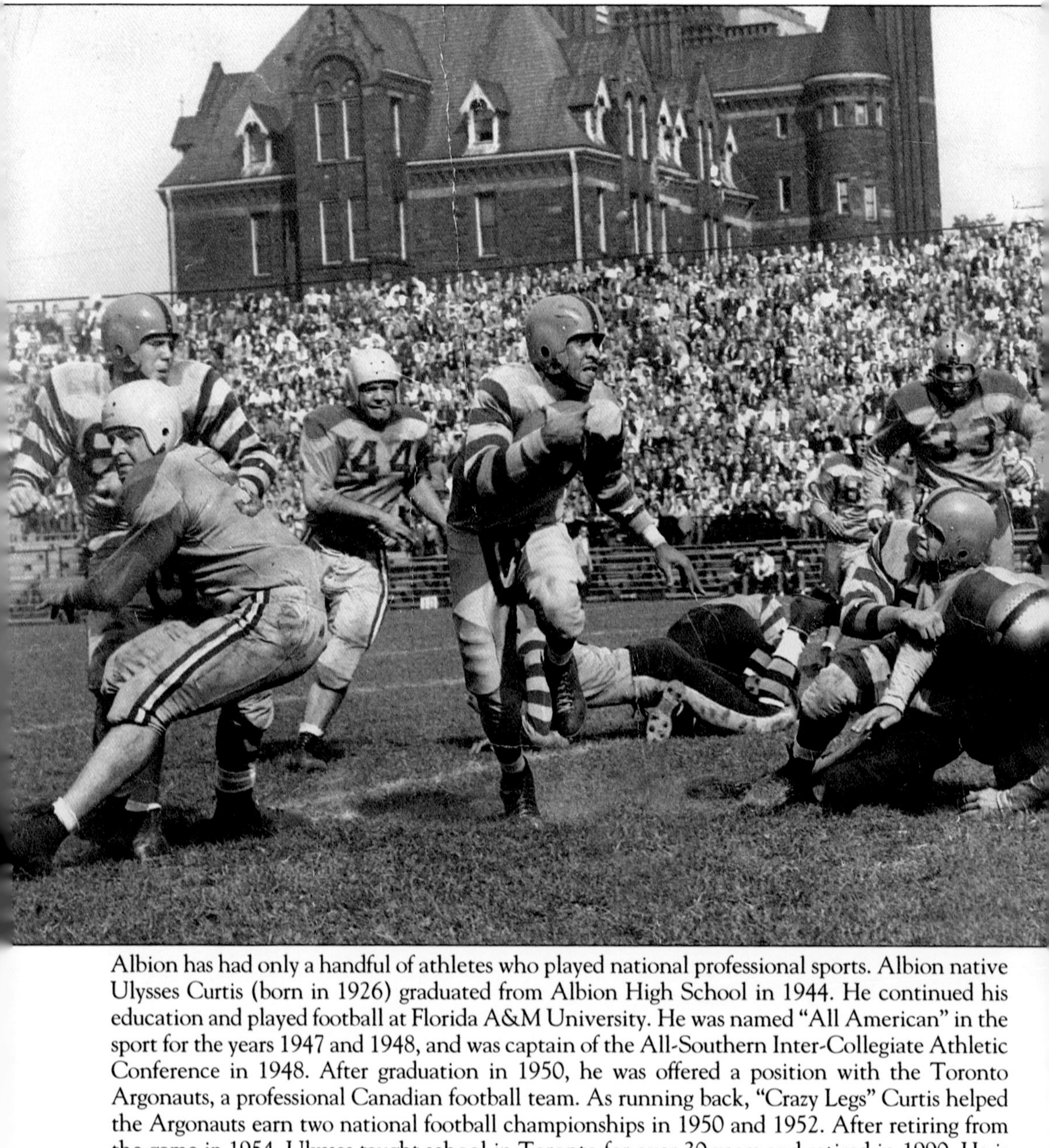


Albion has had only a handful of athletes who played national professional sports. Albion native Ulysses Curtis (born in 1926) graduated from Albion High School in 1944. He continued his education and played football at Florida A&M University. He was named "All American" in the sport for the years 1947 and 1948, and was captain of the All-Southern Inter-Collegiate Athletic Conference in 1948. After graduation in 1950, he was offered a position with the Toronto Argonauts, a professional Canadian football team. As running back, "Crazy Legs" Curtis helped the Argonauts earn two national football championships in 1950 and 1952. After retiring from the game in 1954, Ulysses taught school in Toronto for over 30 years and retired in 1990. He is pictured above (center) carrying the ball for the Argonauts in this 1952 photograph.

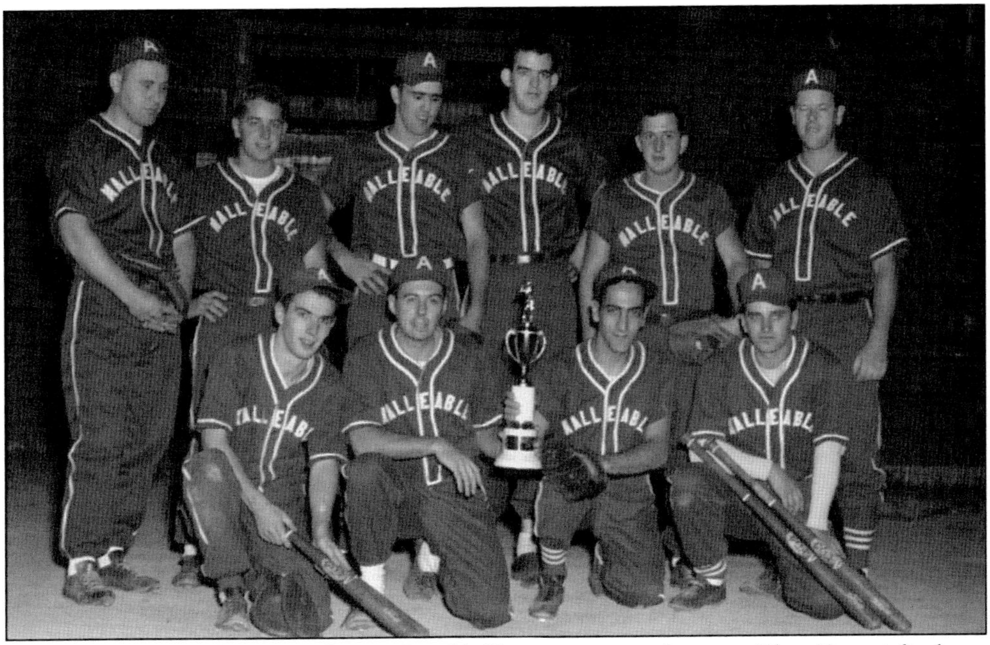

The Albion Malleable Giants fast pitch softball team went to the state Class D semi-finals on Labor Day weekend in 1956, and took third in the state. The team members are, from left to right: (front row) John Putnam, Kenneth King, Joe Bommarito, and Bud Herzog; (back row) Sam Markovich, Allen Winchell, Ed Putnam, Harley Transue, Bruce Nichols, and Lou Bachinski.

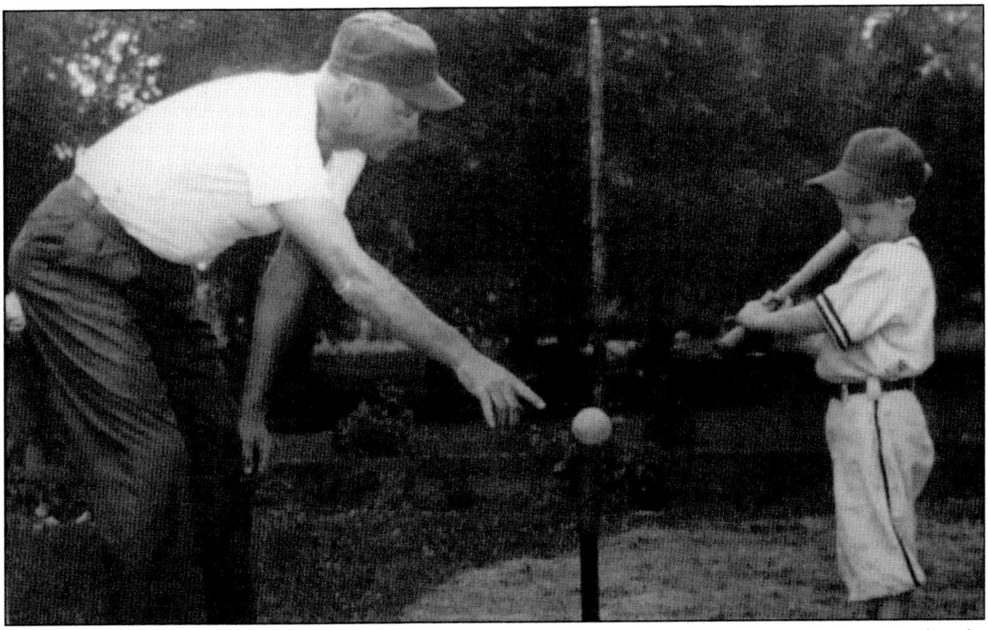

T-Ball baseball as an organized sport was invented in Albion, Michigan by coach Jerry Sacharski under the name of Pee Wee Baseball in the summer of 1956. It was designed so boys 6, 7, and 8 years old could safely learn the fundamentals of the game, complete with a specially designed baseball diamond. Coach Sacharski instructs 6-year-old Craig LeClair about hitting the ball on the tee in this 1958 photograph. The base reads, "Pee Wee Tee." (Photo courtesy Jerry Sacharski.)

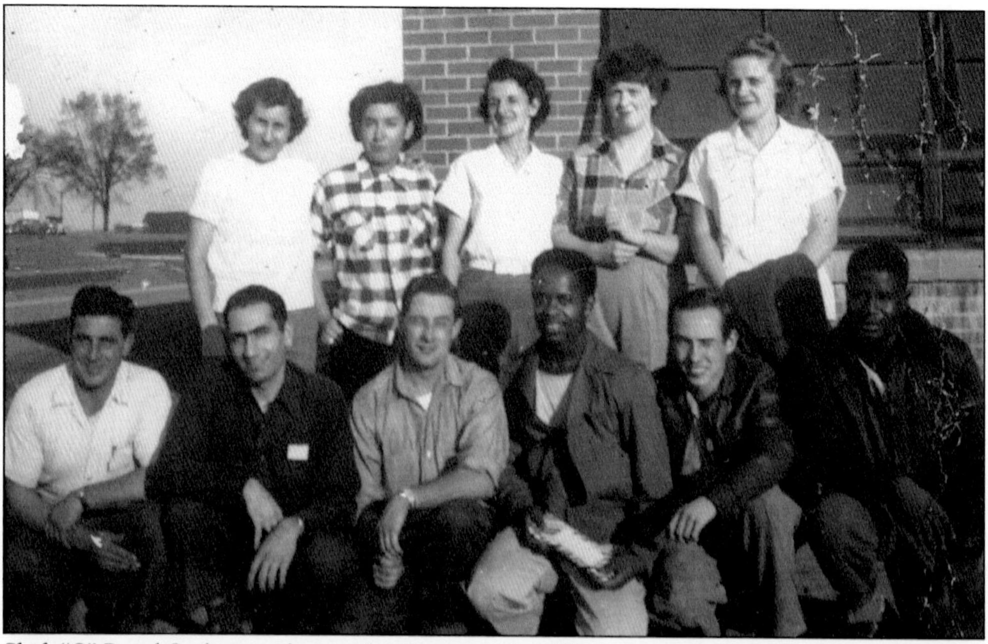

Shift "C" Panel Sealing workers at the Corning Glass Works present co-worker George Hawkins with a gift on the occasion of his return to active duty with the Army in 1951. The workers are, from left to right: (front row) Guy Vitale; K. John Hovnanian, foreman; Herbert Conley; George Hawkins; Wayne Miller; and Robert Simpson; (back row) Wilma Snyder; Julia Rivera; Pauline (Kulikowski) Passic; Twila Frank; and Julia Pohachuck. (Photo courtesy of Guy Vitale.)

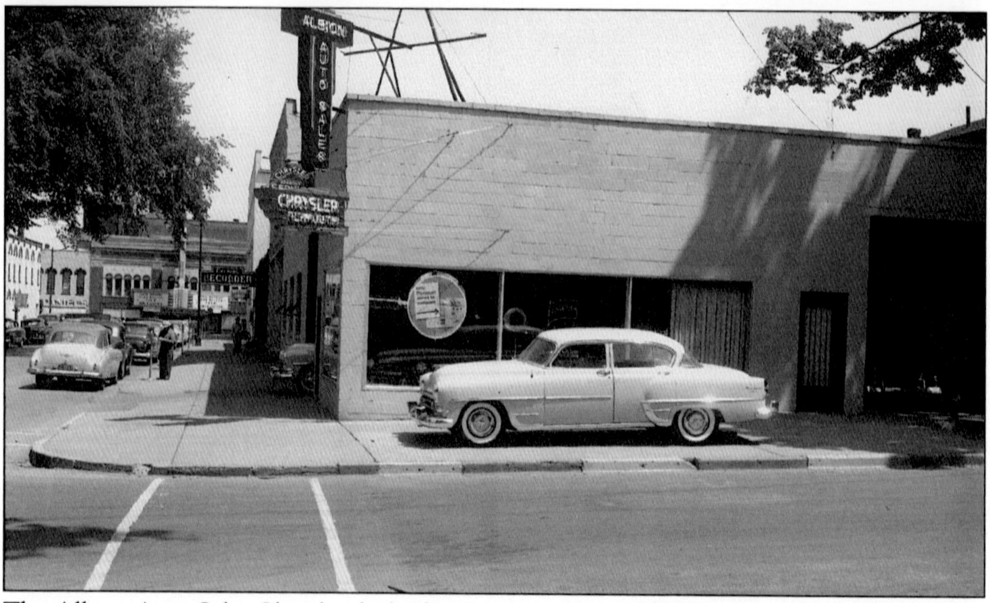


The Albion Auto Sales Chrysler dealership on the corner of South Clinton and West Center Streets was one of several dealerships that were located in downtown Albion, as shown in this 1954 photograph. In the distance can be seen the *Albion Evening Recorder* newspaper sign and the Bohm Theatre. Downtown parking meters kept customers moving, as shown by the gentleman on the left who is feeding the meter.

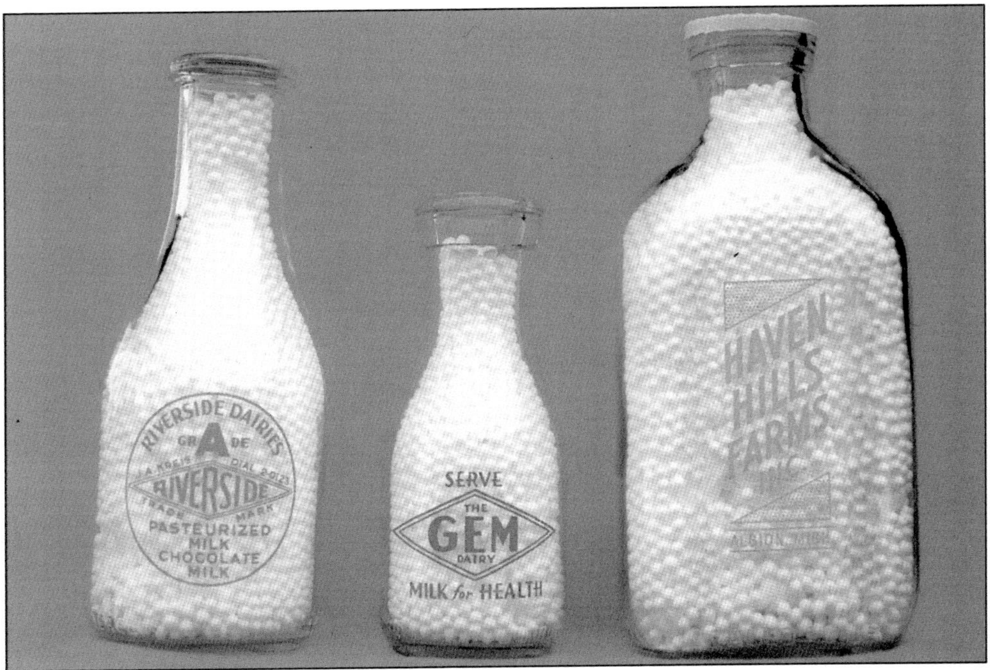


Raw milk was once brought into town from area farms and processed at several local dairies through the early 1960s. It was packaged in pint, quart, and half-gallon bottles, and delivered to homes throughout Albion. Three popular brands were Riverside Dairy, the Gem Dairy, and Haven Hills Farm, whose bottles are shown here. (Bottles courtesy of Mike and Carol Egnatuk.)

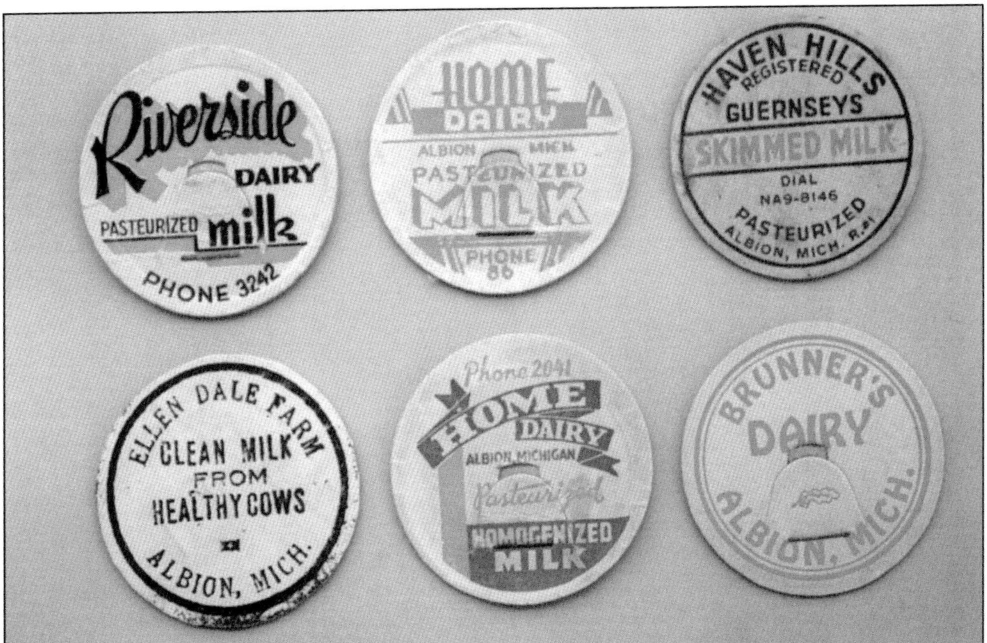


Milk bottles were sealed with locally-labeled milk caps, as shown here, from left to right: (front row): Ellen Dale Farm, Home Dairy, and Brunner's Dairy; (back row) Riverside Dairy, Home Dairy, and Haven Hills. (Caps courtesy of Mike and Carol Egnatuk.)

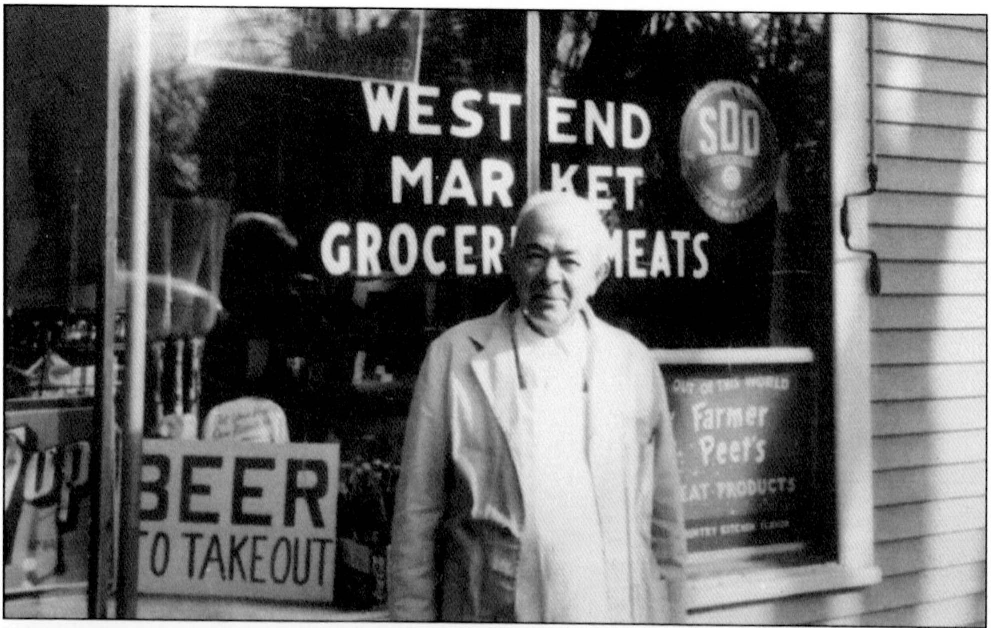

John Mymochod (1884–1961) owned and operated the West End Market grocery at 500 Austin Avenue for three decades, beginning in 1926. A Ukrainian immigrant, John came to the United States in 1911. He is shown standing in front of his store in this 1957 photograph. (Courtesy of Lucille (Mymochod) Wickens.)

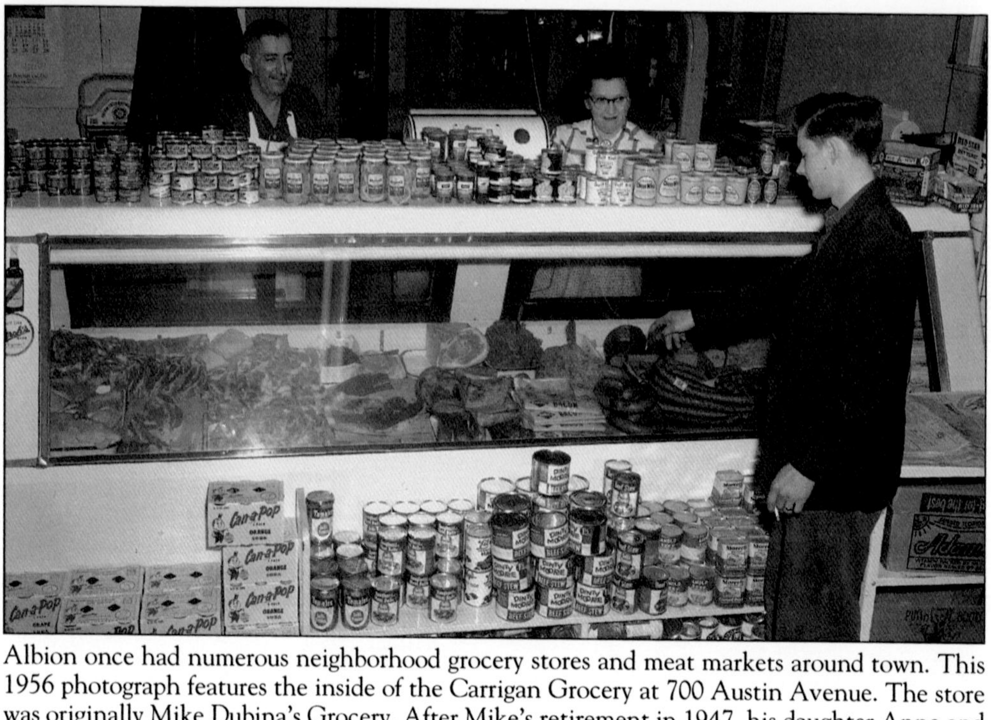

Albion once had numerous neighborhood grocery stores and meat markets around town. This 1956 photograph features the inside of the Carrigan Grocery at 700 Austin Avenue. The store was originally Mike Dubina's Grocery. After Mike's retirement in 1947, his daughter Anne and her husband Leland Carrigan took it over. It operated until 1968. Leland and Anne are shown waiting on customer Melvin Harris.

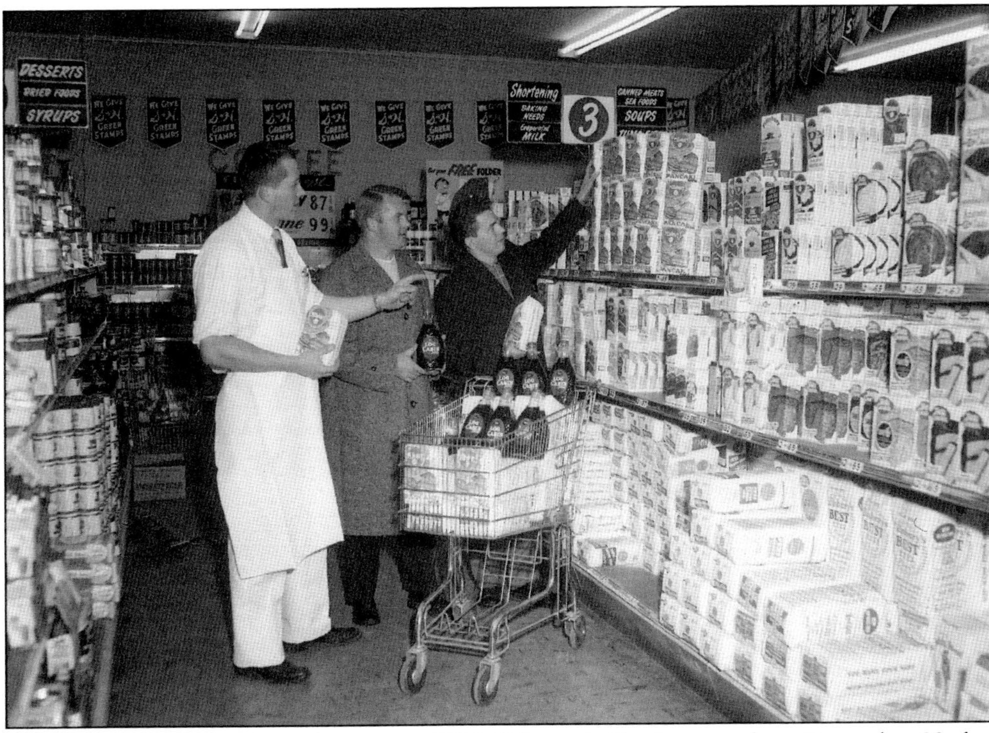


Albion entered the supermarket era in 1954; Felpausch Foods opened on November 23 that year. Tom Feldpausch (left) is shown assisting company representatives with Log Cabin syrup and Pillsbury flour prior to an annual pancake breakfast, which Felpausch Foods sponsored. (Photo c. 1958 courtesy of the Greater Albion Chamber of Commerce.)

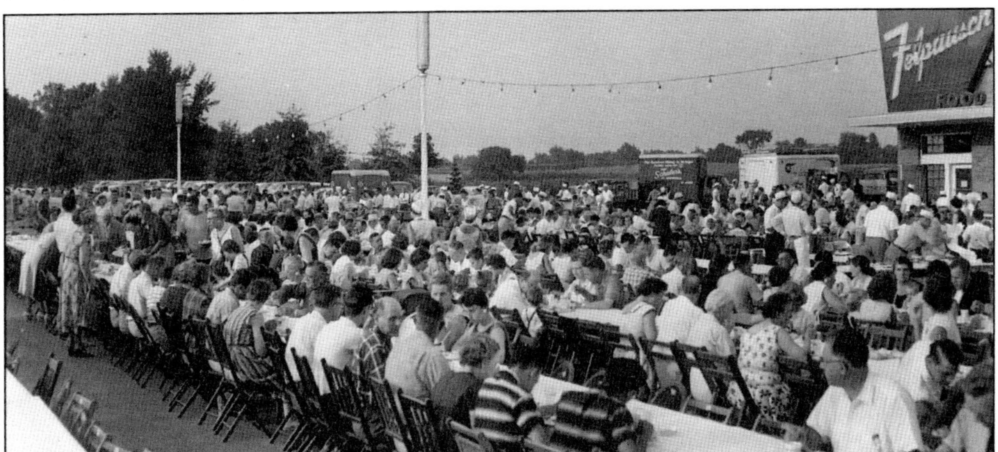

Over 1,500 persons attended an outdoor smorgasbord dinner at Felpausch Foods on August 8, 1956, as part of Youth Booster Day. Two thousand five-hundred dollars was raised to benefit the local community youth fund. Numerous organizations participated in the event, including the Rotary Club, Kiwanis Club, Exchange Club, Jaycees, American Legion, Boy Scouts, and City of Albion. The menu included 1,098 pounds of beef, 360 pounds of ham, 100 pounds of hot dogs, eight cases of celery, 390 pounds of cottage cheese, 580 pounds of potato salad, and 1,970 servings of soft drinks. (Photo courtesy of the Greater Albion Chamber of Commerce.)

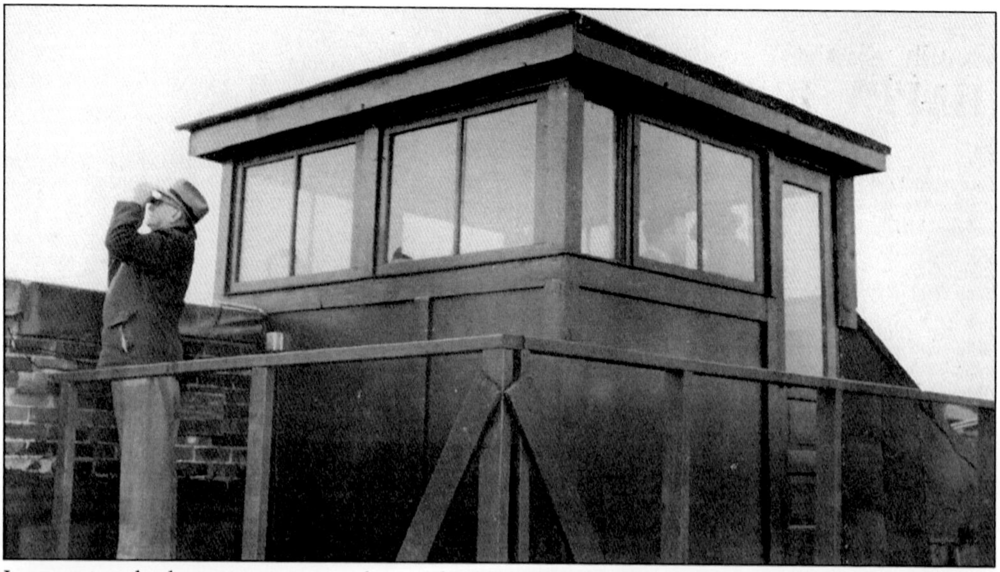

International relations were tense during the "Cold War" of the 1950s and 1960s. Civil Defense signs were placed on sturdy buildings in town, which identified them as a safe place to run to in case of a nuclear attack. A local Ground Observer Corps was established, and the American Legion coordinated the construction of an observation tower on the roof of City Hall. A round-the-clock group of volunteers was assembled to spot any enemy aircraft flying over Albion, and to immediately call the Air Force Filter Center at Grand Rapids if a plane had more than two engines. GOC observer Ralph Wilkinson alertly scans the skies around Albion atop the City Hall observation tower in this 1956 photograph.

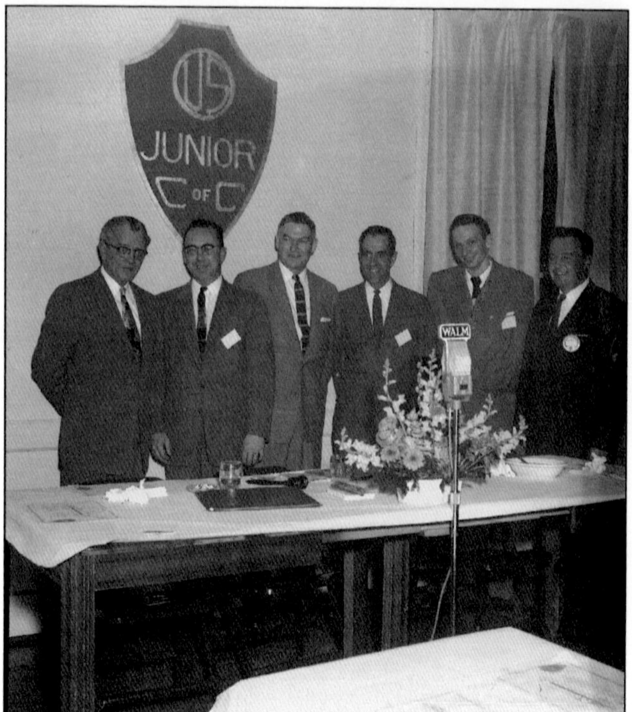


The Albion Junior Chamber of Commerce was organized in 1939, and served the business and promotional needs of the community until the present Greater Albion Chamber of Commerce was formed in 1960. Pictured at left are several Junior Chamber officials at an event broadcast on WALM in the late 1950s From left to right: Jack C. Bedient, unidentified, Frank Costello, George Elyea, Jim Casey (Kukowski) of WALM, and Robert Schultz. (Photo courtesy of the Greater Albion Chamber of Commerce.)

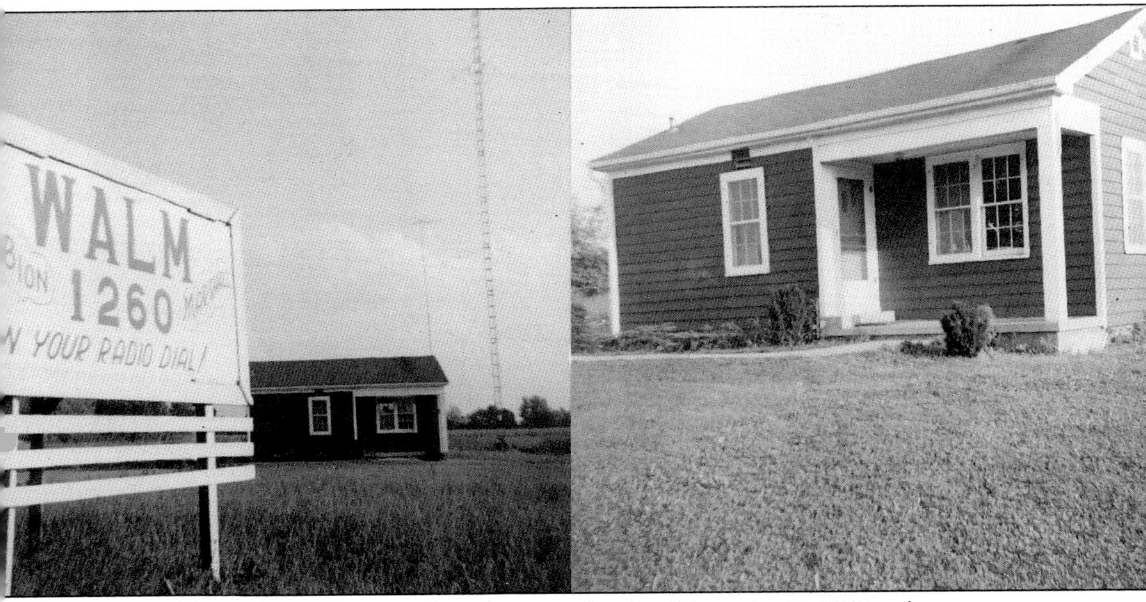


Albion's WALM radio station signed on the air on Sunday, November 2, 1952 and was a source of local news and information for many years. It was first located on Austin Avenue as pictured in this August 1956 photo. The station later moved to Irwin Avenue. WALM went off the air in 1995. (Photo courtesy of Dave Eddy.)

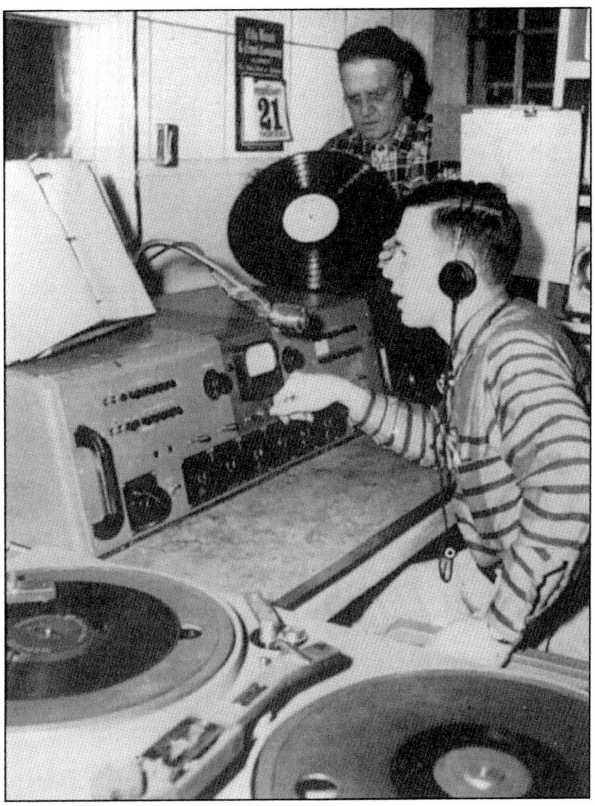


Noted radio personality Dave Eddy began his career at WALM while a teenager in 1956 following his graduation from Albion High School. His popular teenager program "The Pop Shop" aired in the late afternoons. Dave subsequently joined WBCK in Battle Creek in 1960, where he eventually became known as the "morning mayor," announcing there for over 40 years. Dave is shown here spinning records while his father Hewitt looks on in this 1957 photograph.

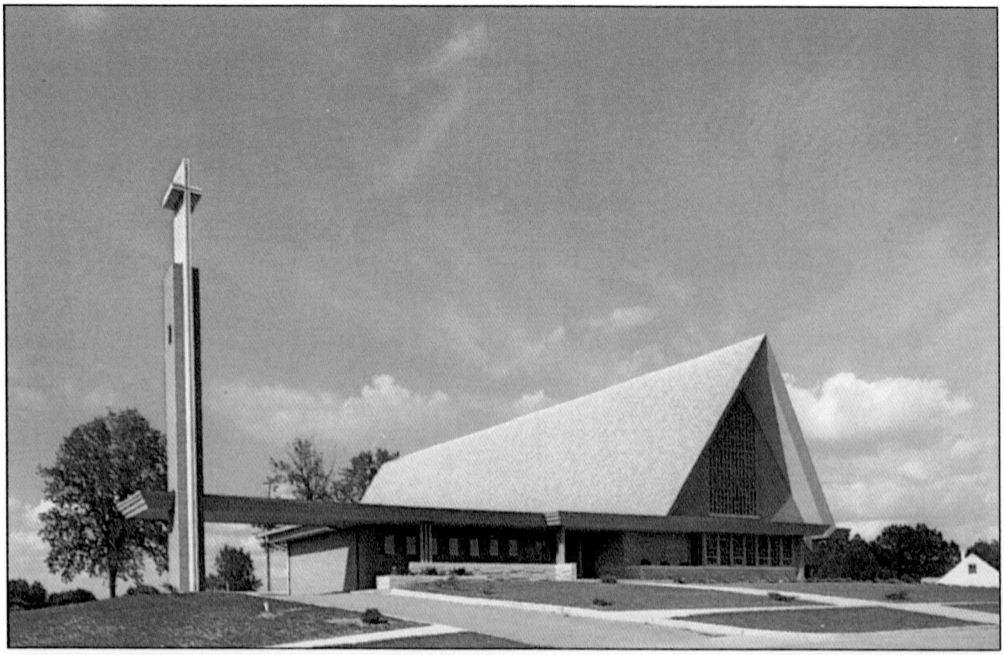

The congregation of St. Paul's Lutheran Church moved into their new $420,000 building in 1958 under the direction of Rev. Paul J. Foust. Chairman of the building committee was Albion Mayor Hugo Rieger. The new church was dedicated on July 13, 1958.

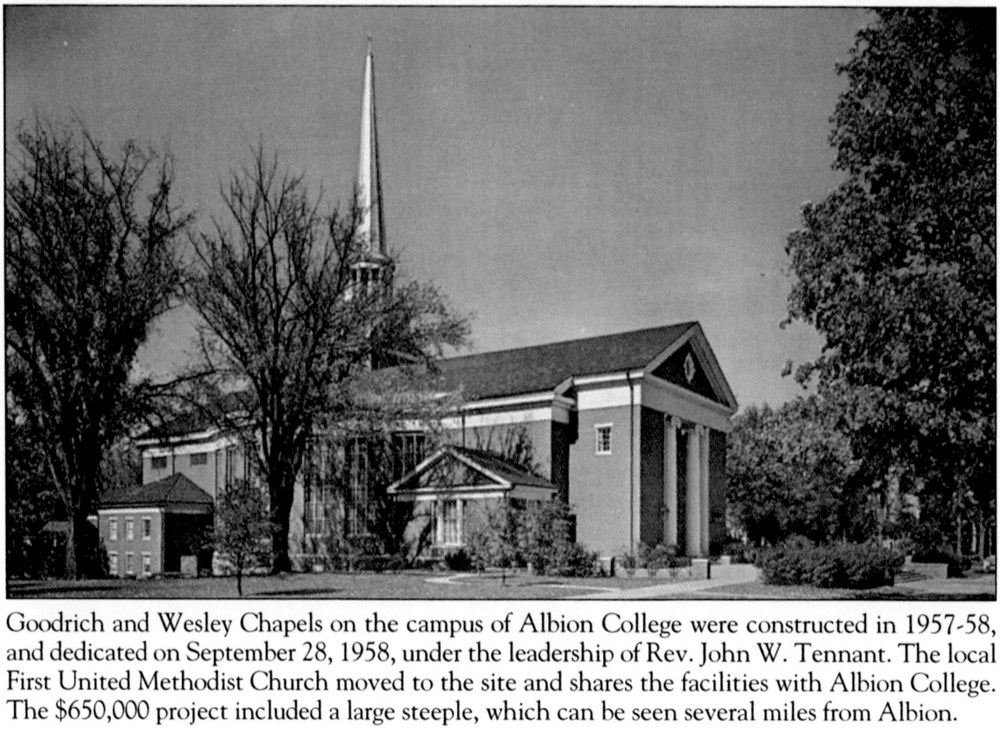

Goodrich and Wesley Chapels on the campus of Albion College were constructed in 1957-58, and dedicated on September 28, 1958, under the leadership of Rev. John W. Tennant. The local First United Methodist Church moved to the site and shares the facilities with Albion College. The $650,000 project included a large steeple, which can be seen several miles from Albion.

# *Four*

# TIME OF TRANSITION

## 1960–1979

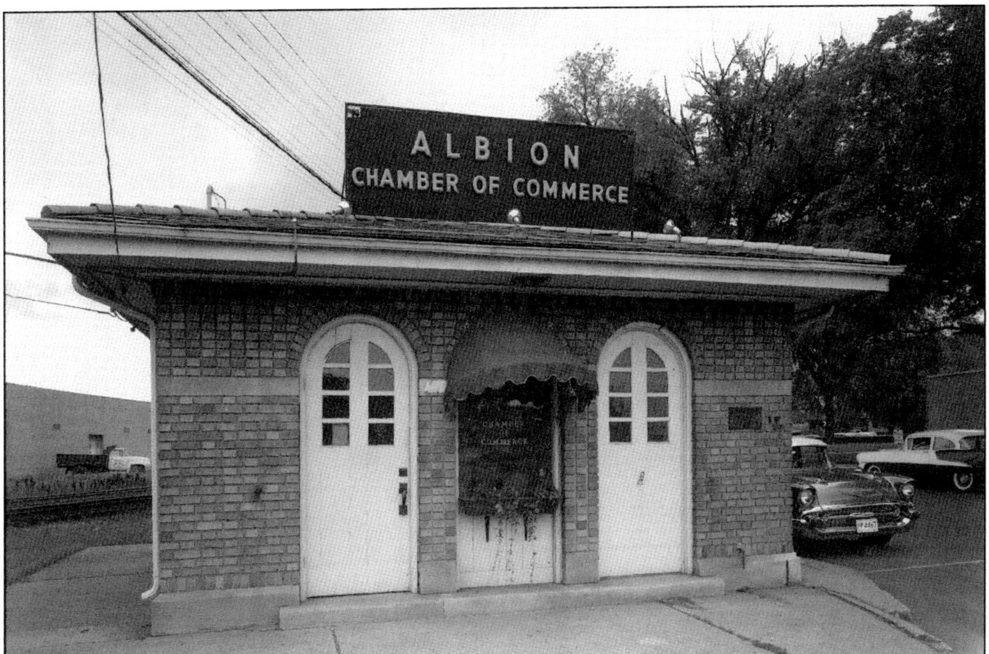


The Albion "Public Comfort Station" was located on the southwest corner of North Superior Street and Michigan Avenue. It provided relief for thousands of motorists on busy U.S. 12 for many years. Warren S. Kessler, president of the Albion Malleable Iron Company, had donated the facility as a gift to the City of Albion in 1924. The opening of the Interstate-94 highway on July 1, 1960, significantly decreased traffic through town, and the facility was deemed obsolete. It was closed on July 15, and subsequently remodeled into the new home of the Albion Chamber of Commerce, which opened here in August 1960. (Photo courtesy of the Greater Albion Chamber of Commerce.)

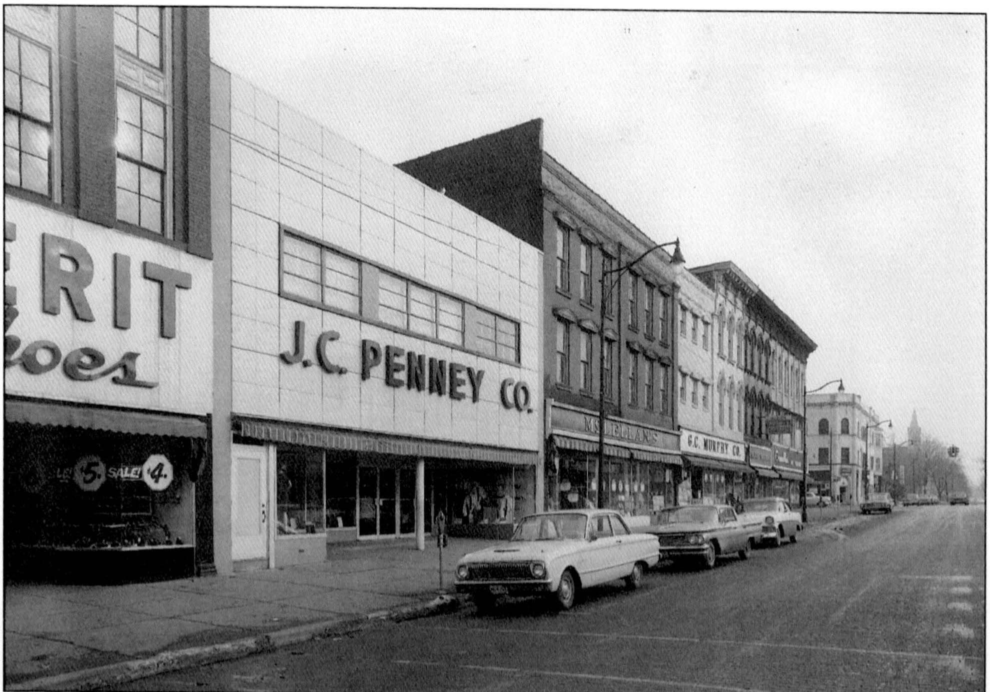


Downtown Albion once contained numerous "national chain" stores, such as J.C. Penney, McClellan's, and G.C. Murphy, as shown in this 1962 photograph of the east side of the 300 block of South Superior Street. Parking meters helped regulate the steady flow of customers.

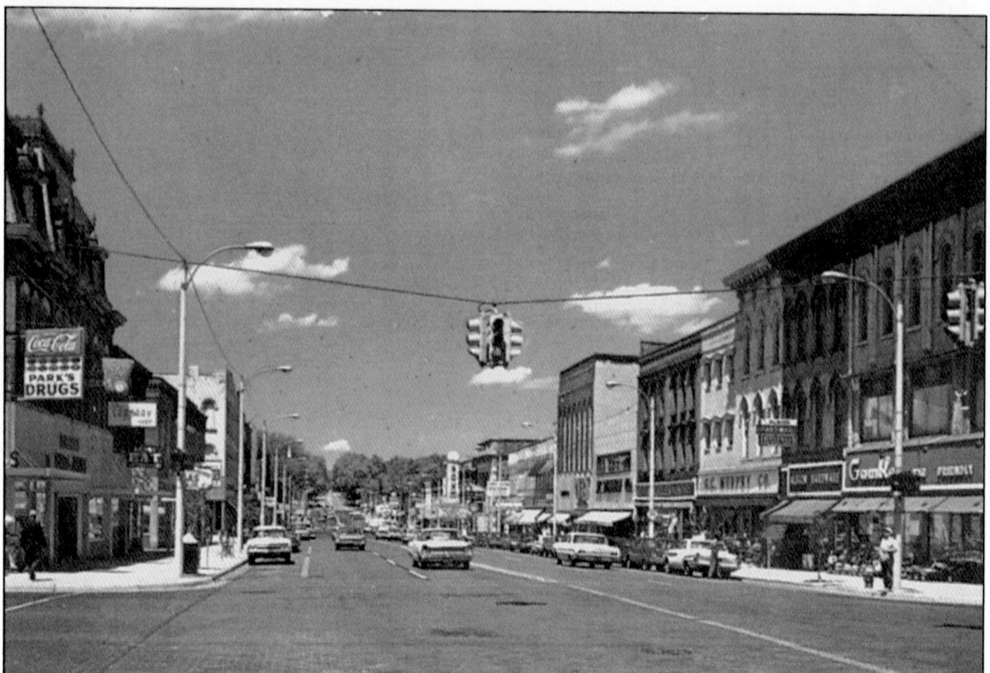


A thriving downtown Albion is depicted in this mid-1960s photograph, looking north from Erie Street.

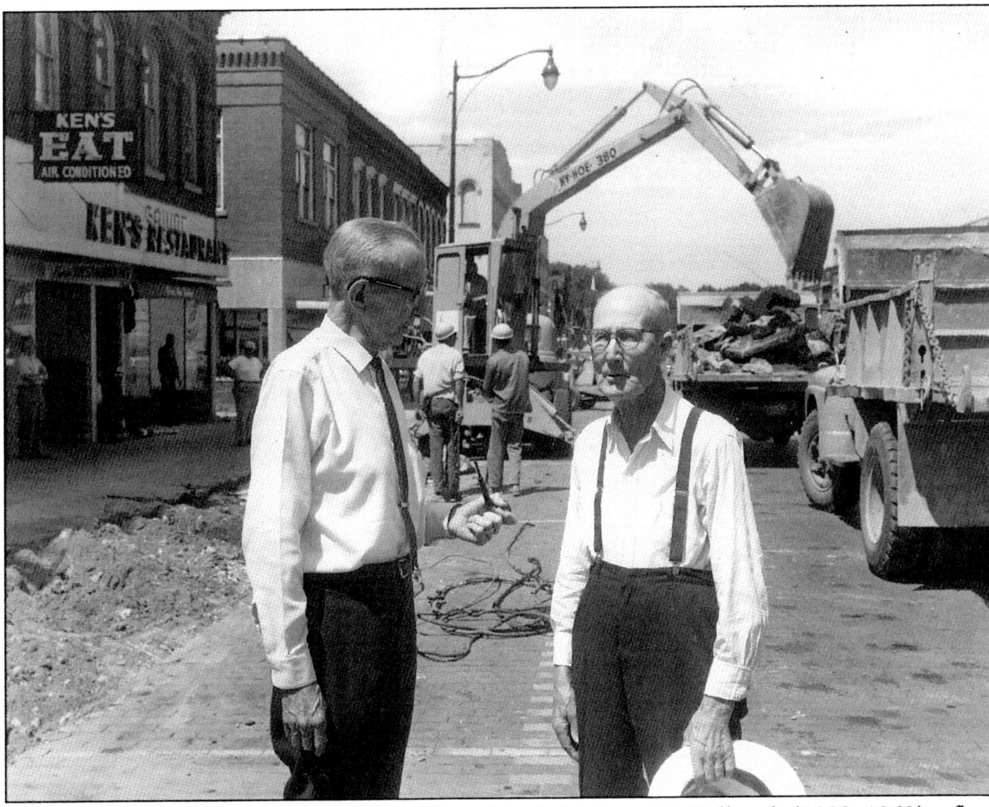


Old-timers (left) Floyd Parks (1890–1967) and (right) Hiram McCullough (1882–1969) reflect upon the new sidewalk project in downtown Albion in August 1964. The former coal storage areas under the old sidewalks were removed and filled in as part of the project, which also included new curbing, and new streetlights.

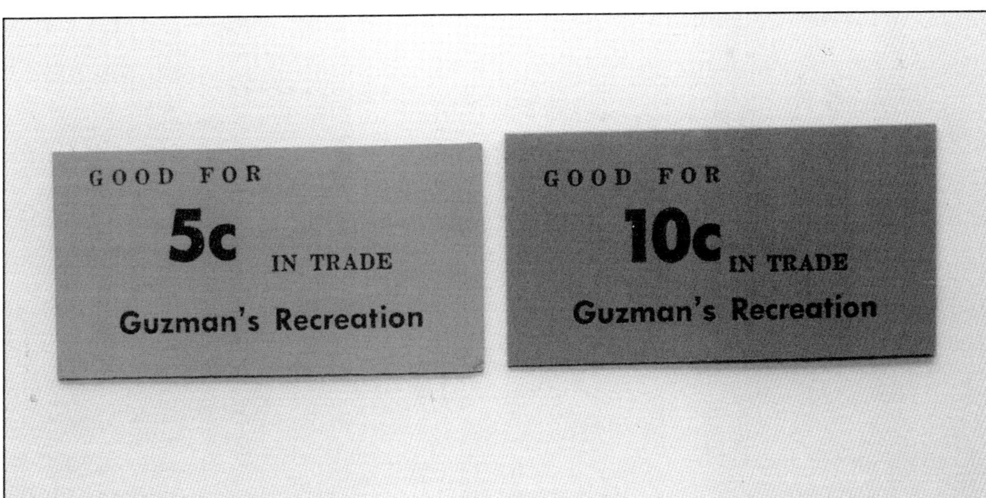


Joe Guzman opened his recreation establishment at 129 North Superior Street in 1960. Guzman issued these cardboard "good fors" worth 5¢ and 10¢ respectively, which were used throughout the 1960s.

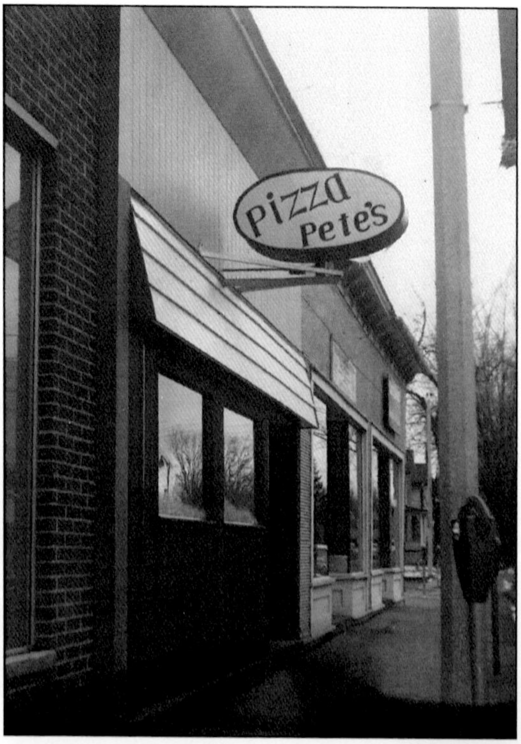


Albion's first pizza establishment, Pizza Pete's, opened on July 8, 1960, at 113 West Cass Street, across from City Hall. Pizza Pete's was owned by Peter Asaro Sr. (1922–1995) and Frank Passic Sr. (1919–1974), and they operated the establishment as a take-out with delivery service. On November 22, 1960, the duo made and delivered 25 pizzas in 20 minutes. The store was remodeled in the late 1960s and featured a redwood exterior, shown here.

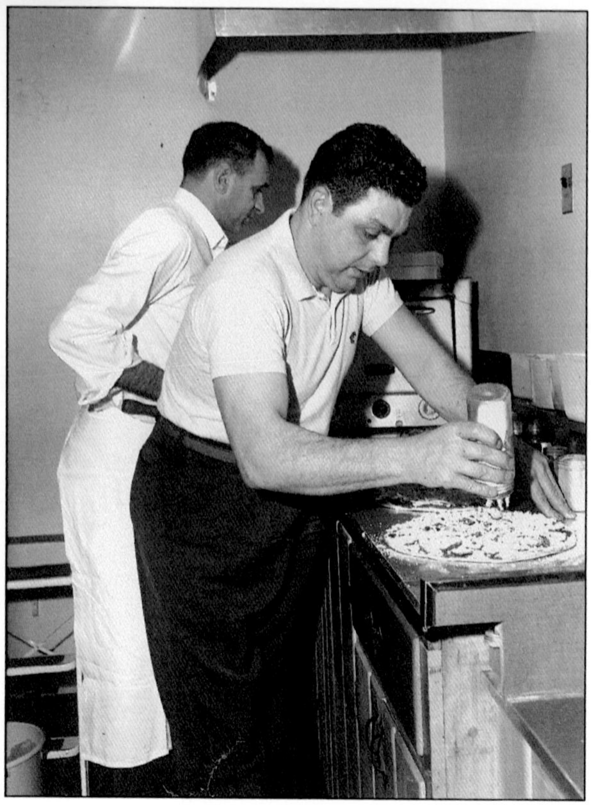

Pete Asaro (left) and Frank Passic (right) diligently prepare pizzas in the fall of 1960.

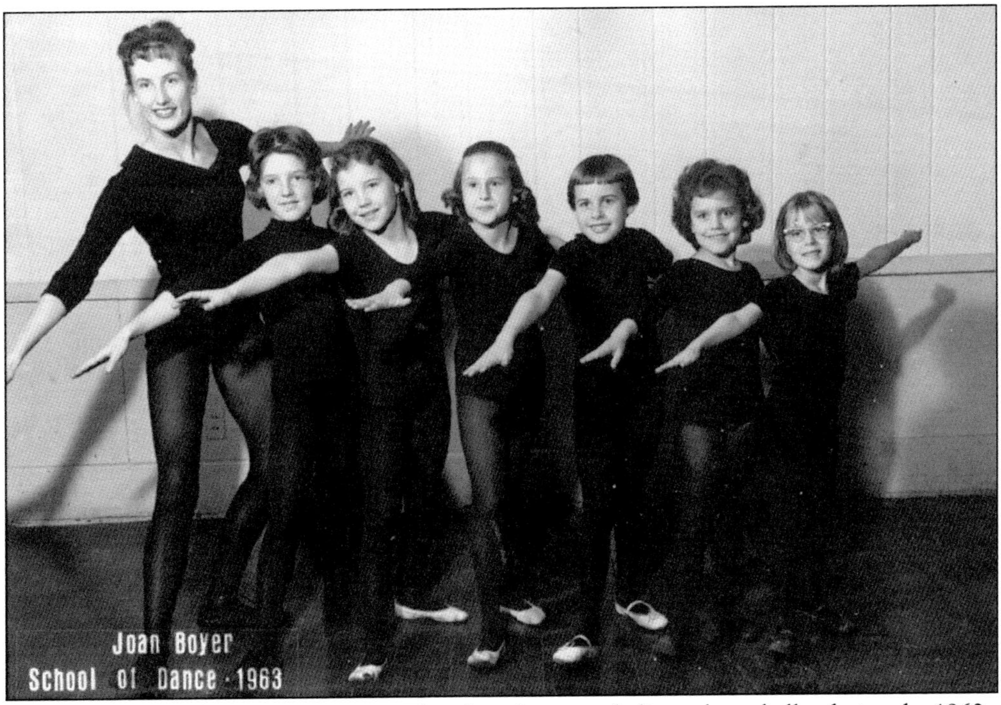

Joan Boyer's School of Dance was a popular place for young ladies to learn ballet during the 1960s, as shown in this 1963 class photograph. The little dancers are, from left to right: Joan Boyer, Jackie Klein, Terry Ward-Bentley, Jackie Warson, Amy Passic, Diane Torrey, and Nancy Lutzke.

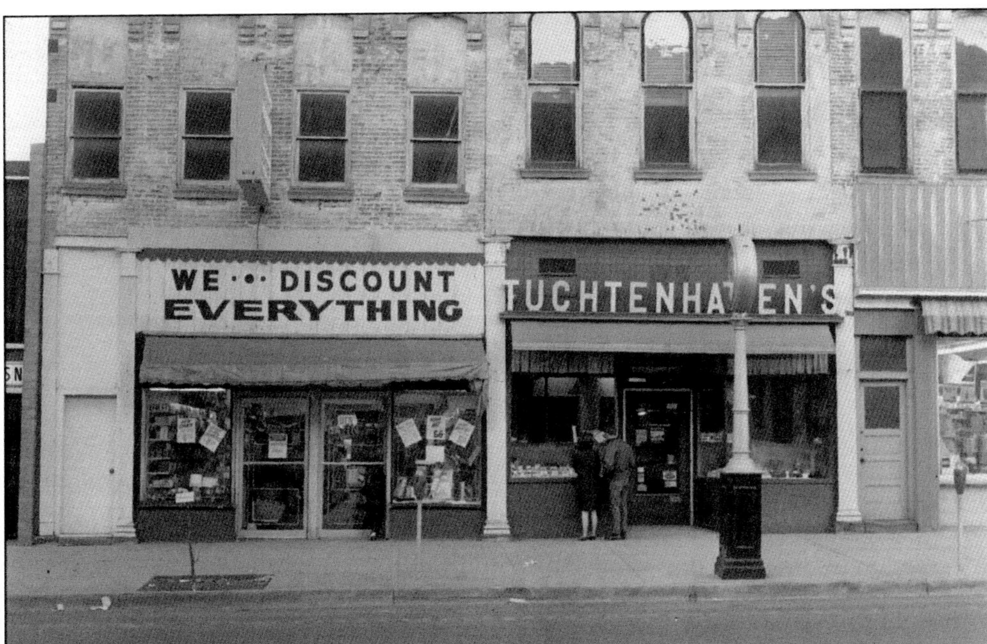

An antique clock once stood in front of Tuchtenhagen's Jewelry at 215 South Superior Street, as shown in this 1964 photograph. To the left is the Federal Discount Company (FEDCO), which opened on October 17, 1963.

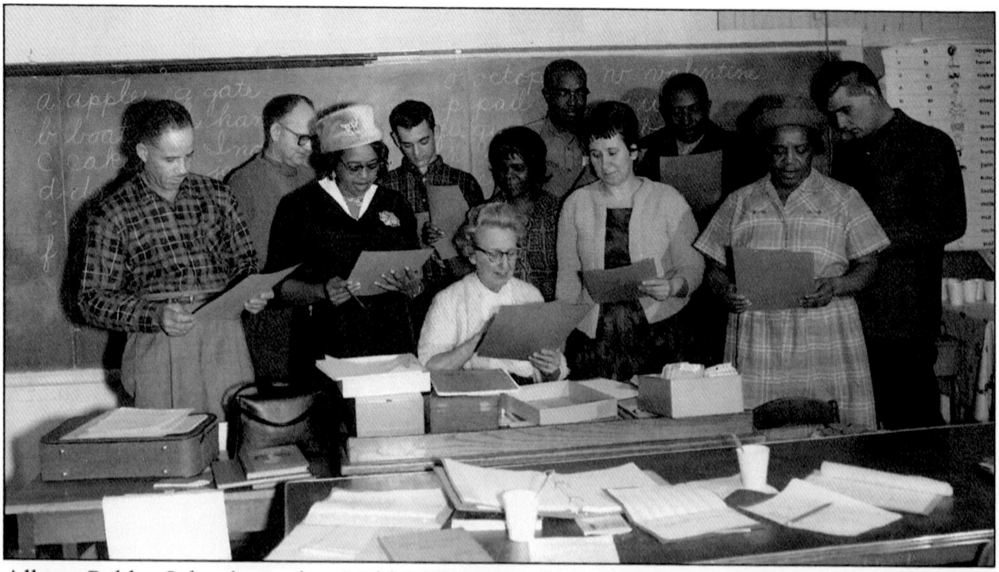

Albion Public Schools teacher Mildred Duckworth leads a group of Albion Malleable Iron Company employees and spouses in an adult reading class. In this March 1965 photo are, from left to right: David McCreary, Lewis Castle, Celesta McCreary, Joel Castle, (below) Mrs. Duckworth, (up) Laree Jackson, (up) Lilbern McKinney, Efrosina Jaskiw, Willie Lane, Lucy Warren, and John Elushik.

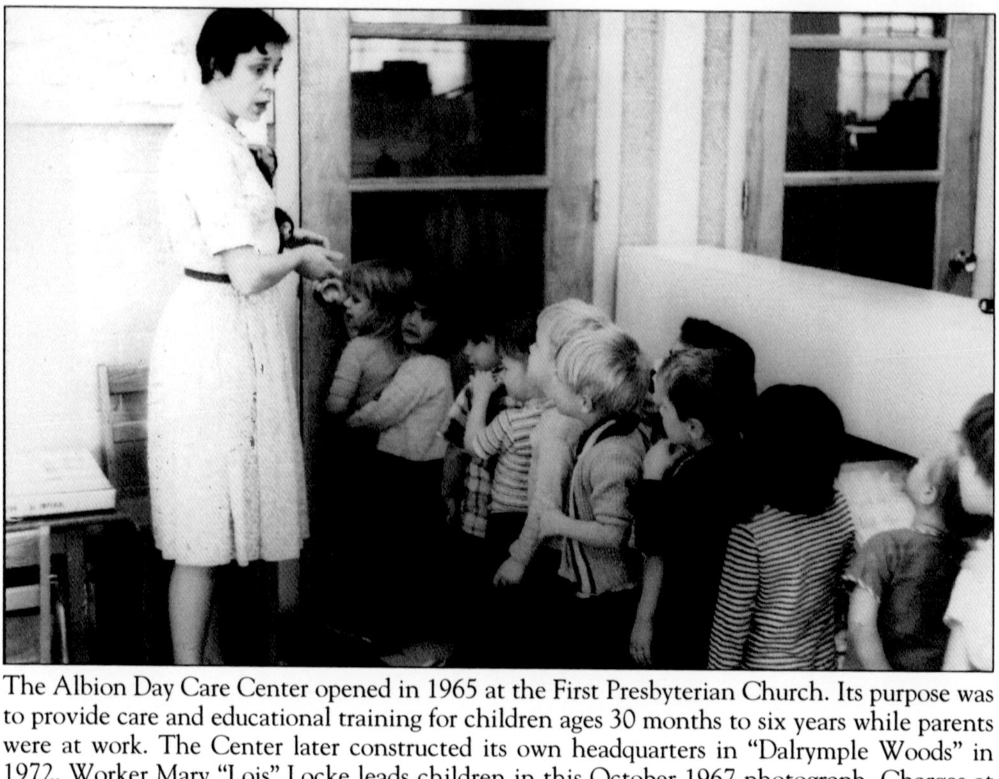

The Albion Day Care Center opened in 1965 at the First Presbyterian Church. Its purpose was to provide care and educational training for children ages 30 months to six years while parents were at work. The Center later constructed its own headquarters in "Dalrymple Woods" in 1972. Worker Mary "Lois" Locke leads children in this October 1967 photograph. Charges at the time were 50¢ an hour, or $4 per day.

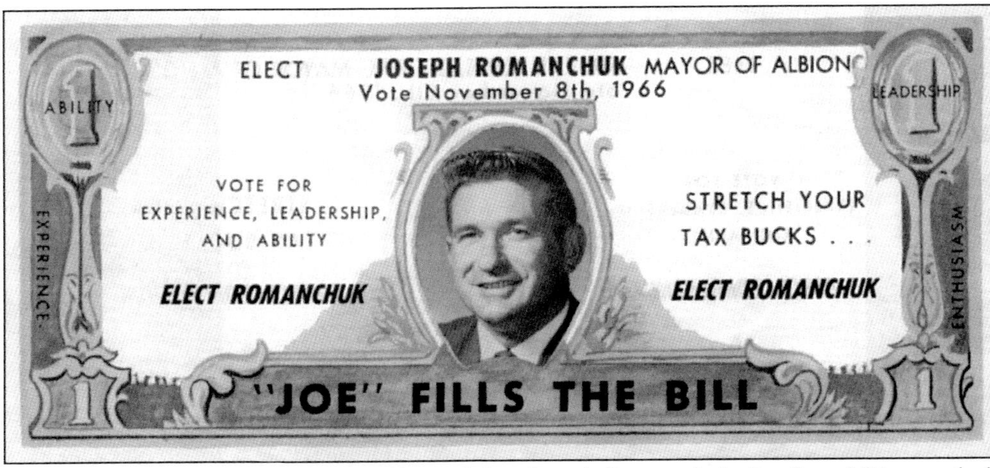


While campaigning for mayor in 1966, candidate Joseph Romanchuk distributed "Romanchuk dollars" across the city to promote his run for the mayoral office. It was a hotly contested campaign, and Romanchuk lost by only 65 votes in the November election. He subsequently served for many years on the Calhoun County Board of Supervisors.

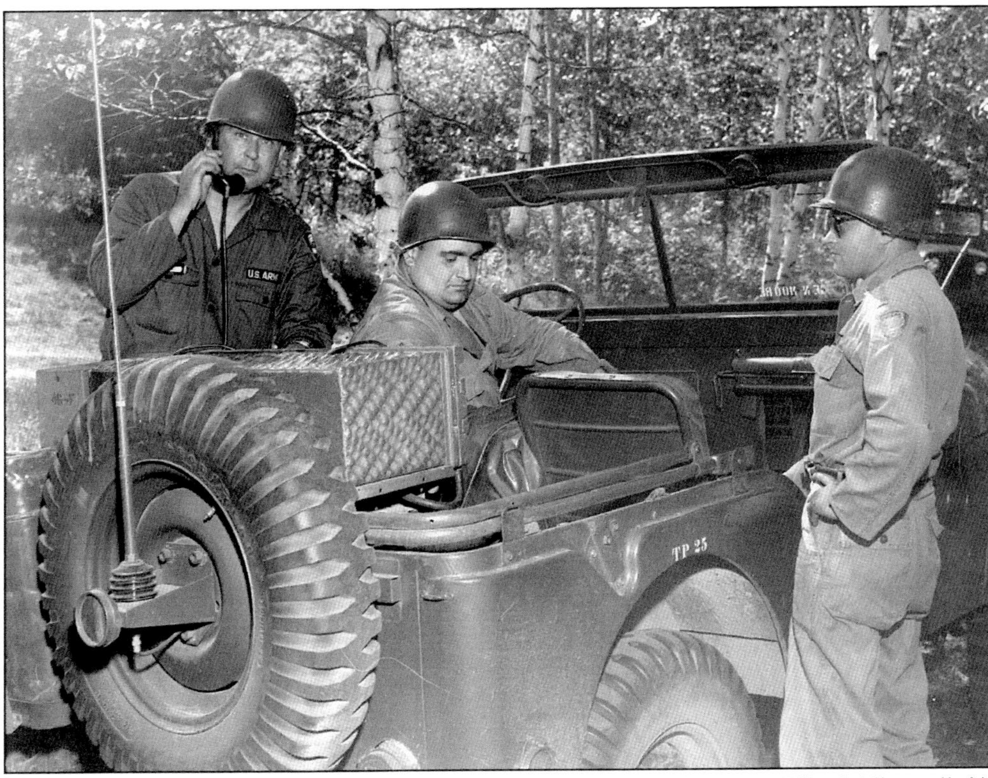

Michigan National Guard Brigadier General Noble O. Moore (1912–1975) of Albion (left), commanding general of the 46th Division Artillery, keeps in phone contact with men under his command during exercise "Mackinaw" at Camp Grayling in August, 1967. Moore was also a command officer during the Detroit riots that summer. An attorney by profession, he served as Albion City Attorney and as Calhoun County Prosecutor. Seated in the jeep is driver Sgt. Major Louis Russo of Tekonsha, and on the right stands 1st Lieutenant J.D. Gotch of Detroit.

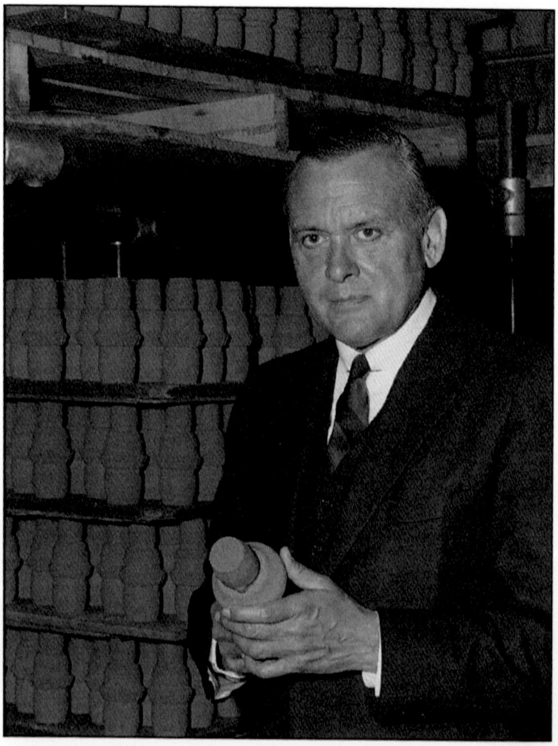

Thomas T. Lloyd (1912–1978) was known as "Albion's Goodwill Ambassador," and began working at the Albion Malleable Iron Company in the 1930s. He assumed the role of vice president in 1938. Lloyd served as executive vice president of the Malleable from 1960 until its merger in 1967. He then became vice president of the new Hayes-Albion Corporation, and executive vice president from 1969 until his retirement in 1974. A civic leader and philanthropist, Lloyd established the Albion Civic (now Community) Foundation in 1968. This is a 1965 photo.

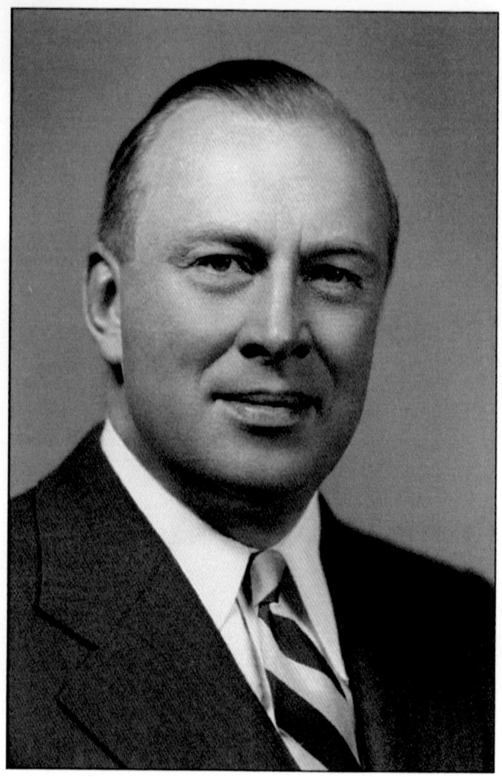

Collins Carter (1906–1983) served as president of the Albion Malleable Iron Company beginning in 1938, and its successor, Hayes-Albion Corporation from 1967 to 1972. Carter strongly believed that industry should be involved in community life, and led the Malleable in its civic efforts here. He was a major supporter of the area Boy Scout movement, and was awarded the Silver Beaver Award in 1961. Carter served on various boards and commissions in both Albion and Jackson. Carter and his wife Mary donated The *American Molder* statue in Molder Statue Park in 1974.

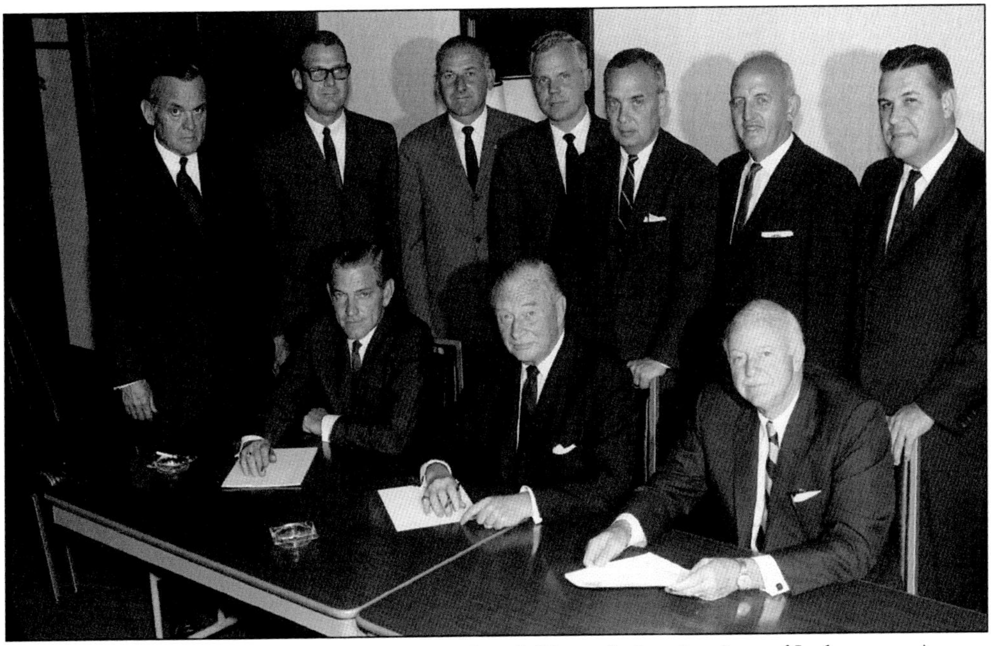

The Albion Malleable Iron Company merged with Hayes Industries, Inc. of Jackson on August 11, 1967, to form the Hayes-Albion Corporation. Officials who participated in the merger signing agreement are, from left to right: (front row) Boyd Vass, vice president and Hayes Group president; Collins Carter, president; and Edwin C. Hetherwick, former Hayes chairman; (back row) Thomas Lloyd, vice president and Albion Group president; Raymond Kurtz, controller; Hugh McVicker, Jackson attorney; unidentified broker; Gardner Lloyd, vice president/secretary; Walter Turner, vice president and treasurer; and Don Davis, former Hayes secretary.

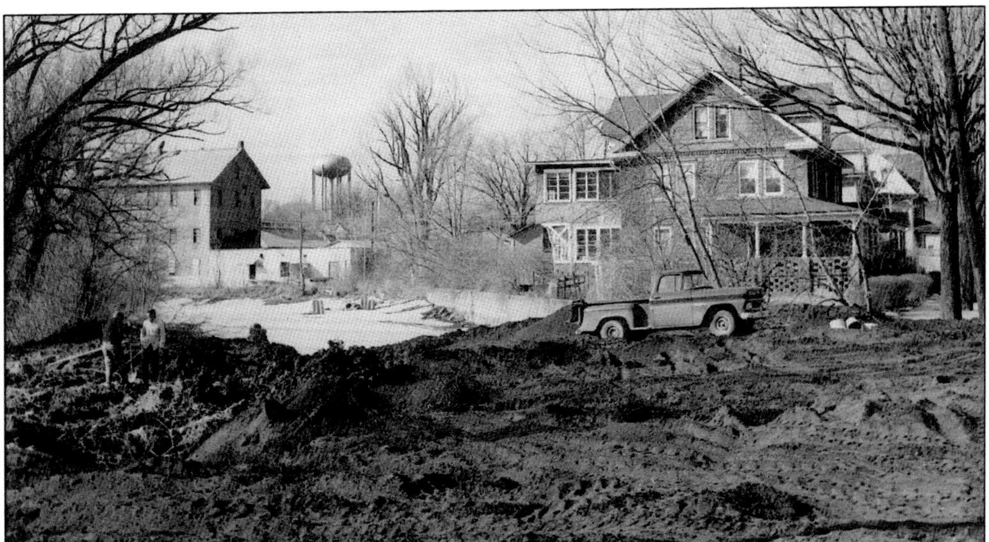

The millrace between East Porter Street and East Cass Street leading to the White Mill (closed in 1957) was filled in, March 1965. The Riverside Apartments were subsequently erected on the site. The Mill was demolished in 1974. The house at 202 South Monroe Street on the right was for many years the home of Audrey K. Wilder, dean of women at Albion College.

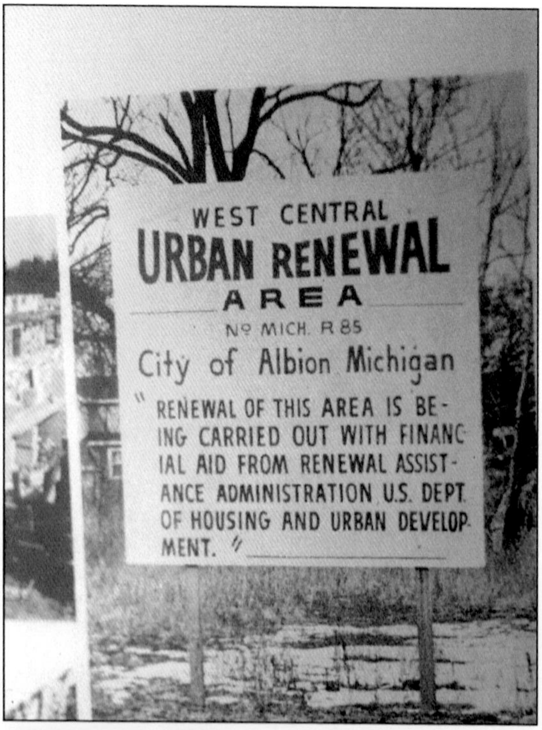


The controversial West Central Urban Renewal project of the 1960s and 1970s displaced many persons living on the west end of town. The program resulted in the acquisition and demolition of about 200 substandard housing units, and the relocation of families into new apartment projects.

The historic David Peabody house (seen in this 1962 photo) on the southwest corner of West Erie and South Eaton Streets was demolished in 1966 as part of the Urban Renewal project. The Peabody Place senior citizens housing facility was subsequently erected on the site.

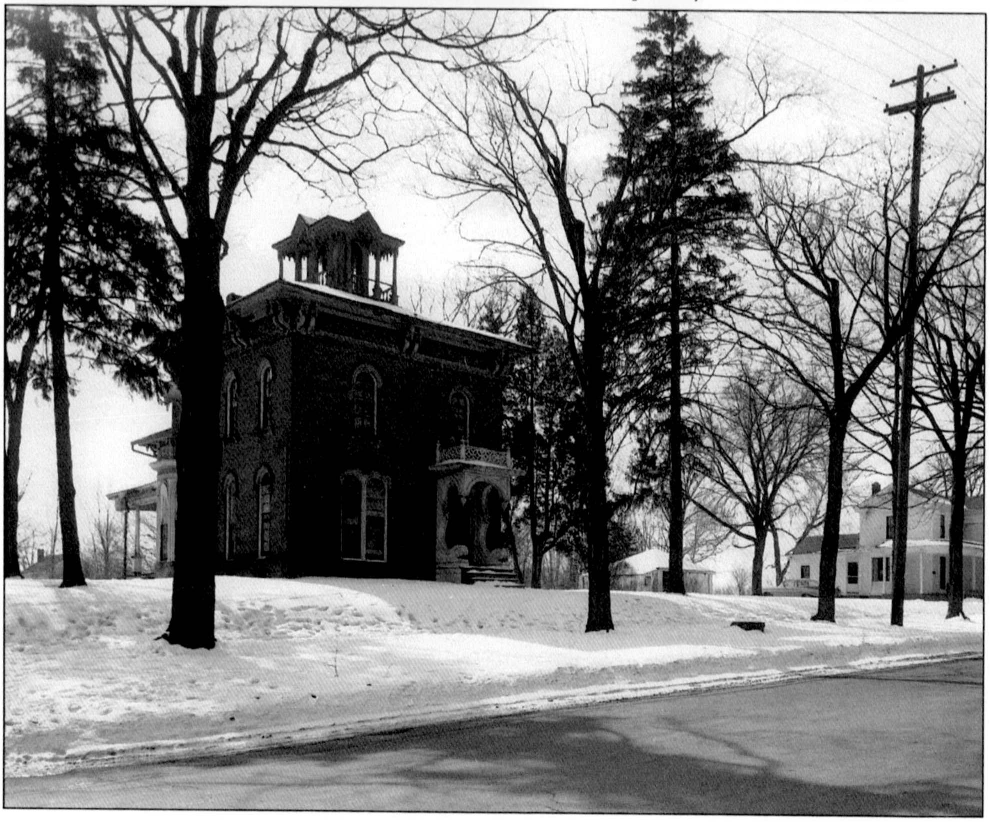

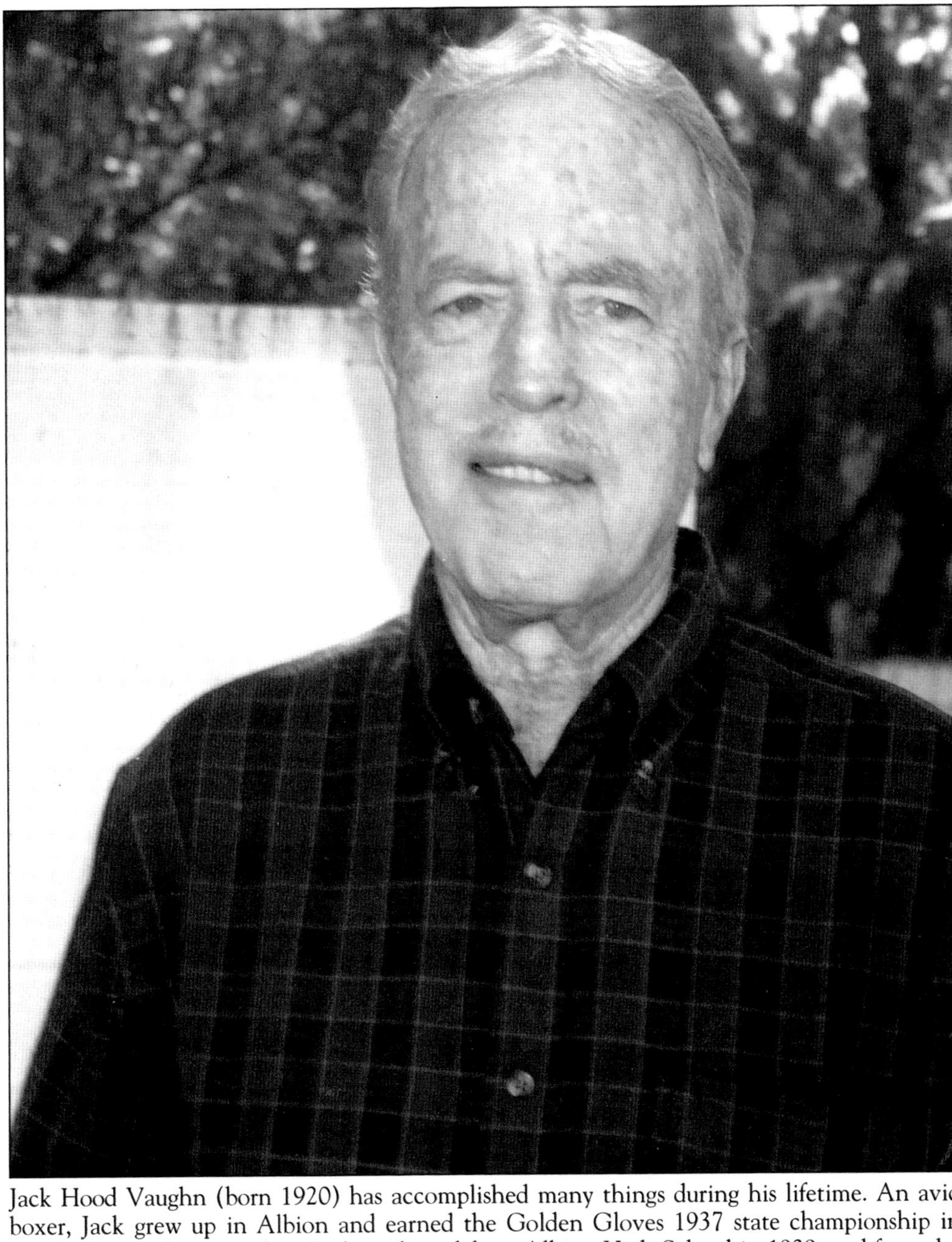

Jack Hood Vaughn (born 1920) has accomplished many things during his lifetime. An avid boxer, Jack grew up in Albion and earned the Golden Gloves 1937 state championship in the featherweight open class. Jack graduated from Albion High School in 1939, and from the University of Michigan in 1943. He subsequently served in the Marines during World War II, and was awarded the Medal of Honor for bravery in action above and beyond the call of duty. Following the War, he was a professional boxer for a brief period of time.

Jack joined the U.S. State Department in 1951 and during the 1950s led work involving government aid programs for foreign countries. He was appointed U.S. Ambassador to Panama in 1964. In 1966, Jack Vaughn was named the second director of the U.S. Peace Corps and served in that position until 1969. He also served briefly as U.S. Ambassador to Columbia. He later served as the president of Planned Parenthood for several years.

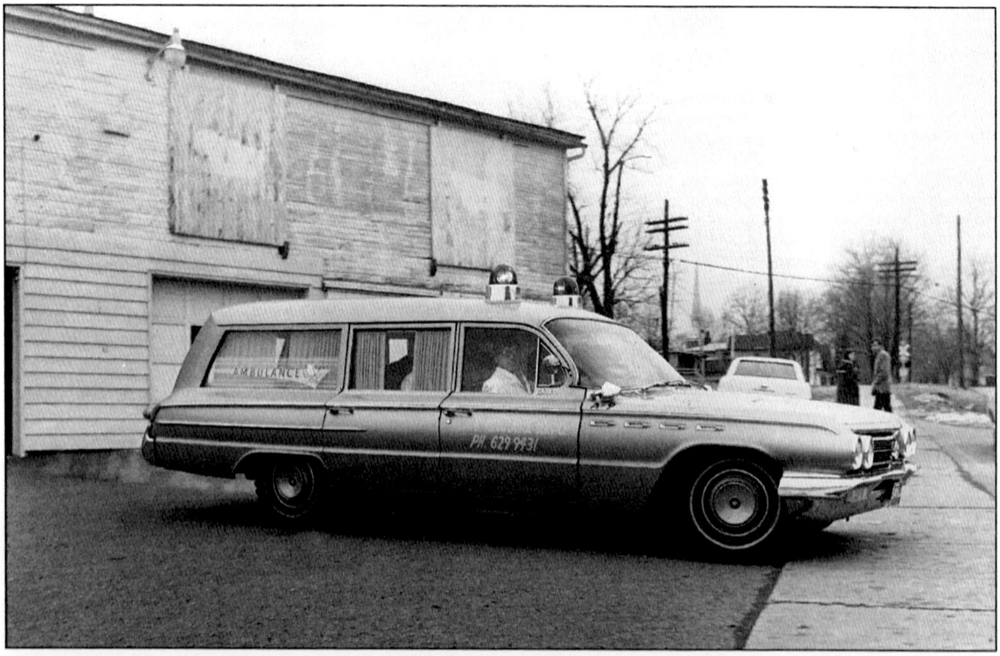


The Albion Area Ambulance Service began operating on December 15, 1966 using two old ambulances obtained from Albion's funeral homes. The Service was first located at 131 East Cass Street, shown above, and the ambulances were stored in sheds of the old Albion Lumber Company. The Service was operated by trained volunteers for many years. It moved to facilities at the Albion Community Hospital on West Erie Street in the spring of 1971.

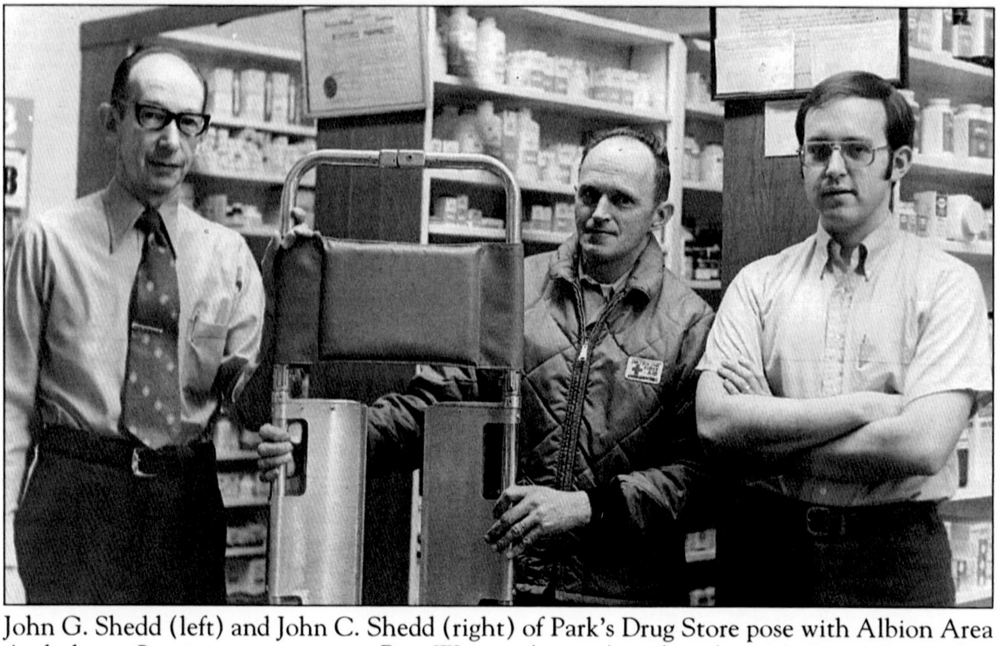

John G. Shedd (left) and John C. Shedd (right) of Park's Drug Store pose with Albion Area Ambulance Service representative Ron Warson (center) as they donate a "scoop" stretcher to the Service, used primarily for back injuries, in this March 1974 photo. (Courtesy of the *Albion Recorder*.)

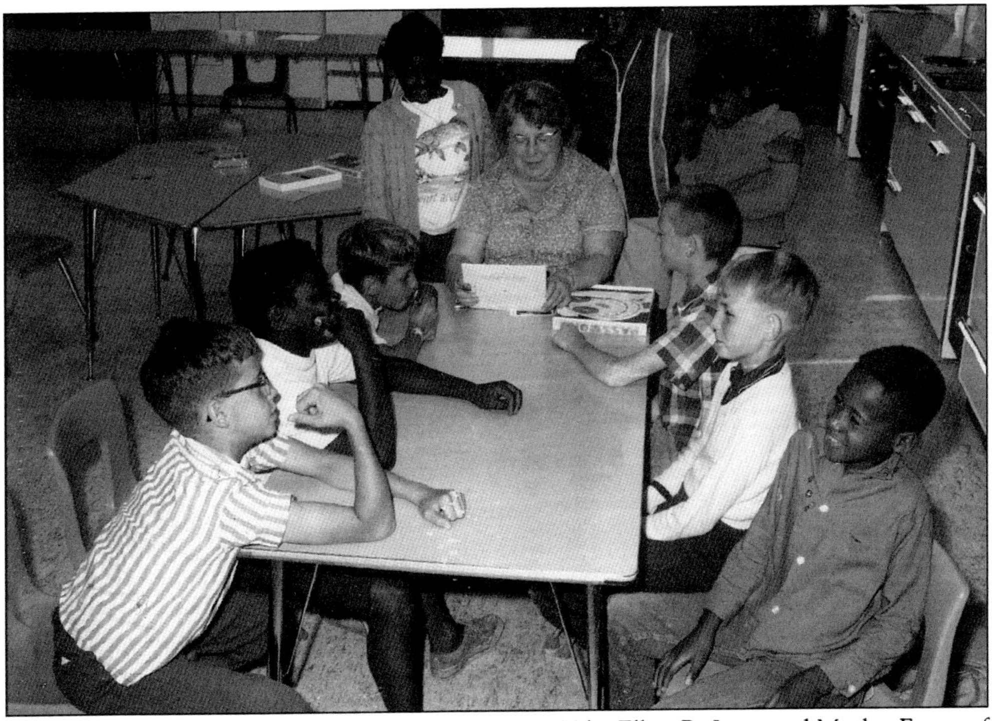

The Earn, Learn, and Play program was begun in 1966 by Elkin R. Isaac and Morley Fraser of Albion College under a grant from the Mott Foundation. Local youth would earn money in community cleaning projects, learn specialized subjects, and participate in team sports. Seen here, teacher Lucille Moore instructs her students in a reading course in a 1968 photo. (Courtesy of Jerry Sacharski.)

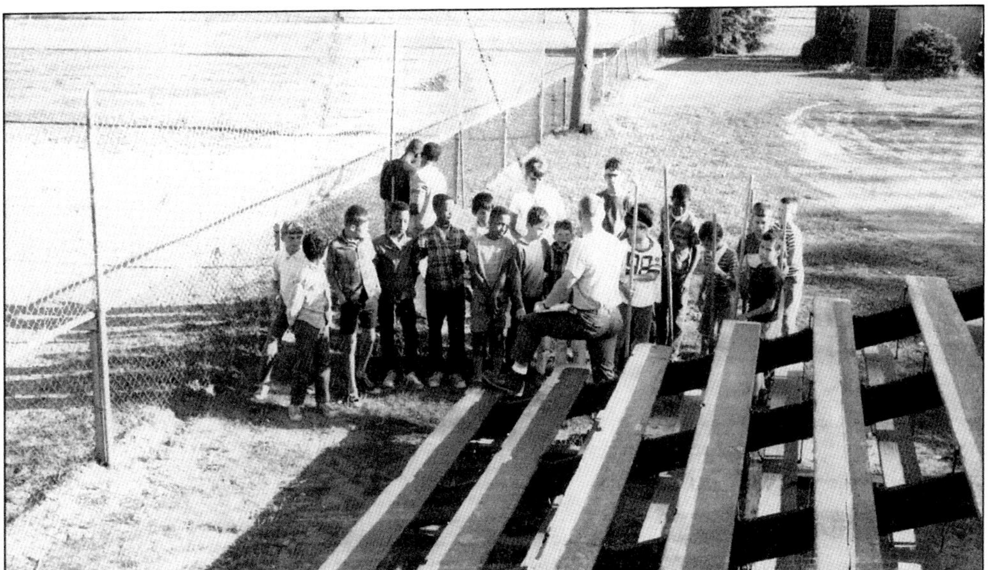

One group of Earn, Learn, and Play participants worked at Ketchum Field under the direction of Joe Curtain. They cleaned and maintained the softball field, cleaned and raked the area, and helped with bleacher repair as shown in this 1968 photo. (Courtesy of Jerry Sacharski.)

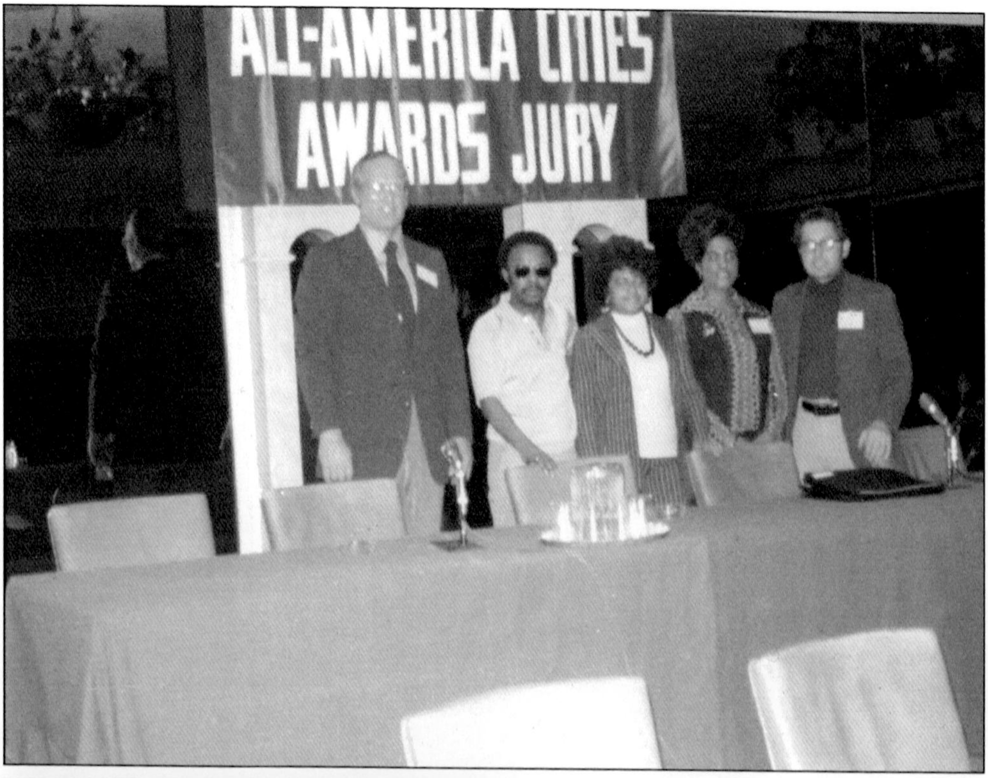


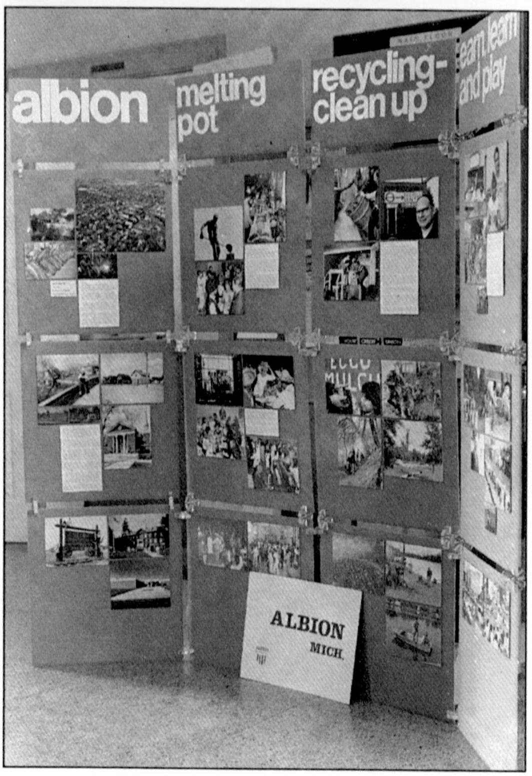


Albion Chamber of Commerce president Don Hull, Mayor Charles Jones and wife Diane, the Melting Pot founder Barbara J. Gladney, and City Manager Neal Godby presented their case for Albion before the National Municipal League on November 10, 1973 in Dallas, Texas. As a result, Albion was one of only ten cities awarded the prestigious 1973 All-America City award out of 400 entries. (Photo courtesy of Tom and Barbara Gladney.)

The 1973 All-America City presentation included this display panel highlighting Albion's accomplishments, such as the Melting Pot organization, the Recycling Center and Kalamazoo River clean up, and the Earn, Learn, and Play program.

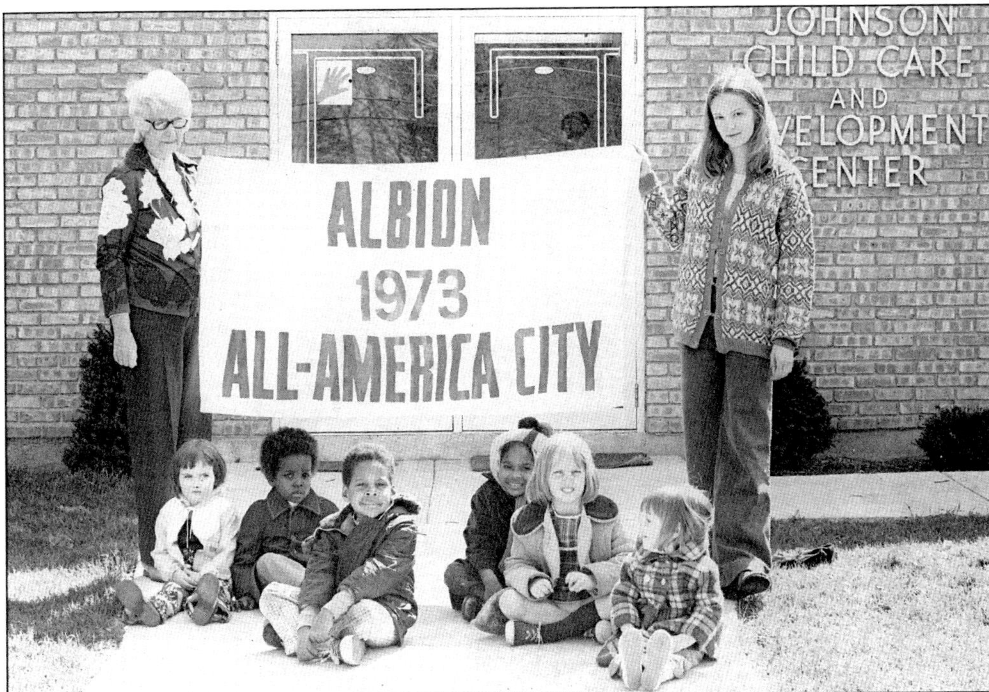


Geraldine Johnson (1902–2000) (left) and worker Lesley Nixon (right) hold the 1973 Albion All-America City banner presented to the City of Albion in May 1974. Mrs. Johnson was the director of the Johnson Child Care and Development Center for many years. The children seated in front are, from left to right: Heather Hunt, Greg Gant, Robin Walker, Kim Lee, Beth Williams, and Nicki Russell. (Photo courtesy of the *Albion Recorder*.)

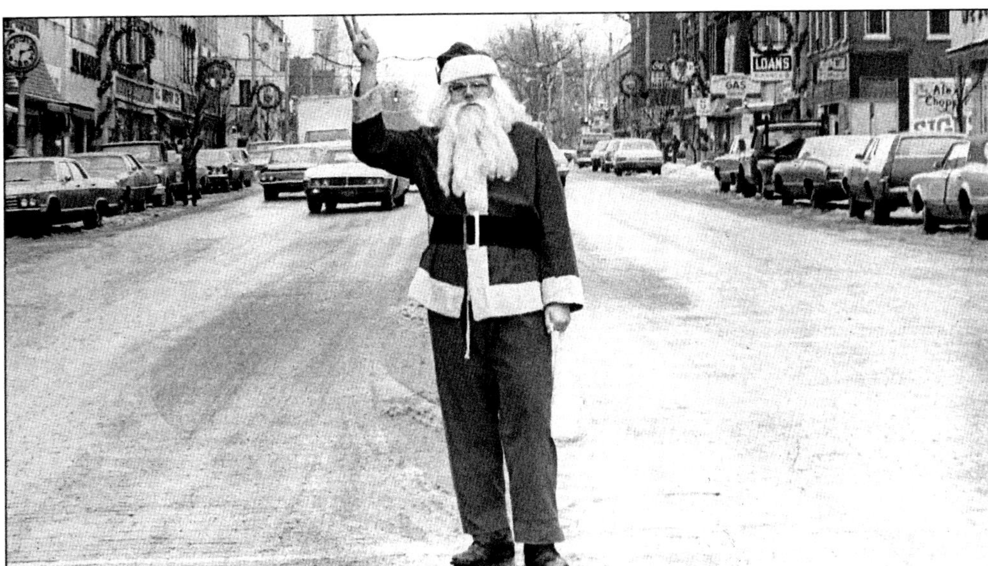


Santa Claus paid a visit to downtown Albion in December 1972 in order to help promote Christmas shopping in the business district. Santa daily walked up and down the street, visiting various stores and distributing candy along the way. (Photo courtesy of the *Albion Recorder*.)

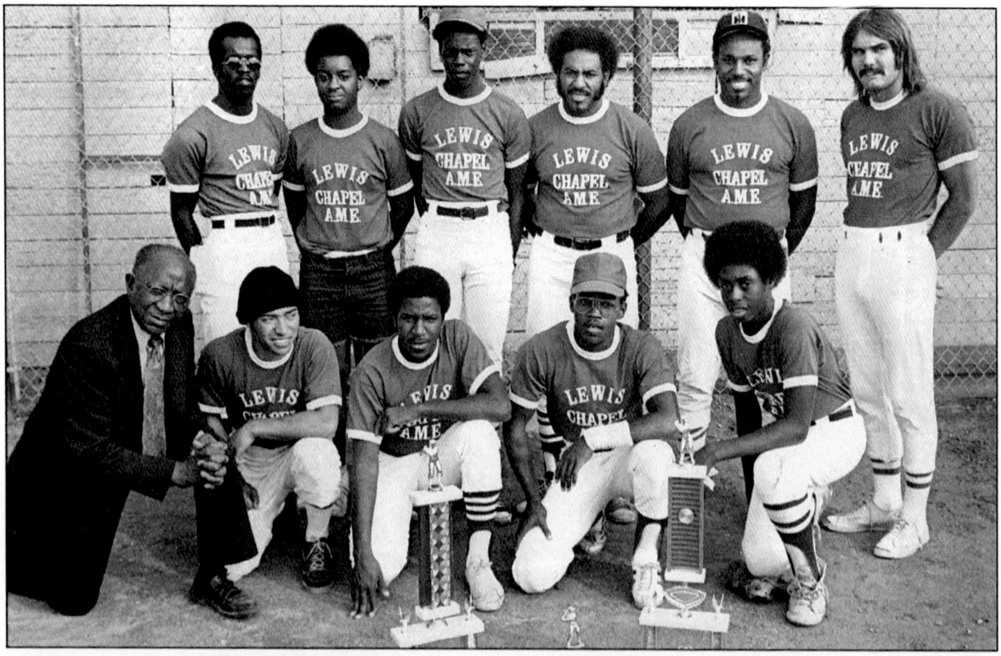


The Lewis Chapel A.M.E. Church softball team took all honors in the 1974 Albion Church Slow Pitch Softball League, winning the regular season and also the league's tournament. The team members are, from left to right: (front row) Rev. Donald Folden, Tony DeJesus, Jerome Collins, Gerald Simpson, and Eric Baldwin; (back row) Don Anglin, George Griffin, Dan Anglin, Charles Clark, Richard Clark, and Larry Hurley. (Photo courtesy of the *Albion Recorder*.)

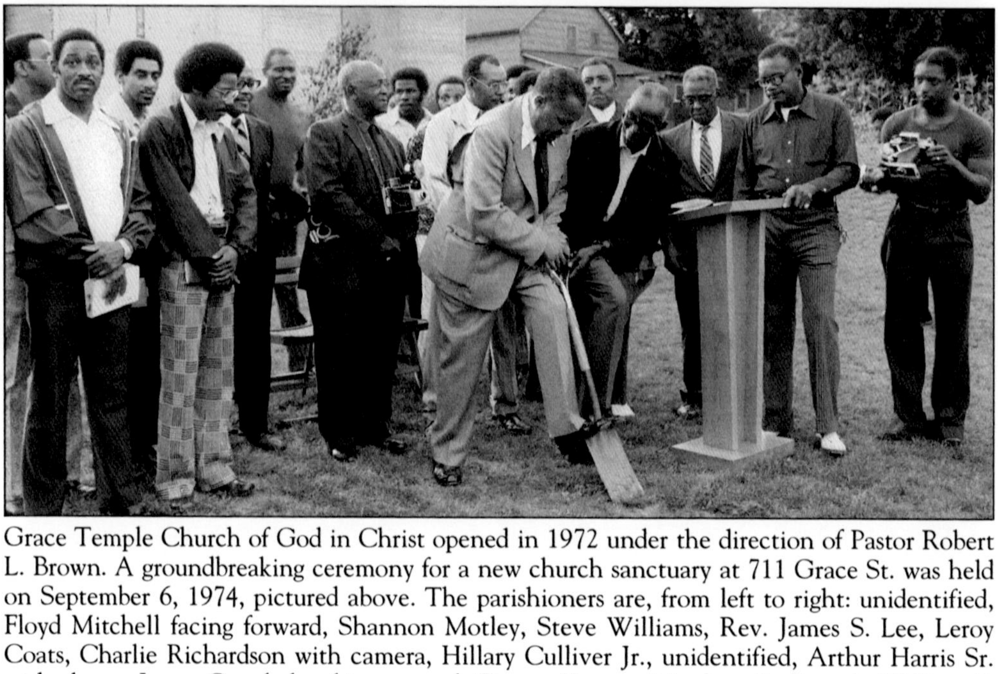

Grace Temple Church of God in Christ opened in 1972 under the direction of Pastor Robert L. Brown. A groundbreaking ceremony for a new church sanctuary at 711 Grace St. was held on September 6, 1974, pictured above. The parishioners are, from left to right: unidentified, Floyd Mitchell facing forward, Shannon Motley, Steve Williams, Rev. James S. Lee, Leroy Coats, Charlie Richardson with camera, Hillary Culliver Jr., unidentified, Arthur Harris Sr. with glasses, James Google breaking ground, George Harvey, Matthew Stallworth, William F. Brown, Jerry Williams, and Jeff Thomas.

Dr. Lawrence J. Heidenreich (1905–1994) operated his dental practice on the second floor of 203 South Superior Street from October 1930 until his retirement nearly 53 years later in May 1983. Generations of families had Dr. Heidenreich as their dentist. He was assisted by his trusted dental assistant, Marjorie Sauer from 1939 to 1983. This March 1974 photo is courtesy of Fred Heidenreich.

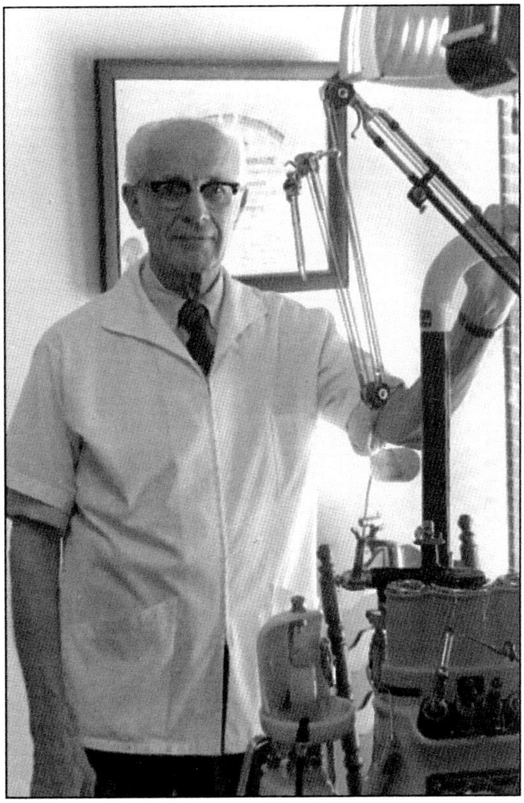

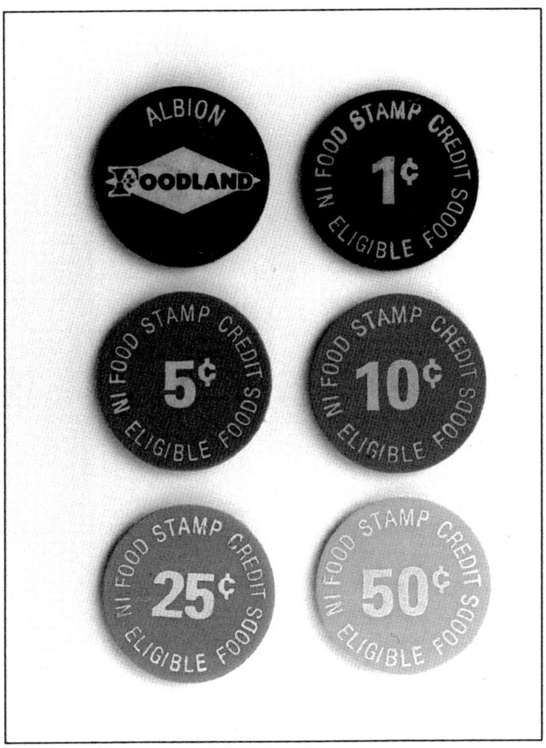


In order to help insure that Food Stamp money was being spent for its intended purposes, Albion Foodland grocery at 110 South Eaton Street issued these Food Stamp Credit tokens in 1977. Users would receive tokens as small change, which could be redeemed for authorized food items on a future visit to the store. The U.S. Department of Agriculture declared such tokens illegal in 1979, and their usage was discontinued in grocery stores across the country.

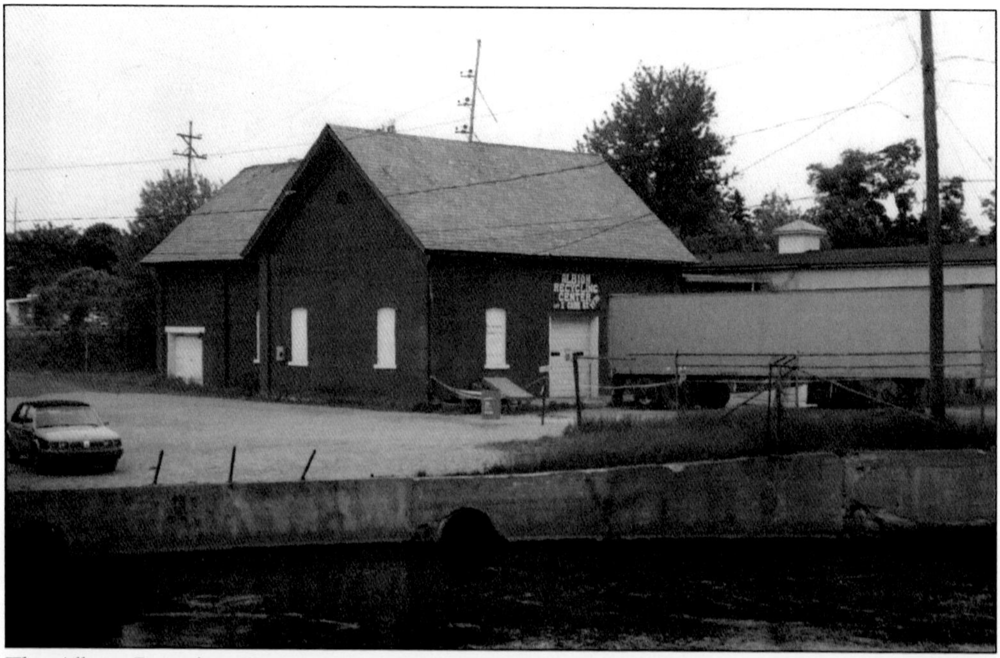


The Albion Recycling Center at 113 East Cass Street shipped tons of recyclable materials from 1970 until its closure on March 27, 1993. Funds raised went towards the dredging of the Kalamazoo River, and other clean-up projects. Director of the Center was Truman L. Barnes (1916–1991), who was assisted by many community volunteers through the years. This photo is from 1993.

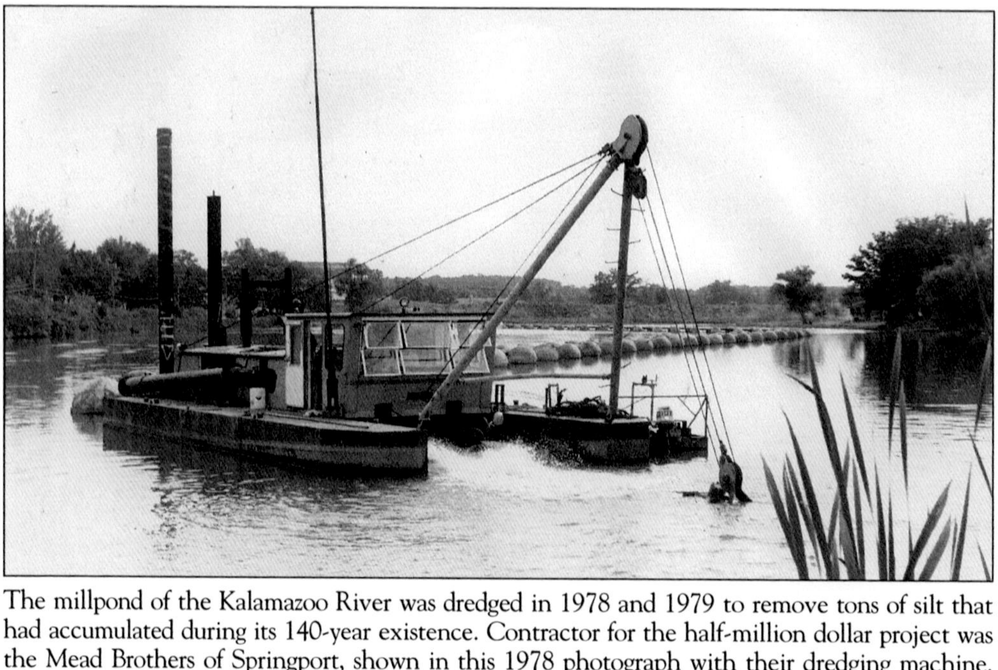

The millpond of the Kalamazoo River was dredged in 1978 and 1979 to remove tons of silt that had accumulated during its 140-year existence. Contractor for the half-million dollar project was the Mead Brothers of Springport, shown in this 1978 photograph with their dredging machine. The egg-shaped flotation devices in the distance held the vacuum pipe that led to a receiving pond where the silt was thereby deposited. The millpond was dredged to a depth of up to eight feet.

*Five*

# Forward Into the New Millennium

## 1980–2002

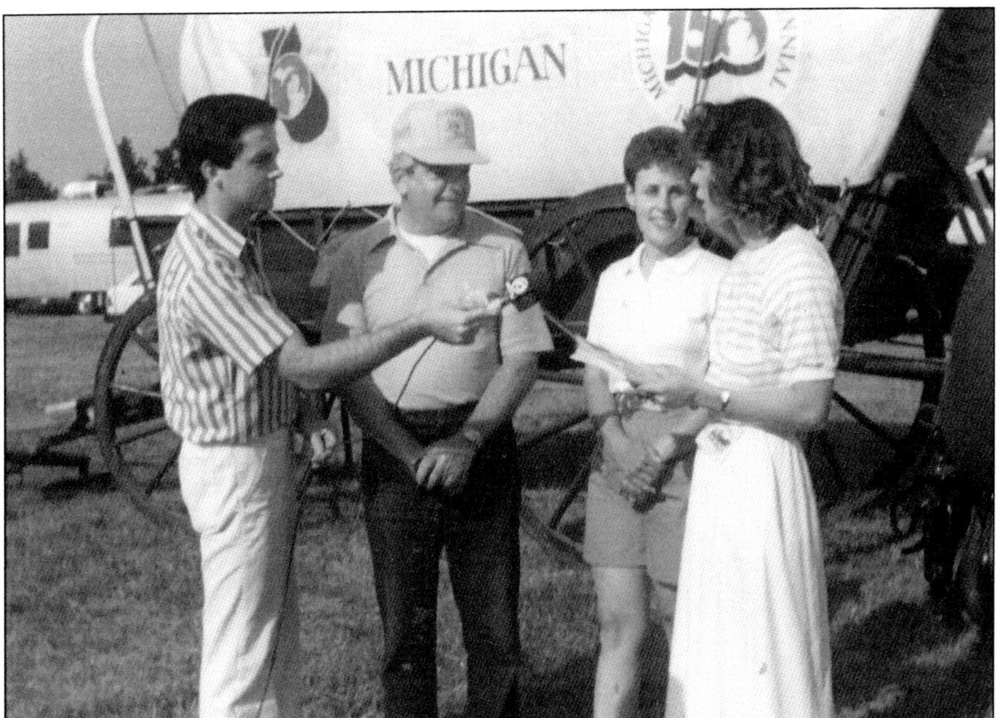


Part of Michigan's 1987 Sesquicentennial celebration included a covered wagon train with horses, mules, donkeys, and oxen that traveled across the state. Albion hosted the entourage at the Albion High School grounds on June 18–19. Participants camped out and were fed free-of-charge courtesy of various local donors and the Albion Chamber of Commerce. CENTER: Co-chairs Ed Maney of Albion College and veterinarian Dr. Amy Bearman are interviewed by WILX-TV10 news anchors (left and right ends). (Photo courtesy Dr. Amy Bearman.)

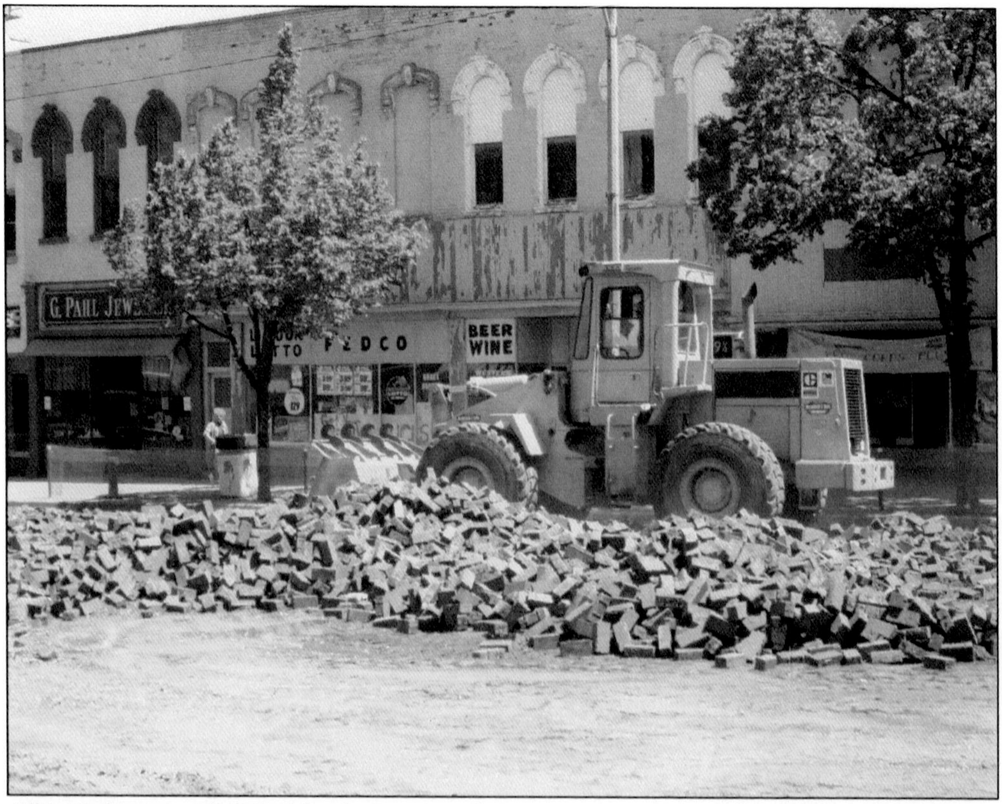


Albion's historic 1940-laid brick Superior Street was removed in the summer of 1993 and replaced with new bricks. Here we see the old bricks being scooped up for removal in front of 217 South Superior Street on May 12, 1993.

ALBION

PAVING THE WAY FOR A SUPERIOR FUTURE

This was a familiar logo in 1993, as the Greater Albion Chamber of Commerce led a promotional effort designed to attract shoppers to downtown Albion during the brick reconstruction project.

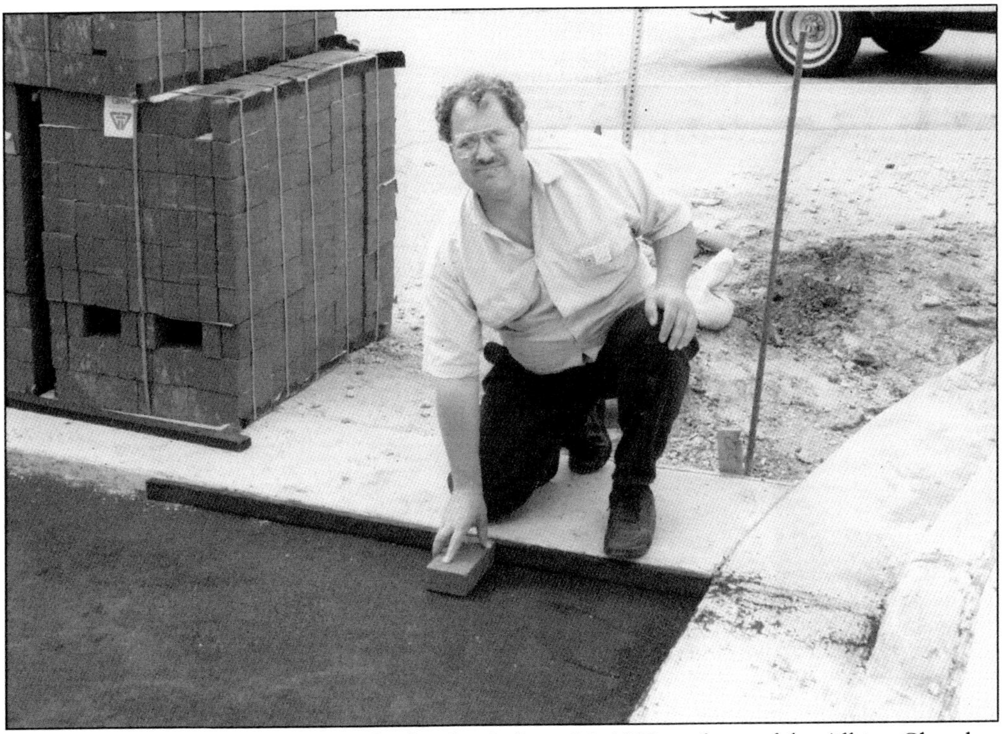

Albion historian Frank Passic lays the first brick, June 18, 1993, in front of the Albion Chamber of Commerce.

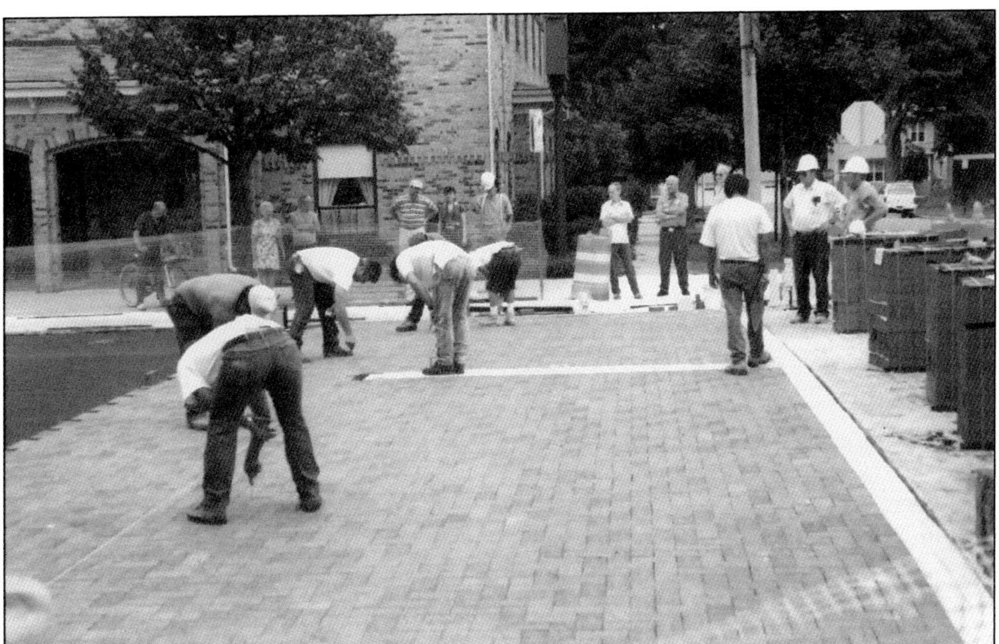

Workers from the Seidl Construction Company are seen here beginning their work of laying the first stretch of paving bricks on South Superior Street at Ash Street on Friday, June 18, 1993.

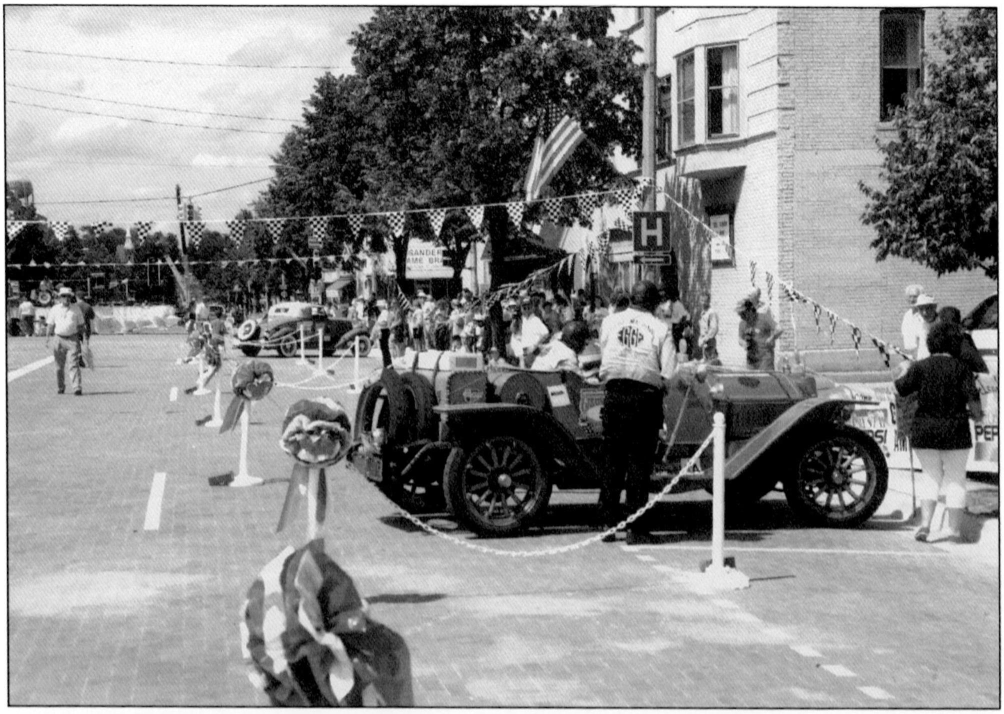

The Great American Car Race passed through Albion on July 6, 1993, and was the first to travel on the new bricks between Erie and Ash Streets. Albion served as one of 20 pit stops on the cross-country course that featured domestic and foreign classic automobiles. Hundreds of persons greeted the race participants, and Albion received a $5,000 award from the Great Race organizers for being the city showing the most enthusiasm.

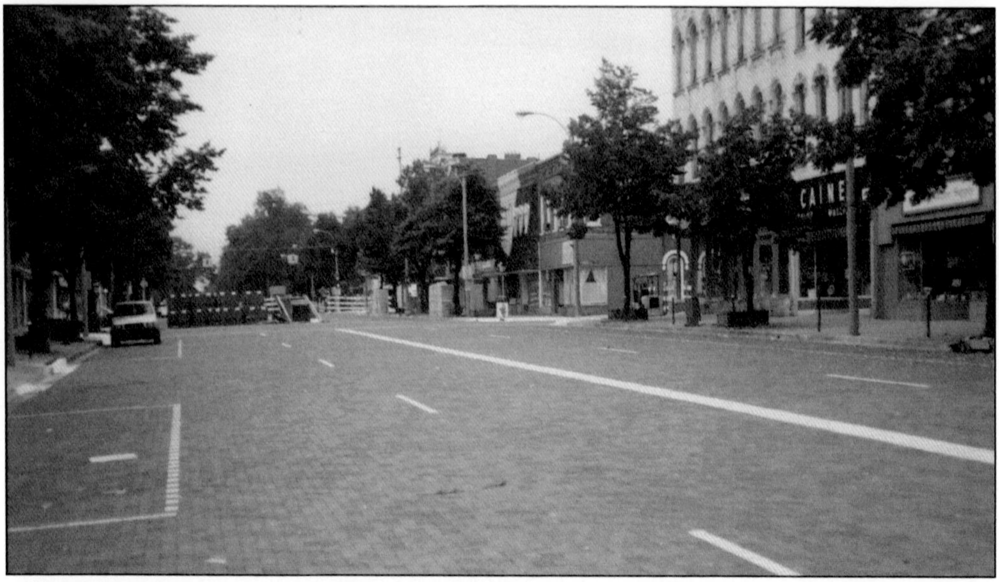

Albion's 1993 brick street included white bricks that were used for centerlines, lane markings, and parking areas boundaries. The paving bricks were manufactured by the Glen-Gery Brick Corporation in Bigler, Pennsylvania.

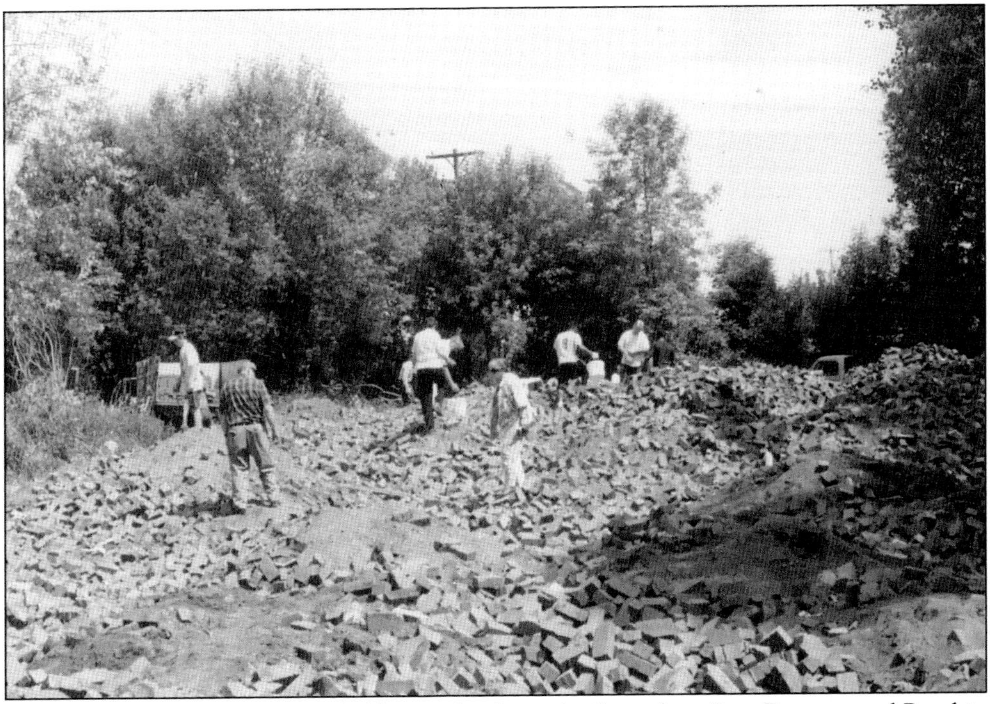

Scavengers comb the mounds of old street bricks at the "tree dump" on Brownswood Road in the summer of 1993, where bricks were being sold for 10¢ each.

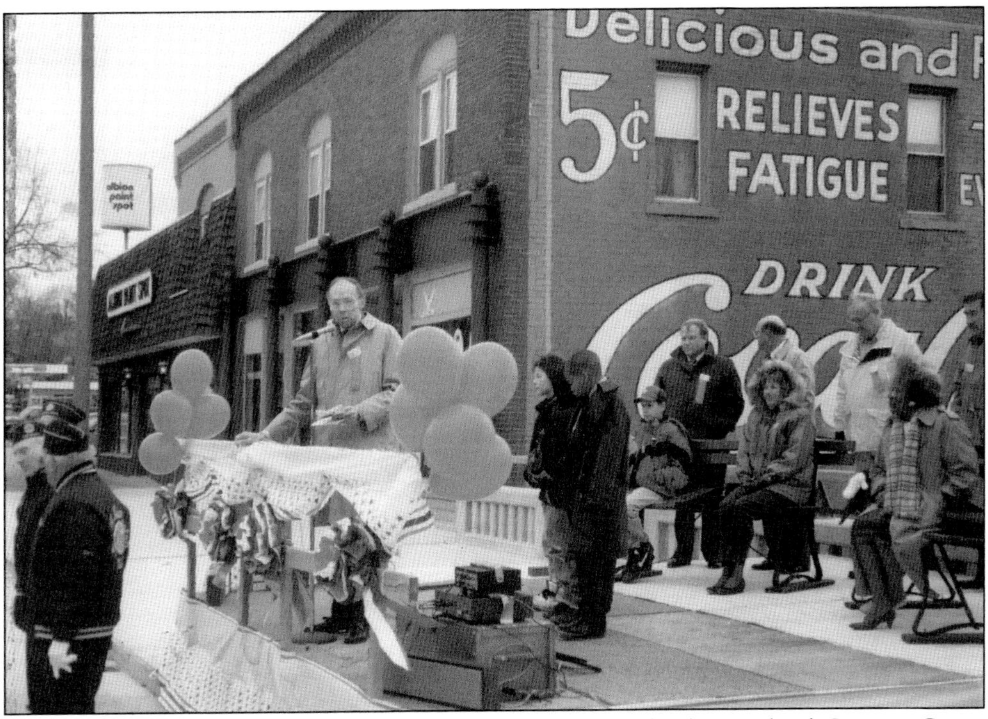


Albion jeweler Gordon Pahl leads the dedication ceremonies for the new brick Superior Street on Sunday, October 31, 1993. The entire street had been re-opened to traffic on October 14.

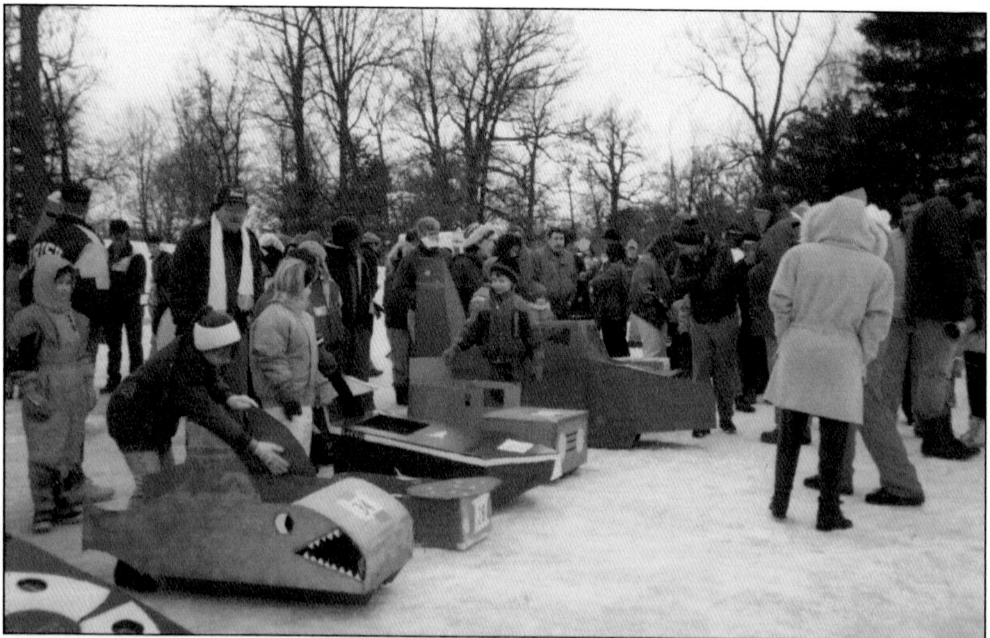

The Cardboard Classic sled race was begun in 1990 by the Greater Albion Chamber of Commerce. It is held each January on the Victory Park sledding hill. The event attracts participants of all ages, who turn ordinary cardboard into decorative and colorful sled designs, as indicated by their enthusiasm in this 1993 photo.

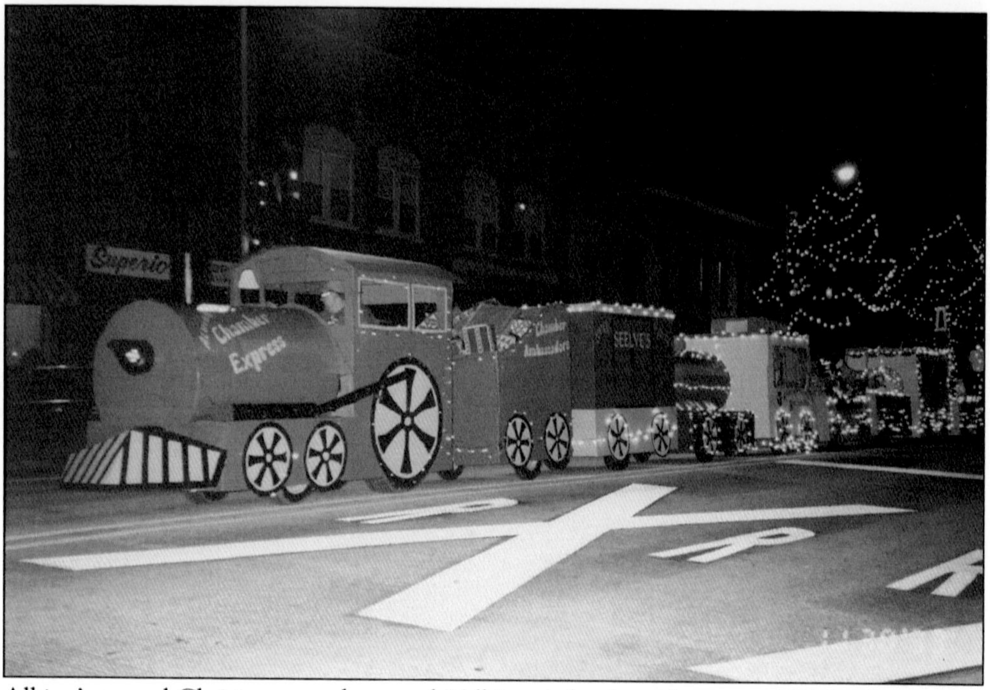


Albion's annual Christmas parade named "Albion Aglow" was begun in 1991 by the Greater Albion Chamber of Commerce. This 1993 photograph shows the "Albion merchants train" float rolling along on the newly laid bricks on South Superior Street.

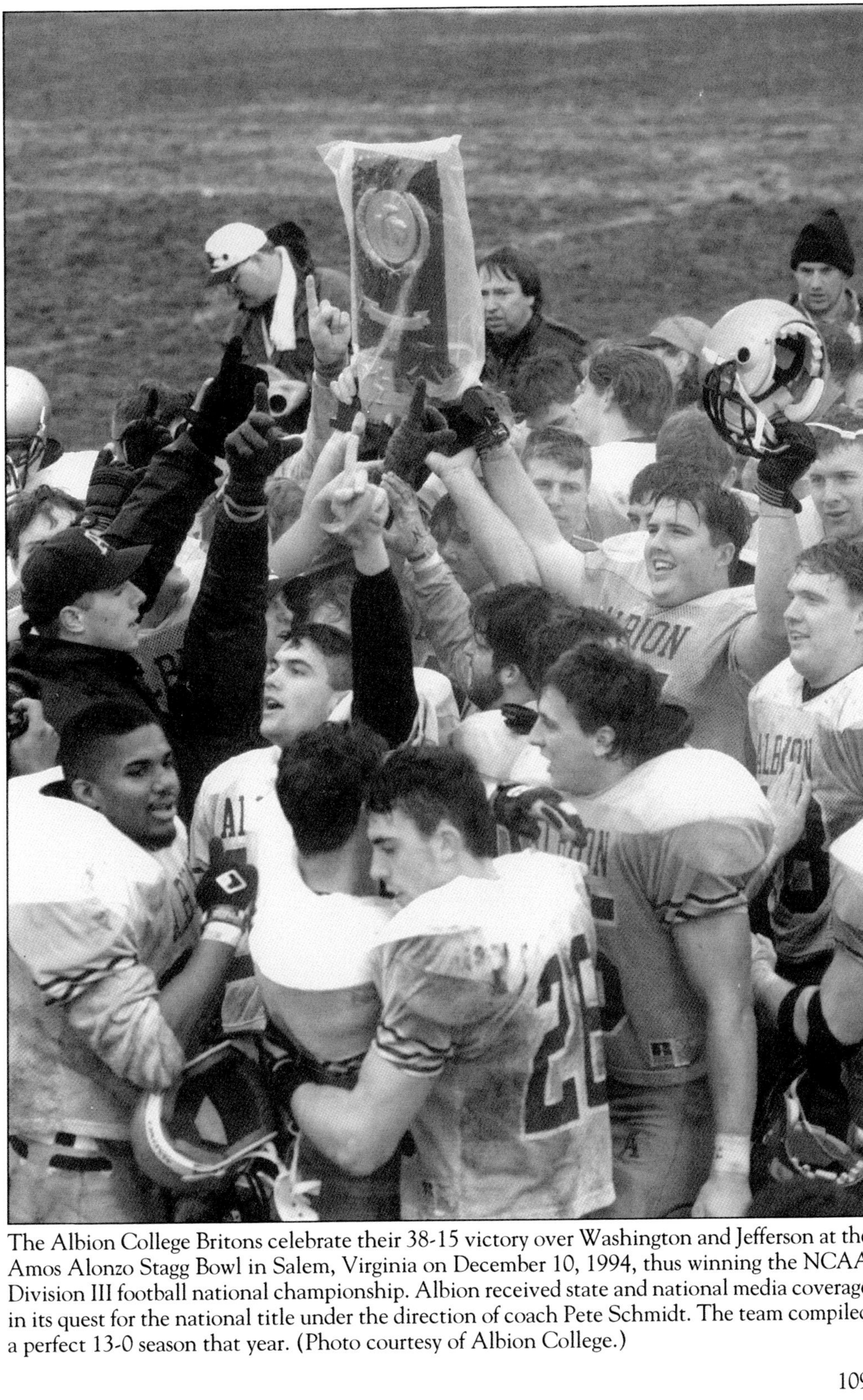

The Albion College Britons celebrate their 38-15 victory over Washington and Jefferson at the Amos Alonzo Stagg Bowl in Salem, Virginia on December 10, 1994, thus winning the NCAA Division III football national championship. Albion received state and national media coverage in its quest for the national title under the direction of coach Pete Schmidt. The team compiled a perfect 13-0 season that year. (Photo courtesy of Albion College.)

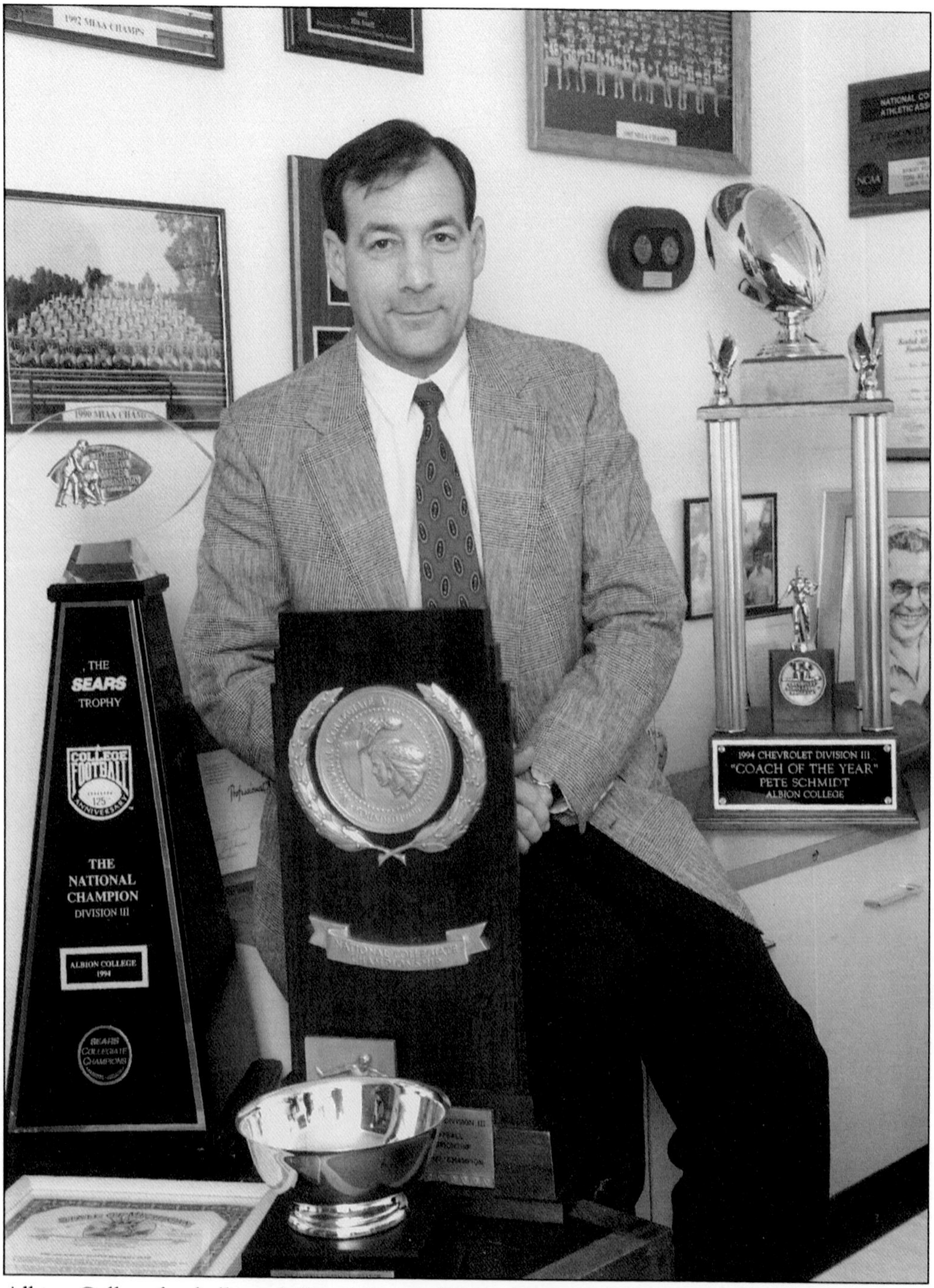


Albion College football coach Pete Schmidt (1948–2000) poses around the several trophies and plaques won by the 1994 NCAA Division III national football champion Albion College Britons. Schmidt was named the 1994 Division III football Coach of the Year by the American Football Coaches Association. Schmidt compiled a 104-27-4 record that included nine MIAA titles during his 14-year tenure as coach from 1982 to 1996. (Photo courtesy of Albion College.)

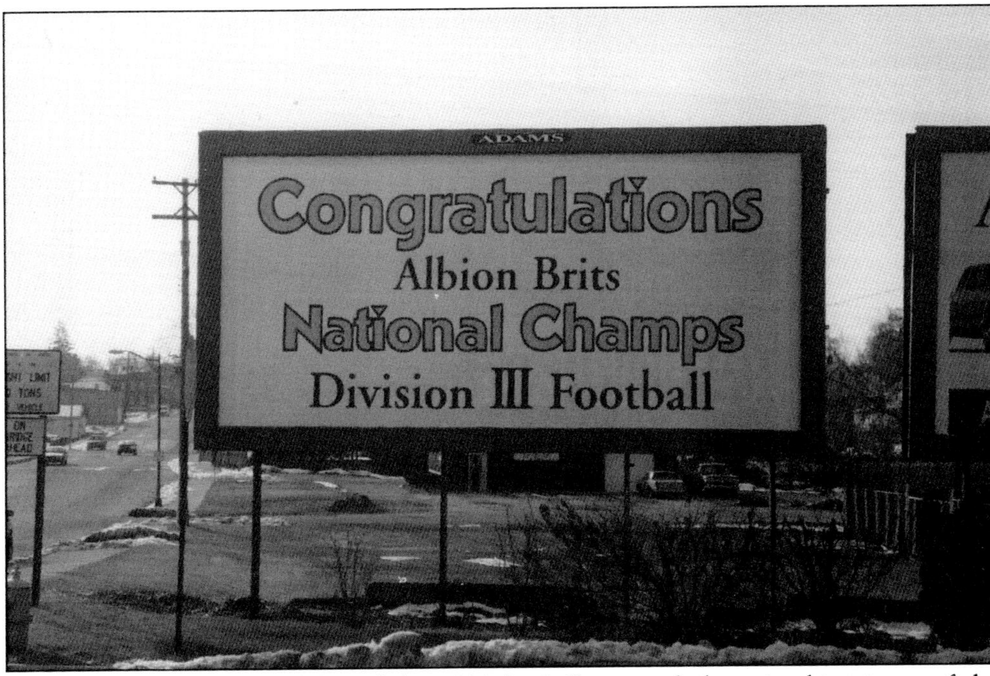


The Albion community celebrated the 1994 football national championship victory of the Albion College Britons, and this billboard was just one of the many signs of community pride around town.

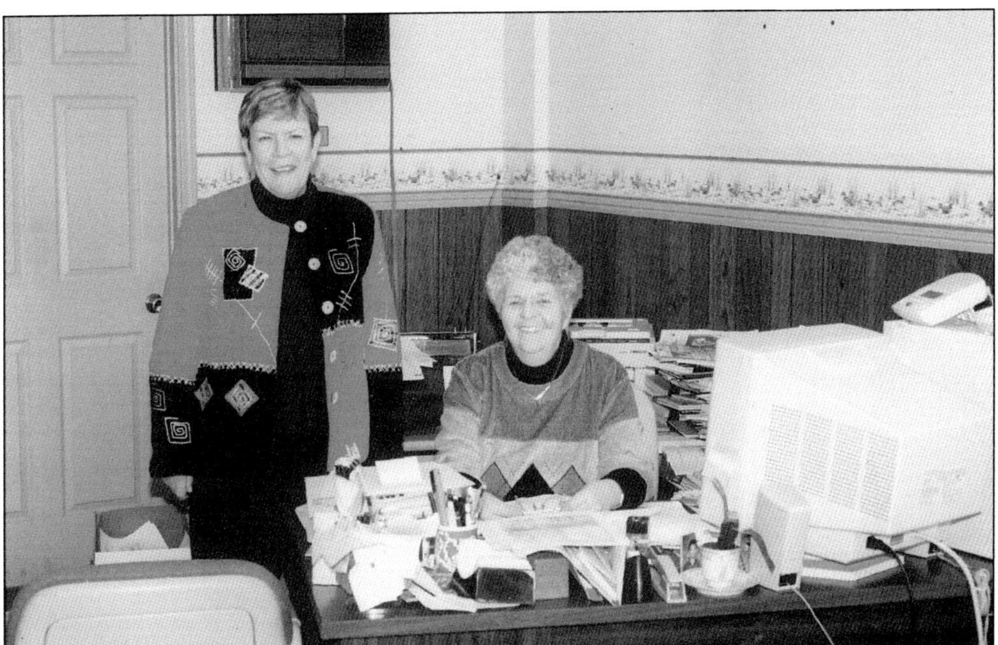

The Greater Albion Chamber of Commerce president Sue Marcos (left) and office manager Peg Eckmyre (right) handle the daily business of promoting Albion and providing assistance with hundreds of inquiries about the Albion area. The duo began their duties in 1985 and 1989, respectively.

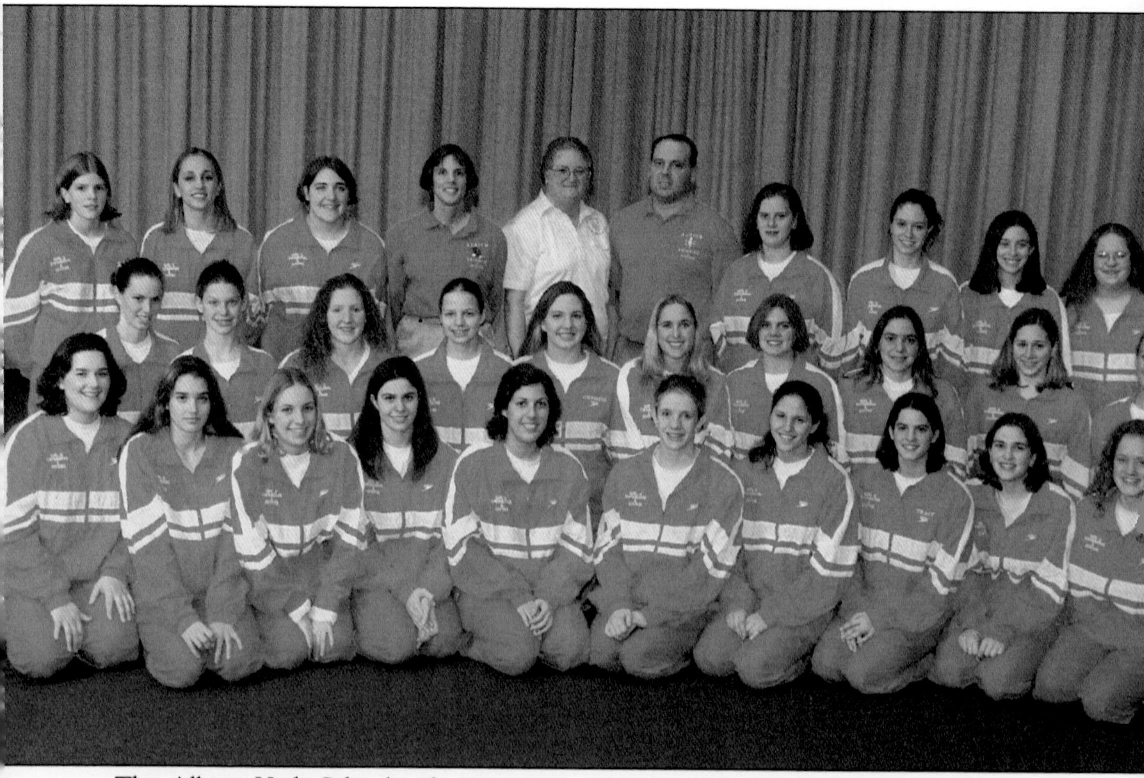

The Albion High School girls swim team won the 1997 Michigan High School Athletic Association Class B-C-D swimming and diving state championship on November 22, 1997. It was the first-ever swimming and diving state championship for the Wildcats, led by swimming coach Mary Ann Egnatuk, and diving coach Ron Face. The team, from left to right, is: (front row) Lisa Bobzien, Claire Wasmund, Katie Garrison, Leeanne Yokum, Michelle Dante, Jordan Longhurst, Sarah Pinkham, Tracy Egnatuk, Erin Nielsen, and Kim Hiatt; (center row) Katie Starkey, Paddy Steinmetz, Emily Dobbins, Mary Christensen, Christie Egnatuk, Kristin Keyes, Kristen Harden, Jamilly Melo, Meagan Flores, and Leslie Purucker; (top row) Marlen Nielsen, Sarah Kovach, April Krause, head coach Mary Ann Egnatuk, assistant coach Barb Shiery, diving coach Ron Face, Kelli Olma, Abby Sharrar, Emily McAllister, and Brandy Michael.

"Albion Across the USA" was the theme of the 1999 Festival of the Forks celebration. Albion, Michigan, is the largest of over a dozen Albions located in the United States. This commemorative elongated cent was issued at the Festival featuring the Festival theme on one side, and a stretched out Abraham Lincoln on the other.

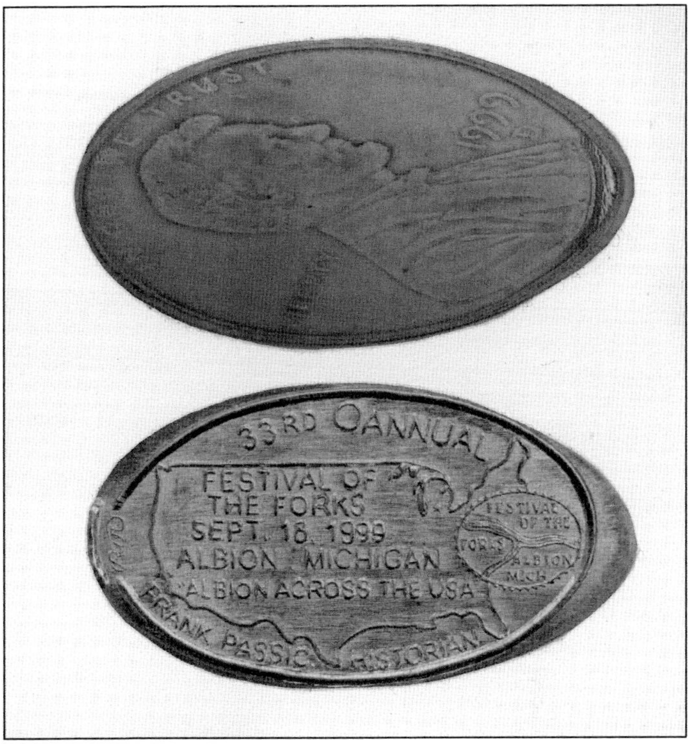


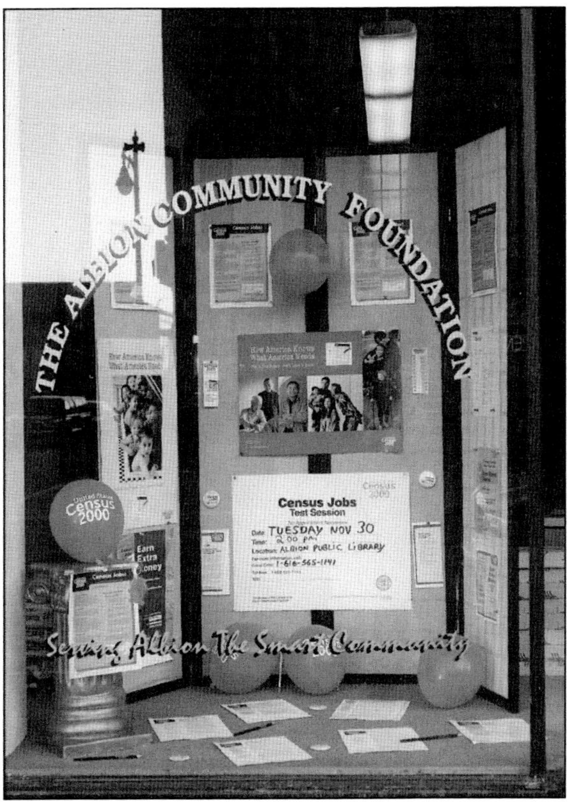


Many Albion residents participated in the U.S. Census 2000 count as enumerators, and received the support of local groups and organizations. This helped achieve a complete and accurate local count of 9,144 persons. The November 1999 display in the window of the Albion Community Foundation pictured here promoted local U.S. Census job recruiting efforts, and public awareness of the importance of filling out the Census form. This author served as the Assistant Manager of Recruiting (AMR) for the seven-county Local Census Office area in Census 2000.

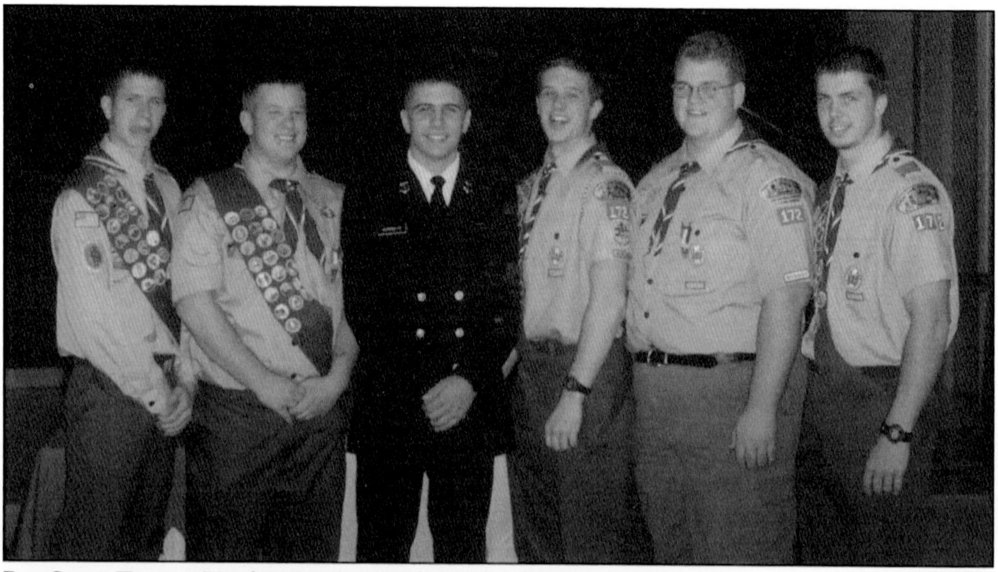

Boy Scout Troop 172 of St. Paul's Lutheran Church has the distinction of having seven eagle scouts in a ten-year period. Their court of honor gathered on November 25, 2000, to induct their newest member, Mark Anderla. The eagle scouts, from left to right, are: Matt Anderla, Mark Anderla, Benjamin Bearman, Michael Anderla, Tim Krause, and Ben Buskirk. (Photo courtesy Michael Bearman.)

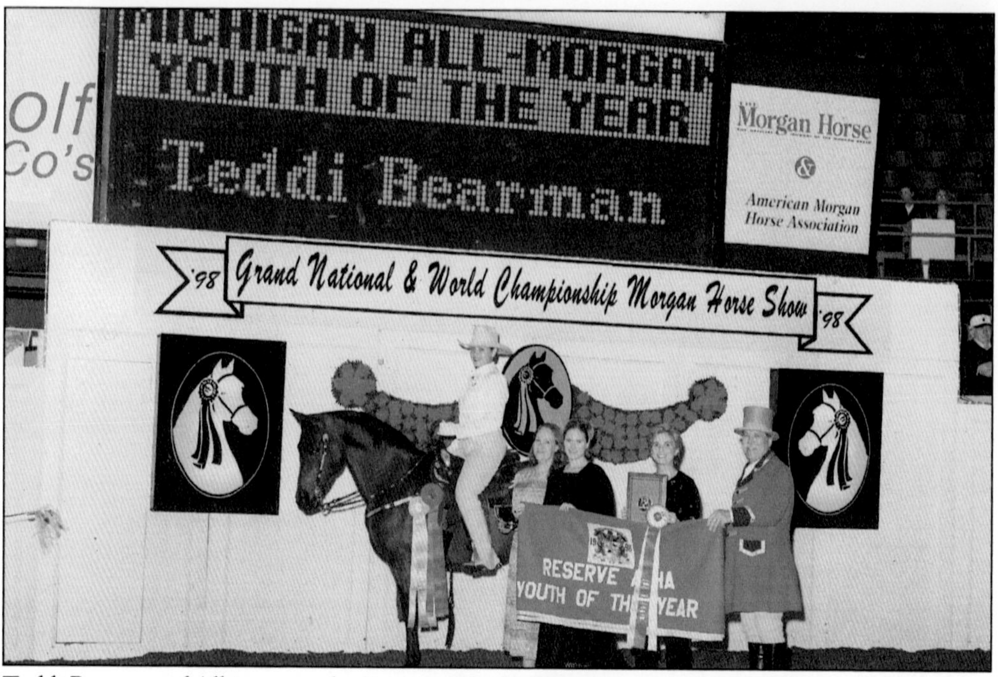


Teddi Bearman of Albion won the Reserve World Champion Youth of the Year award from the American Morgan Horse Association at the 1998 Grand National and World Championship Morgan Horse Show in Oklahoma City, Oklahoma. Teddi is pictured with her horse Battons Maestro and show officials. She had also previously won the Michigan All-Morgan Youth of the Year award for 1998. (Photo courtesy of Howard Schatzberg Photography.)

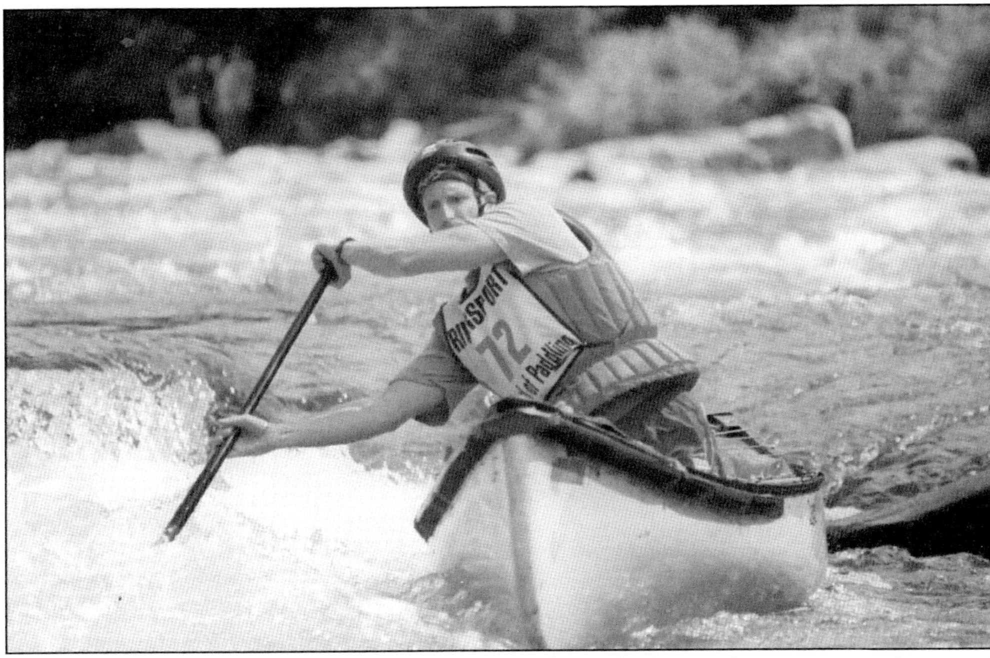

Albion College Aquatic Center director and coach Keith Havens has won several national championships in the National Whitewater Open Canoeing competition. Keith is pictured here in action during the June 1995 event on the Youghiogheny River in Pennsylvania, in which he earned the national championship in the one-person open sprint event.

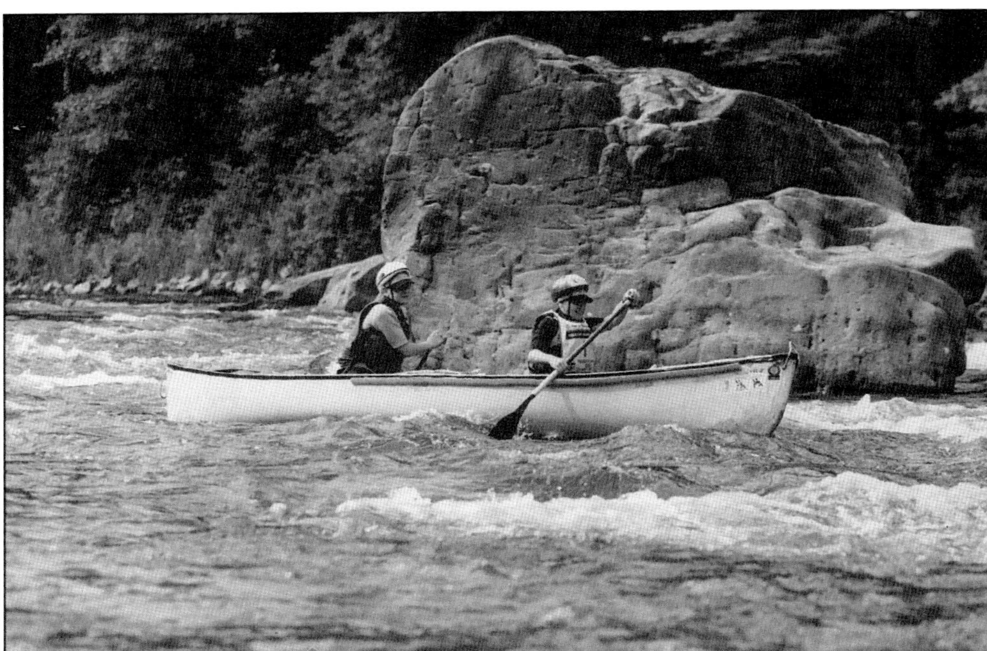

Albion youth Zack (left) and Zane (right) Havens won the 2001 National Championship in Whitewater Open Canoeing in the ages 13–15 division. The event was held on the Youghiogheny River in Pennsylvania. They are pictured here in action during the competition.

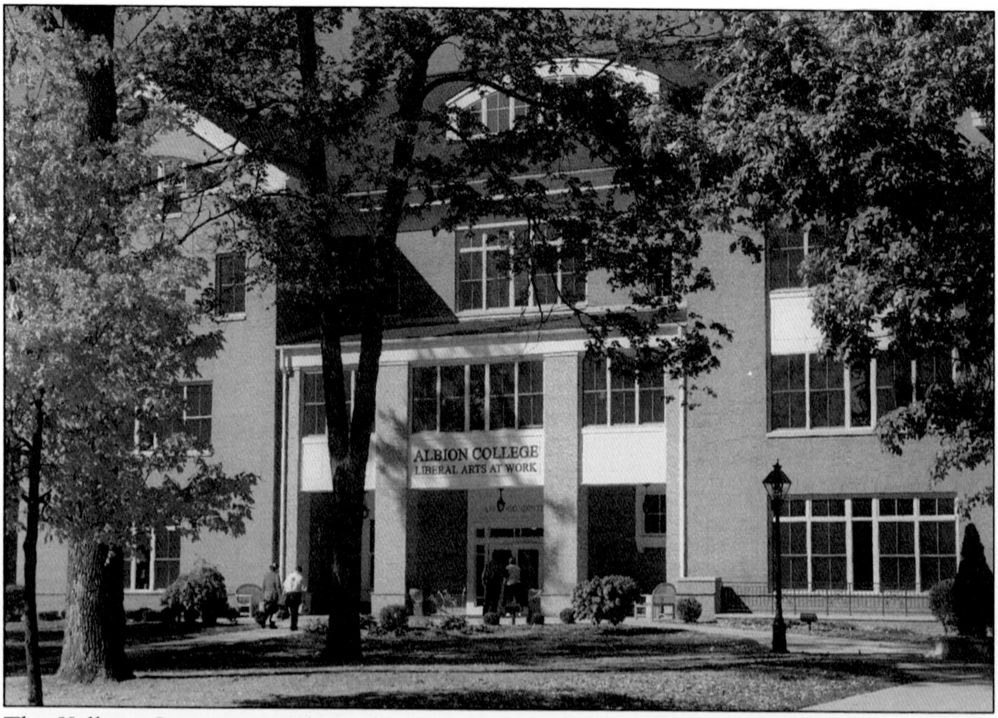


The Kellogg Center opened on the campus of Albion College in 1996 and is used as a meeting place for the entire campus community. The facility includes meeting rooms, student organization offices, campus mailboxes, and the College Bookstore. It was named after the Kellogg Company of Battle Creek, which contributed $6 million toward the project. (Photo courtesy of Albion College.)

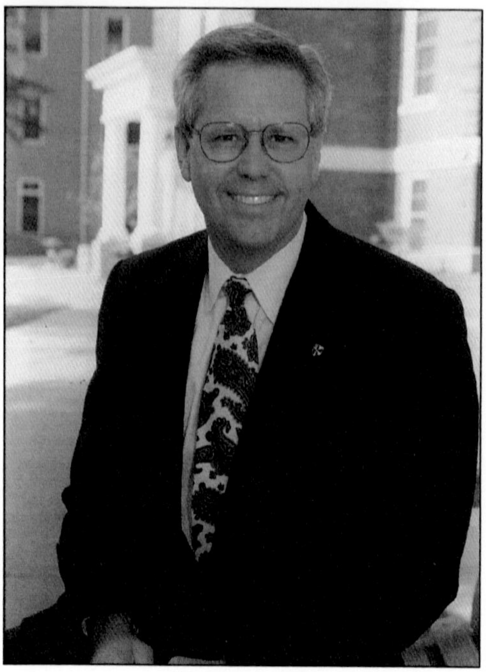

Dr. Peter Mitchell is the 14th president of Albion College, and assumed that position in July 1997. A 1967 Albion College alumnus, Mitchell served as president of Columbia College (South Carolina) beginning in 1988, before returning to Albion. Mitchell has guided Albion College into the 21st century and enhanced its role as one of the country's leading liberal arts colleges. (Photo courtesy of Albion College.)

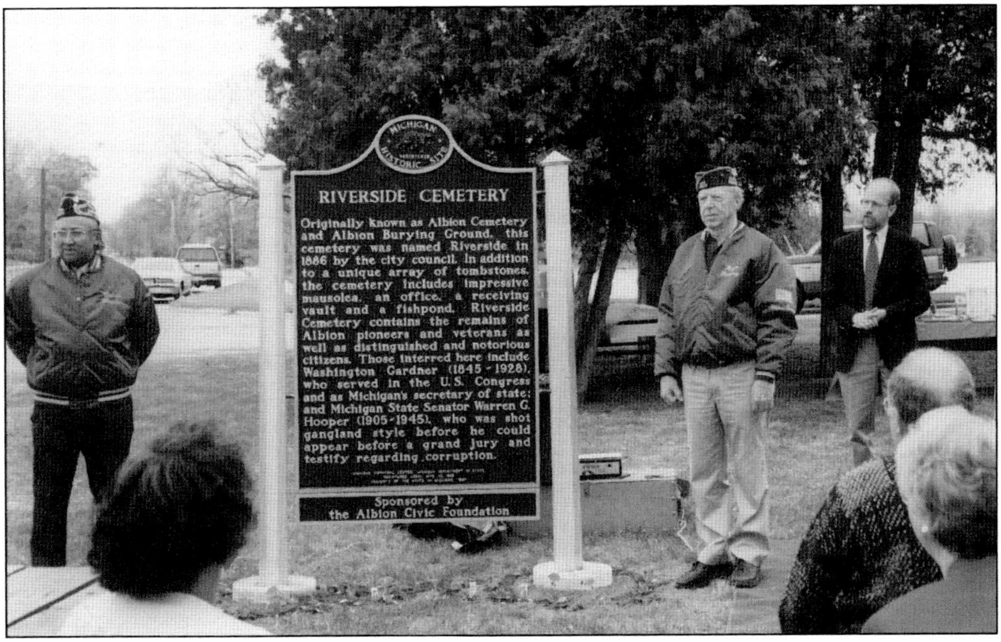


The Michigan Historical Commission placed Riverside Cemetery on the State Register of Historic Sites on August 29, 1996. An historical marker dedication ceremony was held on May 18, 1997. Pictured here, from left to right, are Albion VFW Post No. 3672 members: Calvin Wheeler, Brian Downey, and Albion mayor Kim Tunnicliff, who participated in the event. The marker was funded by the Albion Civic Foundation.

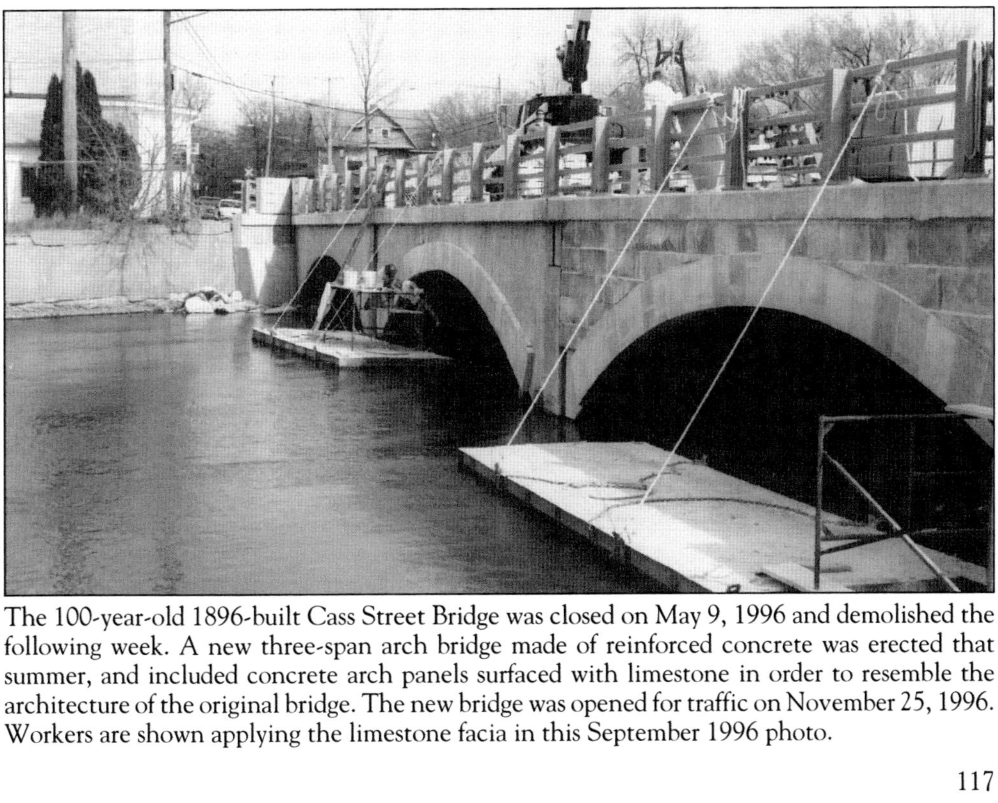

The 100-year-old 1896-built Cass Street Bridge was closed on May 9, 1996 and demolished the following week. A new three-span arch bridge made of reinforced concrete was erected that summer, and included concrete arch panels surfaced with limestone in order to resemble the architecture of the original bridge. The new bridge was opened for traffic on November 25, 1996. Workers are shown applying the limestone facia in this September 1996 photo.

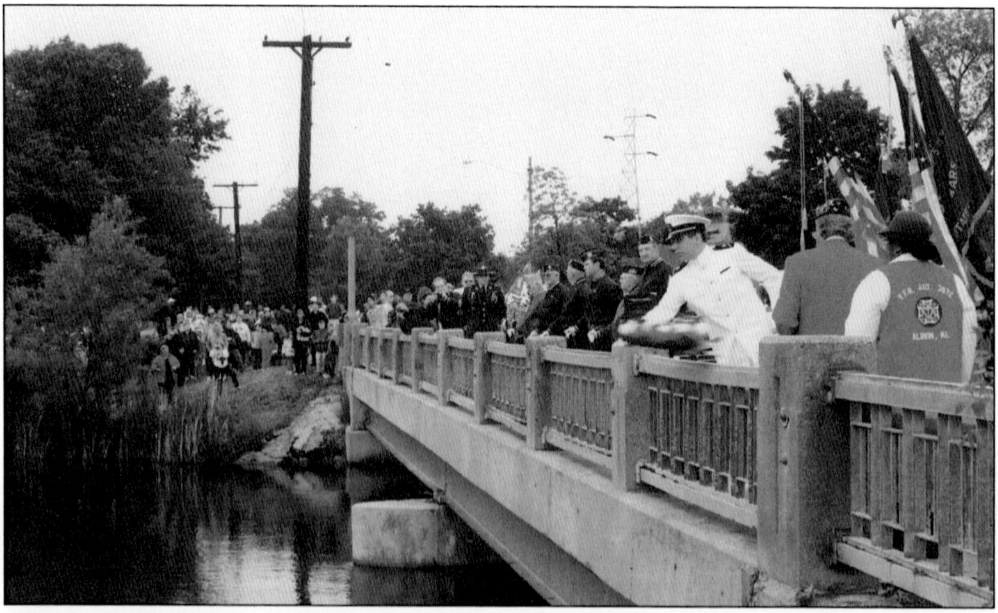

Albion citizens gather at the South Superior Street Bridge over the Kalamazoo River by Riverside Cemetery on Memorial Day to remember its veterans and those who gave their lives in service to our country. U.S. Naval Academy Midshipman Benjamin Bearman of Albion (a 2000 graduate of Albion High School) throws the traditional memorial wreath into the river below during the 2001 service, as members of the Veterans of Foreign Wars, the American Legion, and other officials watch nearby.

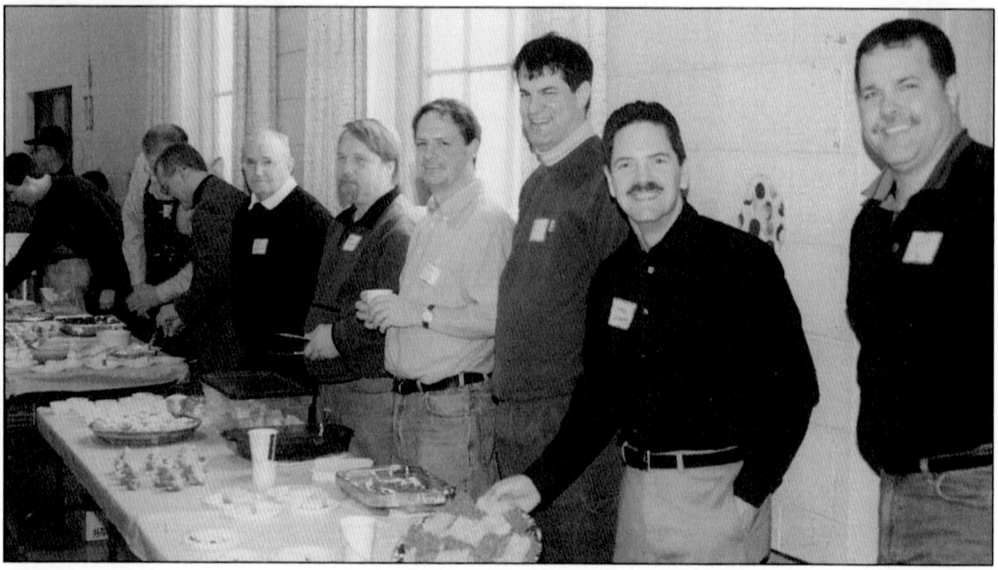

The Citizens to Beautify Albion hold an annual event called "Men Who Cook," which raises money to purchase flowers that are planted along the business route through town each year. Men from throughout the community volunteer their time and homemade food for residents to sample at this well-attended event. The dessert table above is staffed by these chefs looking at the camera, from left to right: Ron Warson, Mike Tymowicz, Thom Wilch, Andy French, Mark Schauer, and Jeff Bell.

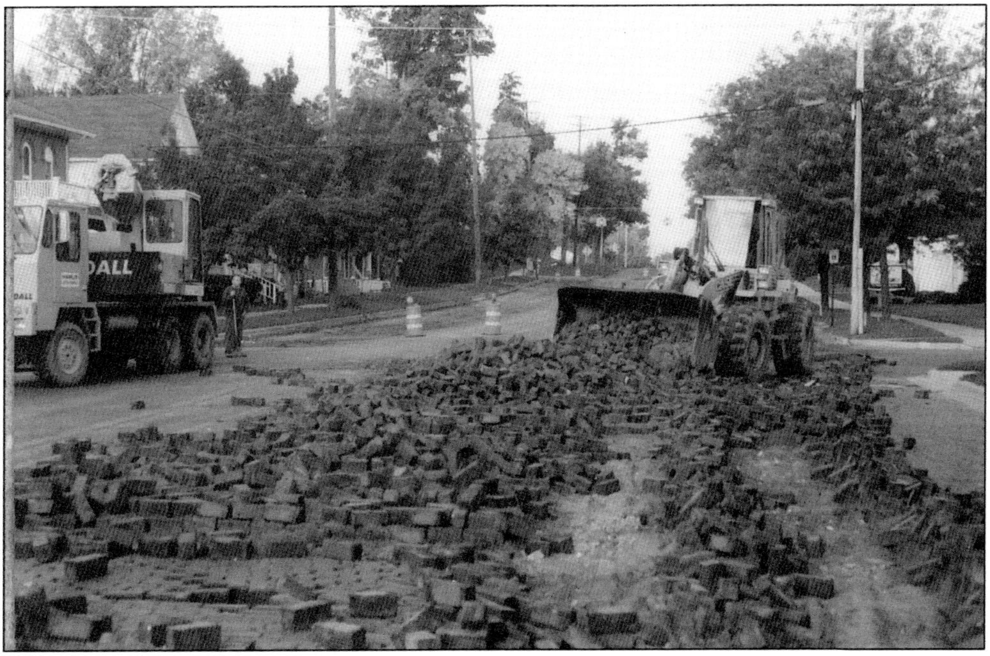

The paving bricks in the 100 block of West Erie Street were removed on October 1, 2001. This scene, facing west, shows the bricks being scooped into a pile prior to disposal. The street was repaved with asphalt.

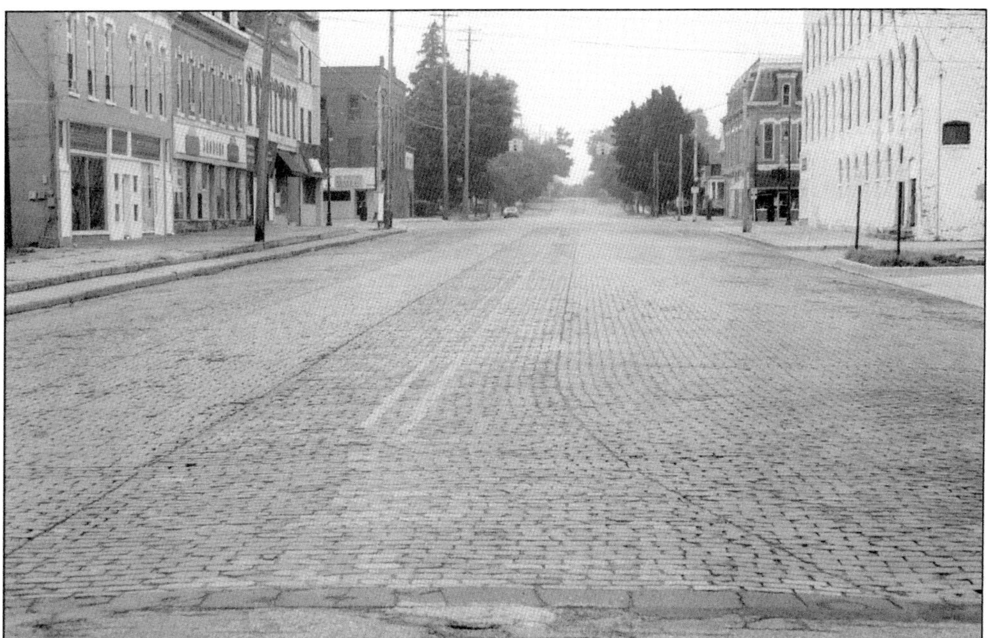

The paving bricks in the 100 block of East Erie Street show the "scar" of the old interurban tracks, which were removed, in the early 1930s. The bricks shown here are scheduled to be removed in 2002 and replaced with asphalt.

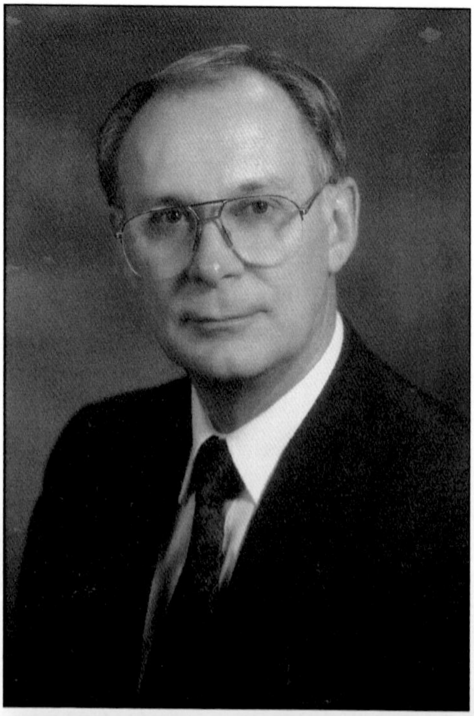

Arlin Ness has served as the third president of Starr Commonwealth Schools since June 1981. Ness is chair of the board of Reclaiming Youth International, and president of the International Association of Social Educators. Starr Commonwealth was founded in 1913 by Floyd Starr, and today provides a broad range of services to children, youth, and families. The Starr Commonwealth campus west of Albion was placed on the State Registry of Historic Sites in 1981.

Co-authors Dr. Larry Brendtro (president of Starr Commonwealth 1967–1981), Arlin E. Ness (current Starr president), and Dr. Martin Mitchell (vice president at Starr) are seen in the back row, from left to right, as they celebrate the publication of their book *No Disposable Kids* in January 2002. Seated in front is legendary boxer Muhammad Ali, who wrote the foreword to the book, and his wife Lonnie. The book offers numerous success stories in working with troubled youth—as a model for educators today.

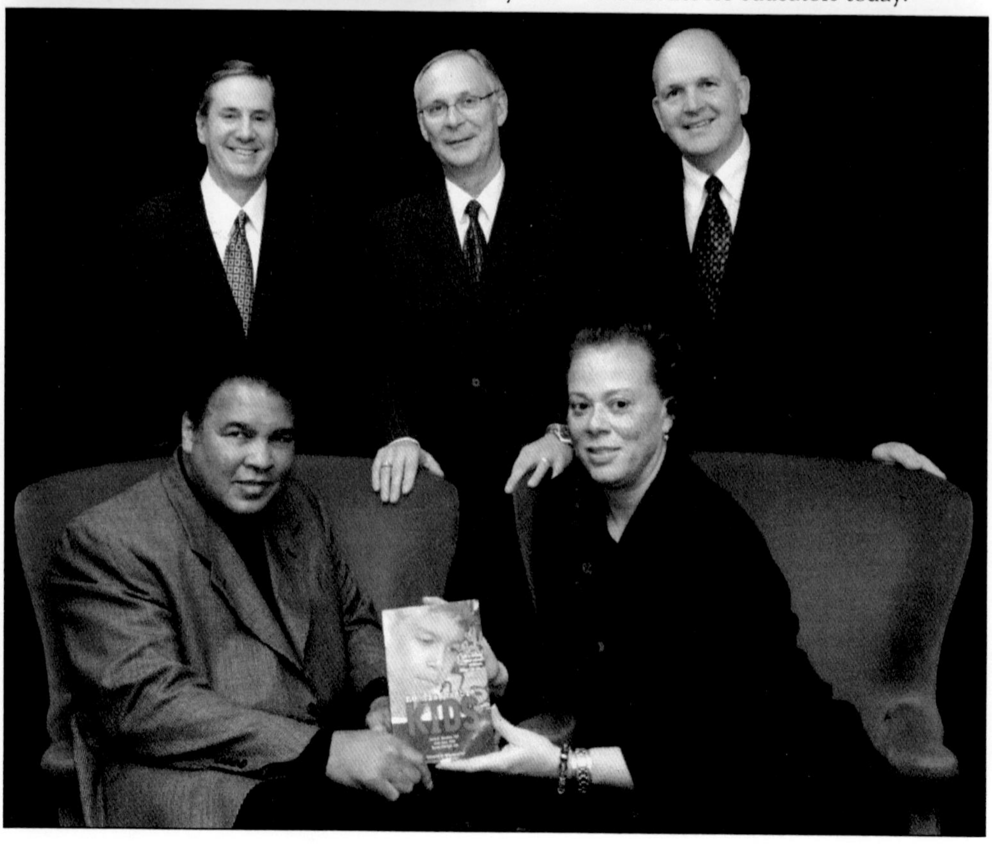

Dr. James L. Curtis M.D. served as associate dean, and clinical associate professor of Psychiatry at the Cornell University Medical School (1970–81), and as clinical professor of Psychiatry at Columbia University College of Physicians and Surgeons (1982–2000). He was chairman of the board of the National Medical Fellowship during the 1970s, and received their lifetime medical career achievement award in December 2001. Dr. Curtis is the author of two books about minorities in the medical field, as well as numerous articles. He is a 1940 graduate of Albion High School.

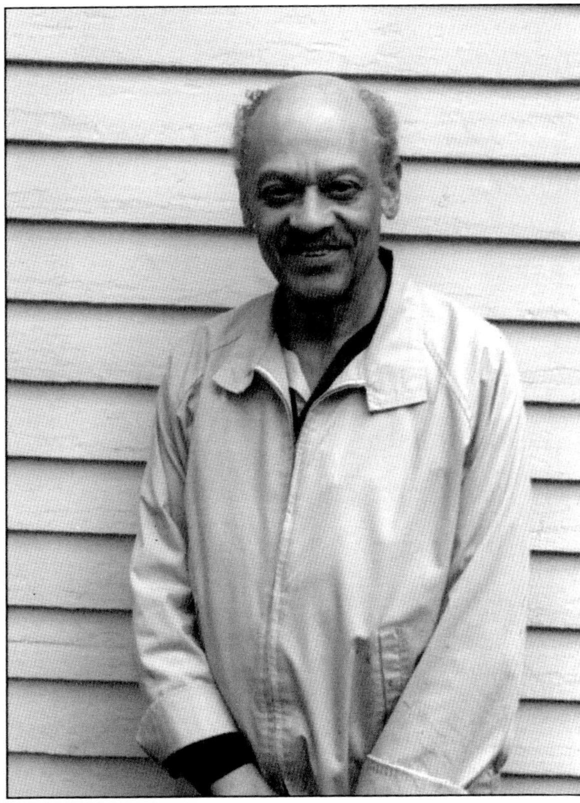

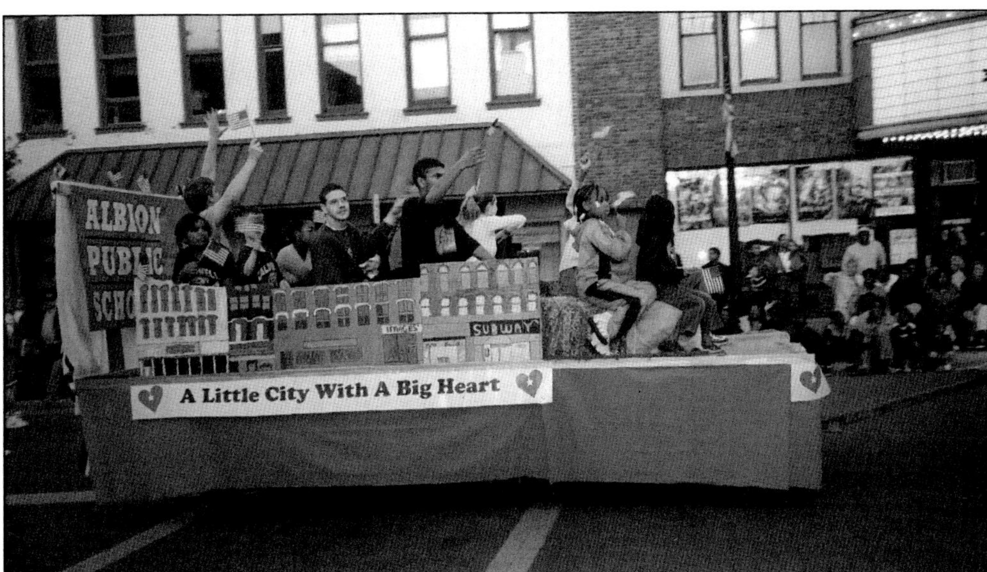

The Albion Public Schools float in the 2001 Festival of the Forks parade represented the theme "Albion—A Little City With a Big Heart." It included students on it from each of the schools. (Photo courtesy of Cathy Campbell.)

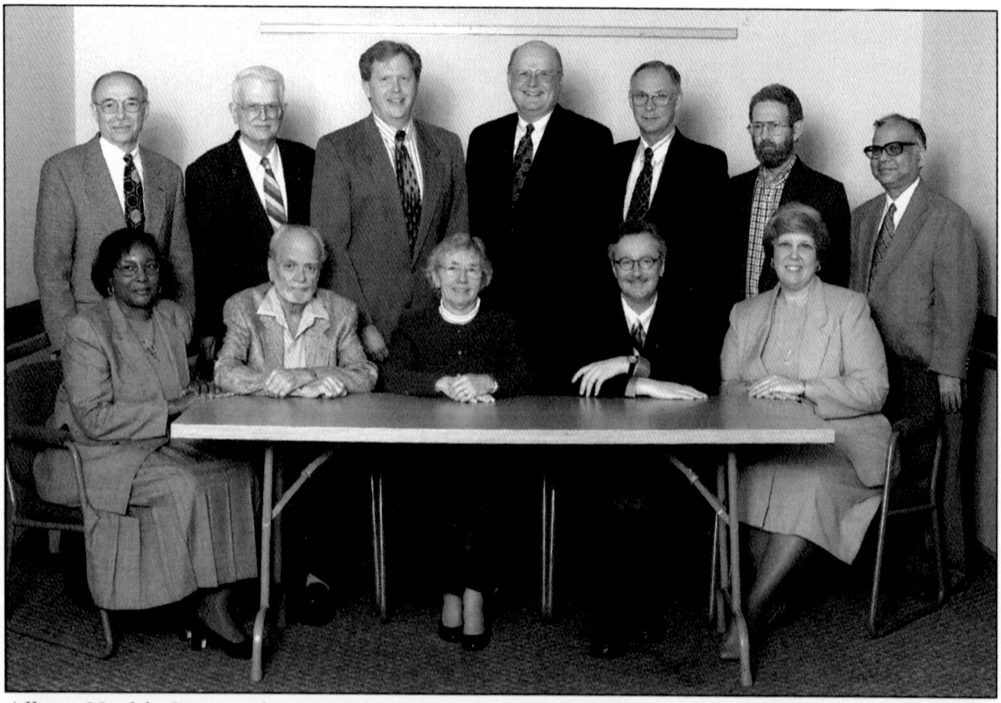

Albion Health Services board of directors, shown in 1999, are, from left to right: (front row) Joyce Spicer, Charles Lentz; Kitty Padget, vice chairman; William Stoffer, chairperson; and Madeline Adie; (back row) Bernard Konkle Sr., treasurer; Ralph Cram M.D.; Mike Boff, president; Chris Miller, secretary; Arlin Ness; Martin Holmes M.D.; and M. Rashid Siddiqui M.D. (Photo courtesy of M. Rashid Siddiqui and Austin Professional Portraiture.)

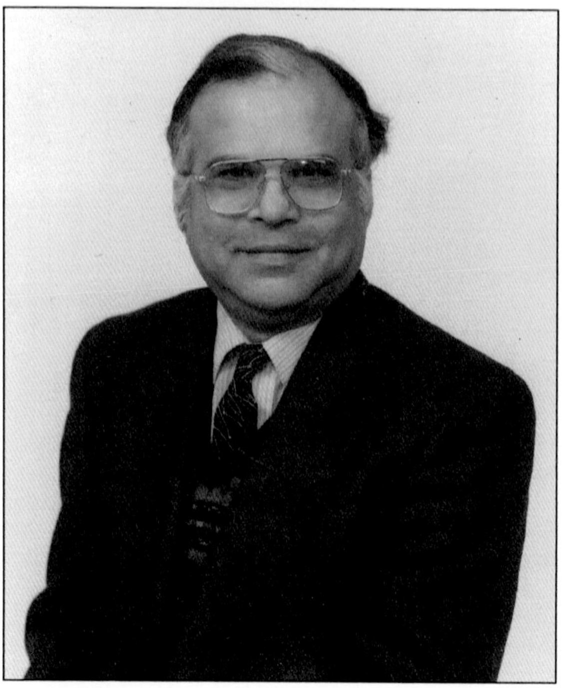

Mohammad Rashid Siddiqui, M.D. began his general practice in Albion in July 1974. He has served as chief of staff, chief surgeon, chairperson of the surgery and anesthesia department, and in other vital roles at Albion Community Hospital and Trillium Hospital through the years. After the closure of Trillium Hospital, Dr. Siddiqui became affiliated with Oaklawn Hospital medical staff and continues his independent practice in Albion today. (Photo courtesy of Trillium Hospital.)

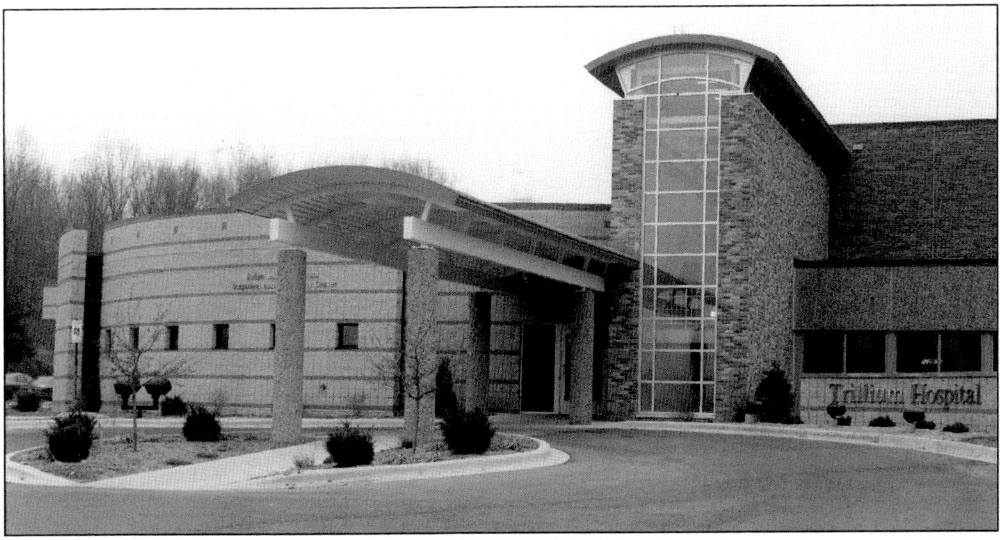


The 1967-built Albion Community Hospital at 809 West Erie Street became known as Trillium Hospital on December 6, 1996. The Ralph and Mary Cram Outpatient and Emergency Center addition was erected in 1999–2000 and opened on December 12, 2000. Trillium Hospital was subsequently closed on February 5, 2002.

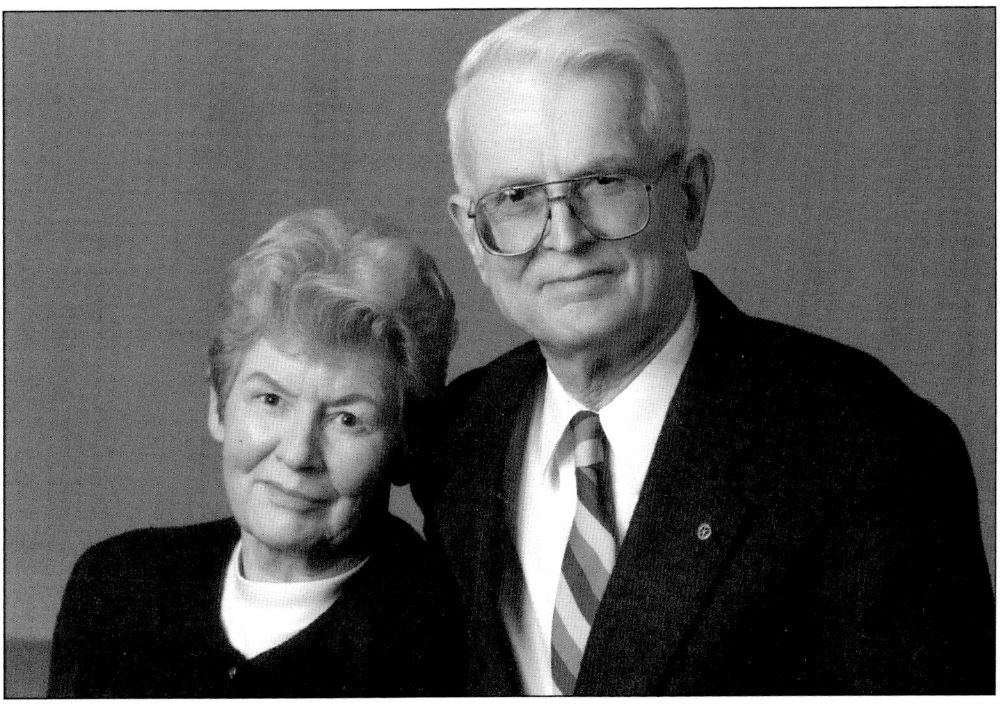

Dr. Ralph Cram M.D. began his family practice in Albion in 1958. He delivered over 3,000 babies over his 40-year career before retiring in 1999. Dr. Cram was named the 1993 Michigan "Physician of the Year" by the Michigan Academy of Family Practice. Dr. Cram and his wife Mary have been very active in community work and civic organizations throughout their careers. Photo courtesy Trillium Hospital and Austin Professional Portraiture.

# RECENT ALBION MAYORS

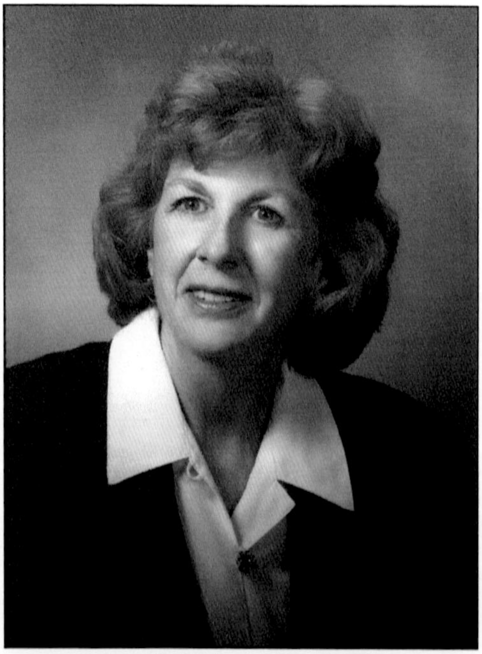

Lois McClure 1992–1994

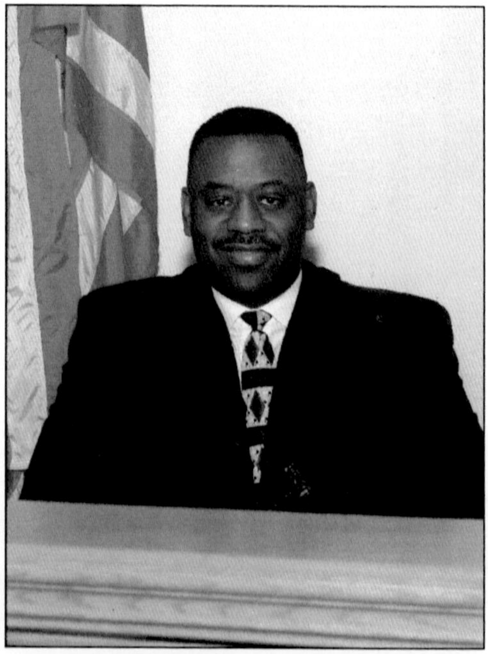

Michael Williams 1994–1997

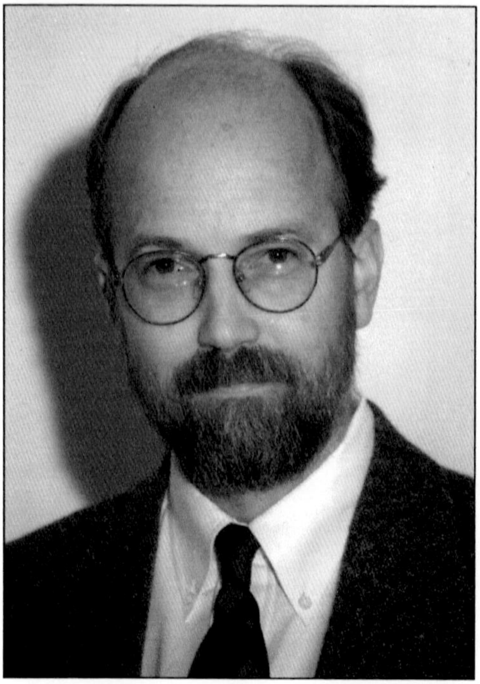

Kim Tunnicliff 1997–1999

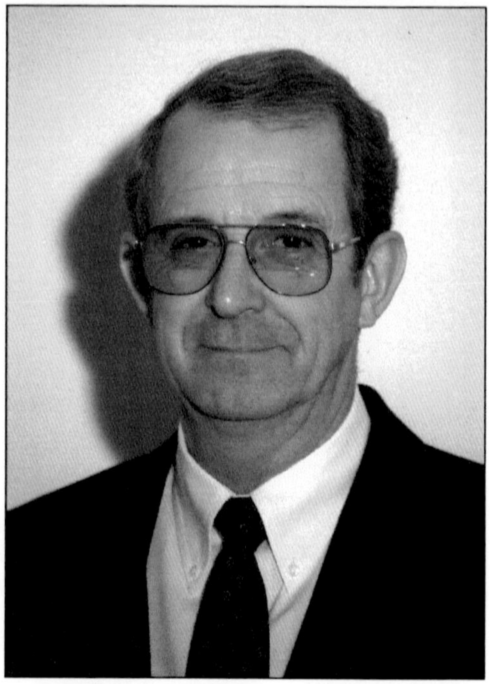

William M. Wheaton, 1999–present

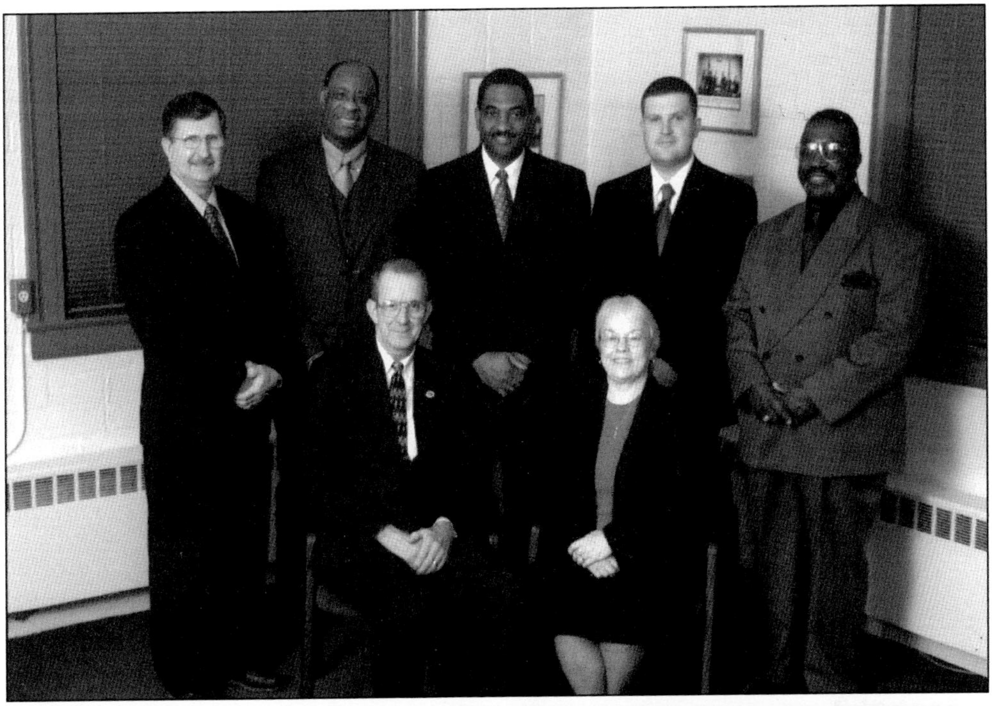

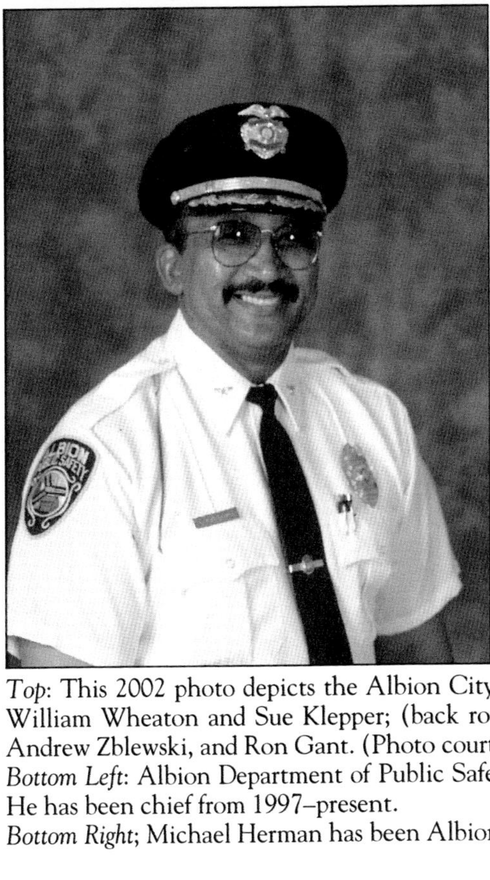

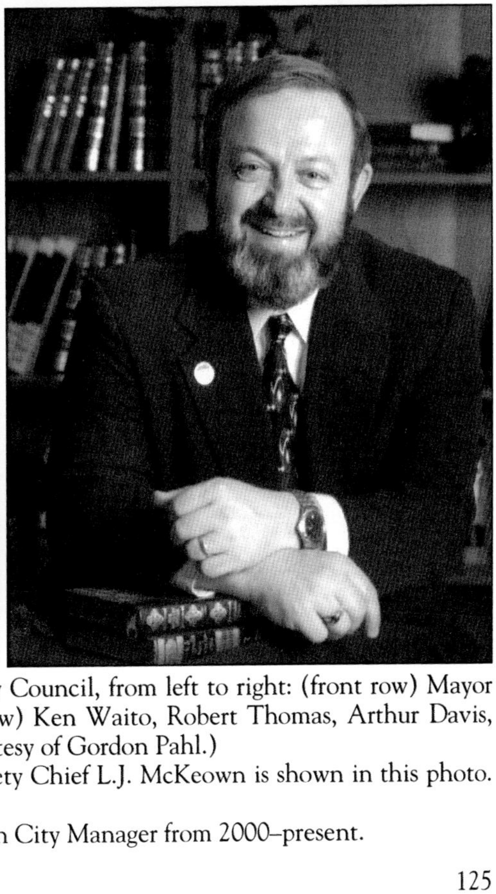

*Top*: This 2002 photo depicts the Albion City Council, from left to right: (front row) Mayor William Wheaton and Sue Klepper; (back row) Ken Waito, Robert Thomas, Arthur Davis, Andrew Zblewski, and Ron Gant. (Photo courtesy of Gordon Pahl.)
*Bottom Left*: Albion Department of Public Safety Chief L.J. McKeown is shown in this photo. He has been chief from 1997–present.
*Bottom Right*; Michael Herman has been Albion City Manager from 2000–present.

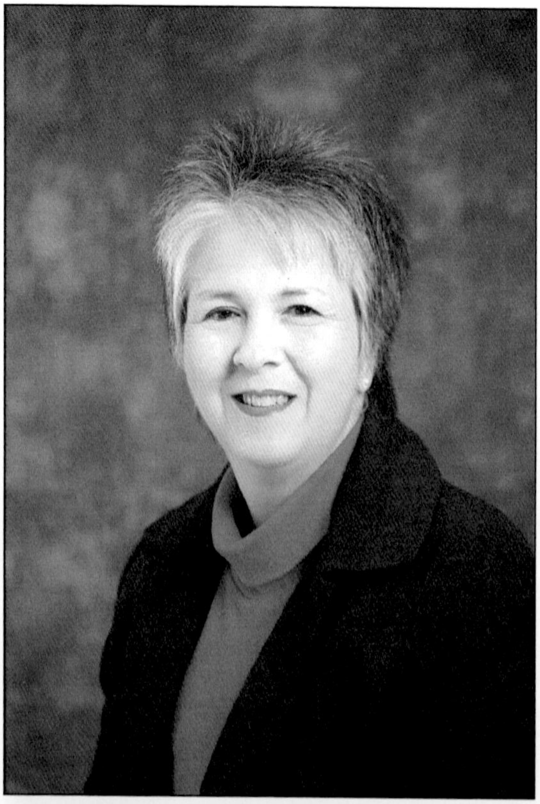

Educator Dr. Carol A. Hansen has served as the superintendent of the Albion Public Schools since 2001. She came to Albion in 2000 from Kansas City, Missouri, where she previously served as the director of the Leadership Institute at the Learning Exchange. Hanson served as assistant superintendent in Albion during the 2000–01 school year before assuming her present position.

The Albion Board of Education, 2001–02 school year, poses for the camera, from left to right: (front row) Kenneth Ponds, treasurer; David Moore, vice president; David C. Farley, secretary; (back row) Alfredia Dysart-Drake; Trisha Franzen; Rebecca Mitchell; and Joyce Spicer, president. (Photo courtesy of Cathy Campbell.)

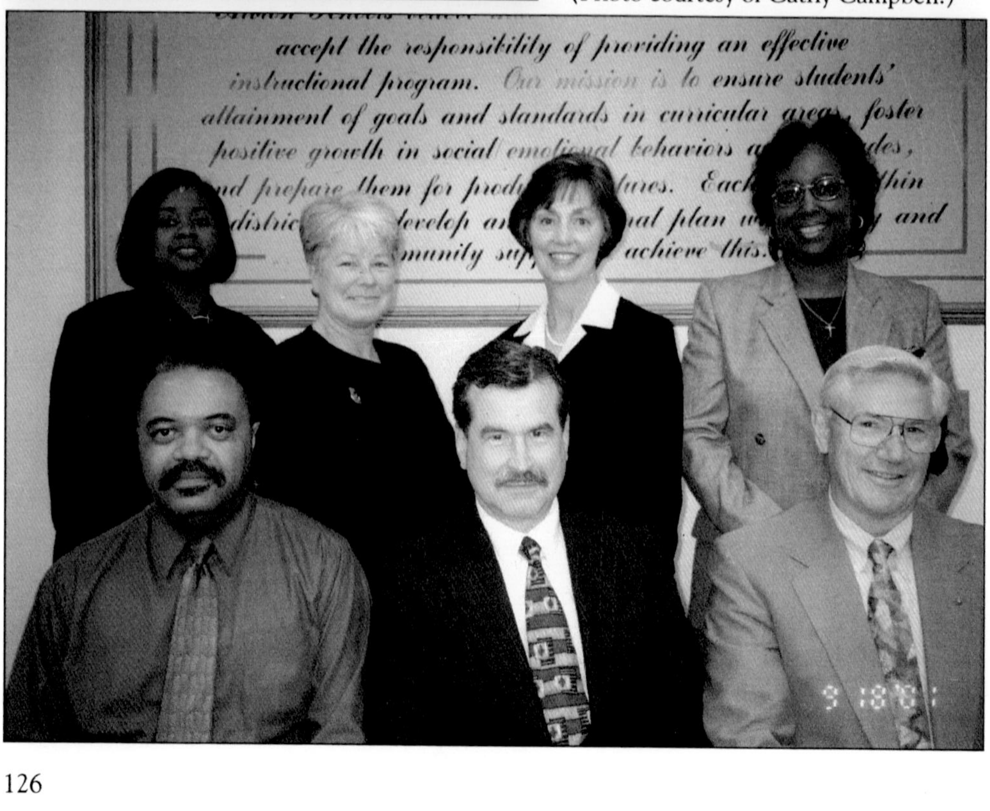

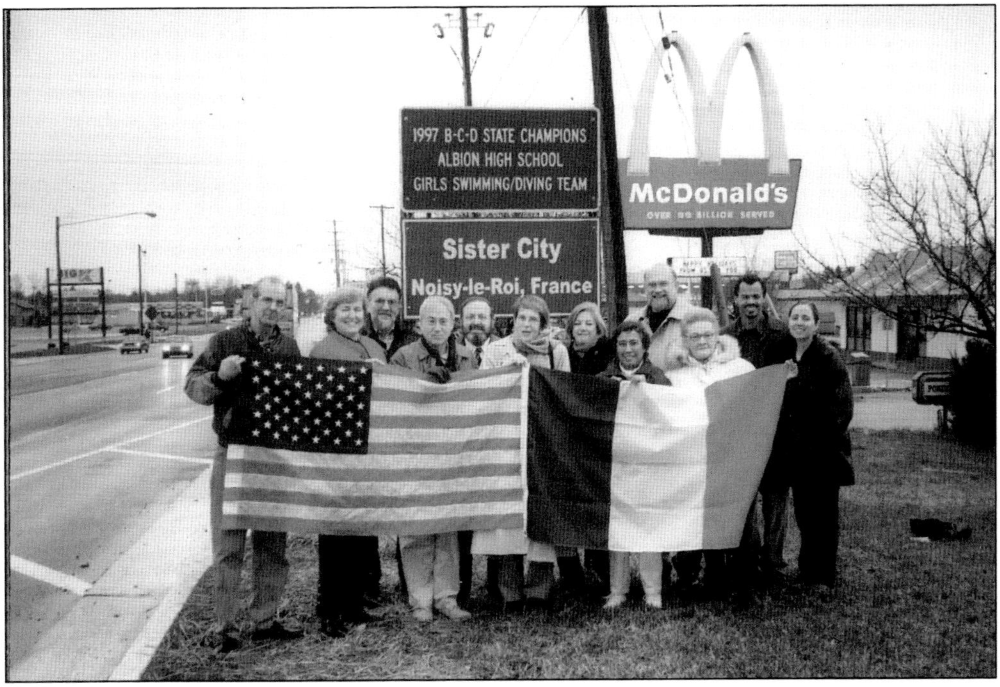


The cities of Albion, Michigan and Noisy-le-Roi, France signed an official Sister City agreement in June, 2001. These Albion representatives celebrate the placement of the Sister City sign at the city limits in December, 2001, and are shown holding the flags of the United States and France, from left to right: Mayor William Wheaton, Marjorie Ulbrich, Mike Soltis, Bruce Borthwick, Mike Herman, Vera Wenzel, Adrian Cargo, Juanita Solis, Charles Robison, Genevieve Underhill, Willie Lewis, and Nancy Lewis. (Photo courtesy of the Greater Albion Chamber of Commerce.)

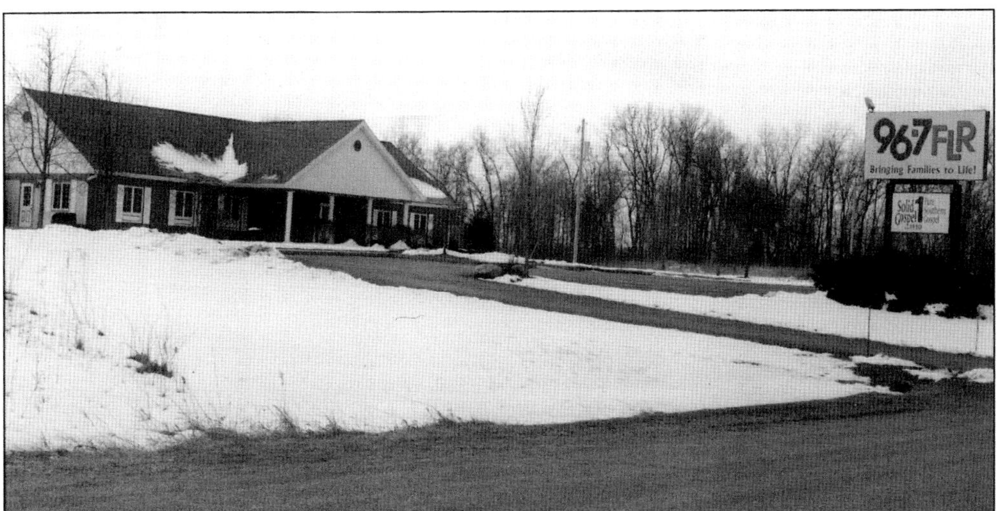


Thousands of cars pass by the studios of Family Life Radio located along I-94 on Donovan Road east of Albion each day. WUFN 96.7 FM Albion signed on the air in 1971, and moved into their present location in the spring of 1992. This non-commercial inspirational station ministers to the Christian community.

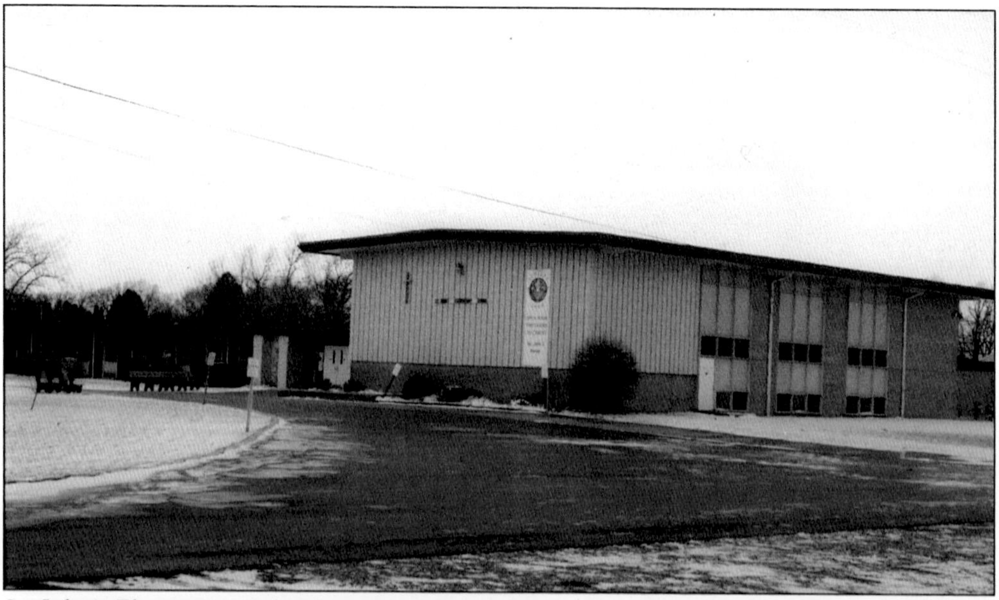

St. John's Elementary School on Irwin Avenue opened in the fall of 1959 as a ministry of St. John's Catholic Church. A parish center is located behind the school. The church moved to the school in the spring of 2002, where services are held today pending the erection of a new church on the property. The school was closed June 7, 2002.

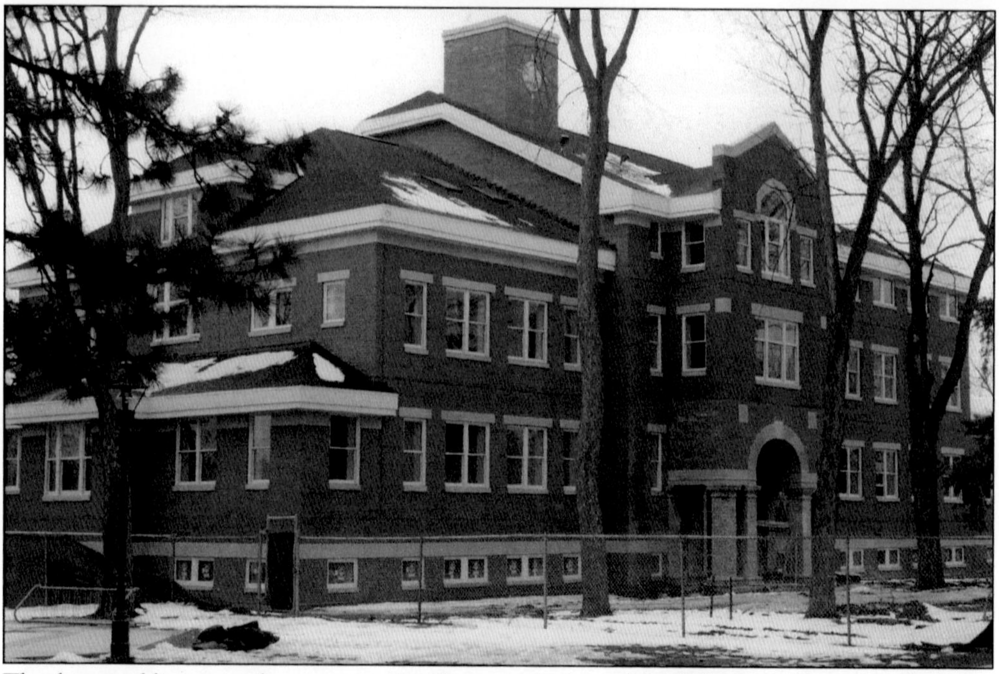

The latest addition to the campus of Albion College is the William C. Ferguson Student, Technology, and Administrative Services Building, which opened in July 2002. Mr. Ferguson is a retired telecommunications executive and a 1952 graduate of Albion College. He chaired the Albion College board of trustees from 1989 to 1996 and served as acting president in the fall of 1995. This February 2002 photograph shows the building in the final stages of construction.